HEINOUS CRIME

HEINOUS CRIME

Cases, Causes, and Consequences

Frederic G. Reamer

COLUMBIA UNIVERSITY PRESS

NEW YORK

COLUMBIA UNIVERSITY PRESS
Publishers Since 1893
New York   Chichester, West Sussex

Copyright © 2005 Columbia University Press
All rights reserved

Library of Congress Cataloging-in-Publication Data

Reamer, Frederic G., 1953–
    Heinous crime : cases, causes, and consequences / Frederic G. Reamer.
        p. cm.
    Includes bibliographical references and index.
    ISBN 0-231-13188-7 (cloth : alk. paper)
    ISBN 0-231-13189-5 (pbk. : alk. paper)
    1. Violent crimes—United States. 2. Violent crimes—United States—Prevention.
3. Criminal justice, Administration of—United States. I. Title.

HV6791.R4 2004
364.15'0973—dc22   2004055136

Columbia University Press books are printed on permanent and durable acid-free paper.
Printed in the United States of America
c 10 9 8 7 6 5 4 3 2 1
p 10 9 8 7 6 5 4 3 2 1

Acknowledgment is gratefully made for permission to reprint from the following:

Coping: Maladaptation in Prisons, by Hans Toch and Kenneth Adams, with J. Douglas Grant.
Copyright © 1989 by the American Psychological Association. Reprinted with permission. Revised
by APA and reissued as *Acting Out: Maladaptive Behavior in Confinement,* by Hans Toch and
Kenneth Adams. Copyright © 2002 by the American Psychological Association.

Prison Madness: The Mental Health Crisis Behind Bars and What We Must Do About It, by Terry A.
Kupers. Copyright © 1999. This material is used by permission of John Wiley & Sons, Inc.

For Deborah, Emma, and Leah

Contents

HEINOUS CRIME

THE NATURE OF HEINOUS CRIME

I have clear recollections of my first close encounter with someone who committed a truly heinous crime. In the fall of 1981, I was meeting with a group of inmates at the Missouri State Penitentiary in Jefferson City, what was then the state's principal maximum-security institution. I was working at the penitentiary part time as a social worker, in conjunction with my full-time duties as a professor at the University of Missouri School of Social Work. All the group members were serving lengthy sentences for serious crimes, including robbery, assault with a deadly weapon, and murder.

When I first met Dale Simpson, I barely noticed him.[1] He was simply part of the inmate crowd, and he made no special effort to stand out. It took quite some time for me to notice him enough to even wonder about him. In time my wonderment turned to preoccupation with his life, its special tragedy, and the broader subject of heinous crime.

Dale faithfully attended the discussion group that I facilitated each week at the penitentiary. He rarely spoke, but he was there. For months I knew nothing about Dale's past or the crimes of which he was convicted. Eventually, I learned a great deal about both but in a most unconventional way. One December evening, as I was about to leave the prison, Dale handed me a paper bag and muttered something like, "This is for you for the holidays—oh, and for your wife too." To my surprise, Dale had hand-crafted two leather wallets for us, customized with our respective initials. I was deeply touched—and puzzled. True, for months Dale had attended the weekly group meetings without exception. But I had virtually no sense of him; he was chronically silent. We had not engaged in a single conversation.

Not one. As I drove north on U.S. 63 toward Columbia, it dawned on me that this was Dale's way of reaching out, perhaps in the only way he could. The gesture, it turns out, was full of meaning.

I wrote Dale a short thank-you note and decided to use this as an opportunity to communicate one-on-one with him for the first time. After letting Dale know how much I appreciated his gift, I told him that I had been wondering about him for some time—about his silence, his participation in the group meetings, his state of mind. Little did I know what his reply would unleash, for him and for me.

Dale began his letter with some mundane comments about quitting his leathercraft business. He then began to respond to my questions.[2]

> You are correct in your observation. I have thoughts I would not share with others in the group. I have thoughts I would voice only to one or two others. I have thoughts I would share with no one. I am sure the others are much the same.

Dale and I continued to correspond about various aspects of his life and imprisonment. Several letters later Dale finally broached the subject of his crimes:

> We have finally come to the part I've been dreading. No matter how many times I think about that night I never quite accept that the person doing the killing was me. There's no doubt it was me, but it's hell to live with. I've been tripping [obsessing] the past two days, trying to figure out how to describe the murders to you. I really don't think I can. I don't think there is any way I could make you feel and see what I did.
>
> I guess I need to start with the purchase of the gun. I bought a .22 caliber pistol from a friend of mine maybe three or four weeks prior to the murders. I bought it for squirrel hunting. Many times you'll think about a squirrel and not kill it. I didn't like to see them suffer a slow death so I got the .22 to shoot them in the head with it. My father-in-law showed me how to club them to death, but that seemed worse than them suffering after being shot. We ate the dead squirrels. They are quite good.
>
> On the night of the murders I went to my friend Jim's house and after that went to my friend Kent's house. Kent was my best friend. We had worked together on two different jobs. I really got into drugs more after meeting Kent. We did a lot of partying together. We also went camping, hunting, stuff like that. Kent was about 24 or 25.
>
> Kent had some sort of nervous breakdown after he was married about a

year. He was on a speed run and something snapped. He was admitted to a hospital nut ward for a while. He lost his memory for a short period of time.

Marla was Kent's girlfriend after his divorce from his first wife. Marla had a daughter, Gina. I did not know Marla at all. She seemed like a nice person from the few times I was around her. Gina was a normal 4-year-old girl. Kent would baby-sit at times and I would drop in. We would play games with Gina until she wore us out. I could never purposely hurt a child, and I find Gina's death hard to cope with even after seven years.

I want you to have some idea as to my state of mind that night. Before arriving at Kent's I had taken eight to ten dime bags of PCP, I don't know how many mini whites, I did one hit of acid, drank a few beers, and smoked many joints. I started at about 1:00 or 2:00 P.M. at a friend's house in St. Charles. It was around 11:30 P.M. or a quarter to midnight when I got to Kent's apartment. It had to be around that time because Marla got off work at midnight, and she got home soon after I got there. I wasn't paying much attention to the time, I guess. If I had realized it was so close to midnight I would have probably never gone to Kent's, knowing Marla would be home. Not that she would say anything or get mad, but because it would have been bad manners. Kent and I were playing cards when Marla got home, or we were getting ready to, at least. Gina was still up so Marla went to put her to bed.

Kent and I did some more PCP while Marla put Gina to bed. We went back to our card game. Marla didn't want to play and sat on the couch reading. Gina got out of bed and came into the living room to tell Marla something, and they both went into the bedroom.

Kent asked me if I wanted something to drink and went into the kitchen. I walked behind him, and I pulled the pistol out and struck him on the head. *I have no idea why.* He turned around and I stepped back and shot him twice. Marla came running in to see what the noise was. She asked what had happened and I told her I just killed Kent. She asked why and I told her I didn't know.

The baby was crying and I remember telling Marla to put her to bed. Gina came in after Marla. Marla put Gina to bed and came back into the living room where I was. I made her strip and I tied her hands and feet. I then began to stab her. I don't remember how many times—10 or 12 maybe. It was sickening. Marla died. I then went and cut Gina's throat and that was even worse.

Scholars have struggled for centuries to understand the nature of crime and its diverse causes. They have focused on offenses as varied as crimes of violence, property crimes, financial and white-collar crimes, and drug-related crimes. Etiological theories abound, as do competing perspectives on the relative merits of punishment, incarceration, restitution and other forms of restorative justice, and rehabilitation.

Certainly, the general public is troubled by all forms of crime. No one wants to be the victim of automobile theft, rape, embezzlement, fraud, shoplifting, or robbery. But what the public is most concerned about, understandably, is that subclass of crime that is so horrific that it shocks our collective conscience: heinous crime. Heinous crimes—offenses that are "utterly reprehensible," according to *Random House Webster's College Dictionary* (1991)—are those that feature remarkably gruesome, odious circumstances that take one's breath away.

It is tempting to explain away all heinous crimes as the consequence of "sick" and "twisted" minds. In my experience, however, this is far too simplistic. In fact, many heinous crimes can be explained much more rationally.

The challenge, which is my focus here, is to examine heinous crimes comprehensively, explore their etiology, and weigh arguments for and against a range of possible responses.

Heinous crimes typically involve some kind of extraordinary personal injury or death. Prominent heinous crimes include murder, forcible rape and sexual molestation, aggravated or felonious assault, robbery, and first-degree arson. For purposes of this discussion these crimes are defined as follows:

- Murder: The unlawful killing of a human being that is willful, deliberate, malicious, and premeditated.
- Forcible rape (first-degree sexual assault): Unlawful sexual penetration (sexual intercourse, cunnilingus, fellatio, anal intercourse, or any other intrusion into the genital or anal openings of another person's body) of another person by the use of force or coercion (for example, by use of a weapon, physical violence, or intimidation).
- Child sexual molestation: Sexual penetration of a minor (sexual intercourse, cunnilingus, fellatio, anal intercourse, or any other intrusion into the genital or anal openings of another person's body) or unlawful sexual contact with a minor (sexual touching of a minor's genital or anal areas, groin, inner thigh, buttock, or the breast of a female) for the purpose of degrading or humiliating the minor or sexually gratifying the perpetrator.
- Aggravated or felony assault: A fierce assault upon another person with a dangerous weapon, acid, fire, or another dangerous substance that causes severe or aggravated bodily injury.

- Robbery: Forcible taking of property of another person by the use of violence.
- First-degree arson: The willful and malicious burning of an occupied dwelling or property used for another purpose. Includes causing, procuring, aiding, counseling, or creating by means of fire or explosion a substantial risk of serious physical harm to any person or to the property of a person that is occupied or in use for any purpose.

Each year thousands of people are the victims of heinous crime. According to Rennison and Rand (2002), 2.3 percent of people aged twelve and older were victims of violent crimes in 2002.[3] The FBI (2003) reports that in 2002 the United States recorded

- 1.4 million violent offenses (including forcible rape, aggravated assault, and robbery)
- 16,204 murders and non-negligent manslaughters
- 95,136 forcible rapes
- 420,637 robberies
- 894,348 aggravated assaults

And these figures include only known crimes that were reported to the police or resulted in arrest. They do not include large numbers of violent crimes that were not reported to the police for various reasons (often involving the victim's fear of retaliation or mistrust of the police).

Data from the National Crime Victimization Survey (NCVS) provide a broader perspective, including many crimes that were not reported to police. Each year the NCVS surveys approximately fifty thousand U.S. households, including nearly 100,000 people, concerning the frequency, characteristics, and consequences of criminal victimization. The survey focuses on a number of serious crimes, including rape, sexual assault, robbery, aggravated assault, theft, and household burglary. The NCVS reports that in 2001, 5.7 million U.S. residents aged twelve and older were victims of crimes of violence. The good news is that despite the data indicating large numbers of victims, in recent years reports of violent and serious crimes have declined. In 1973 individuals aged twelve and older reported about 48 violent crimes per 1,000 respondents. The comparable figure for 2001 was 25 violent crimes per 1,000, a decline of about 48 percent.

The historical trend for violent and serious crime, as reflected in reports of crimes to the police, is more complex. According to FBI (Uniform Crime Reports) data, in 1960 there were 160.9 violent crimes per 100,000

THE NATURE OF HEINOUS CRIME

people in the United States; by 2002 this rate had increased dramatically, to 494.6 per 100,000 (although the rate has declined steadily since the peak years of the early 1990s) (FBI 2003). The historical pattern for individual heinous crimes varies.

MURDER

Murders occur for diverse reasons and in diverse circumstances (Holmes and Holmes 1994). Key categories include partner homicide, murder of children, hate group homicide, mass murder, serial murder, terrorism, sex-related homicide, and children who murder. Occasionally, offenders murder a complete stranger without intent, as in the Texas case of a former nurse's aide who was convicted of murdering a homeless man with her car, after she hit him and drove home with his mangled body jammed in the windshield, leaving him to die in her garage after she spent a night of drinking, smoking marijuana, and taking the drug ecstasy (Brown 2003).

Partner Homicide

A significant percentage of murders involves intimate partners, including individuals who date, formerly dated, live together, are separated or divorced, or live as a married or common-law couple. Most murders involving domestic partners (married or otherwise) are committed by men and occur in the home.

Many women convicted of murder kill an abusive partner. The majority of such women are relatively young (midthirties and younger), mothers, unemployed, have relatively low levels of education, have previous arrest records and a history of suicide attempts, and are involved with men who have drug or alcohol problems (Holmes and Holmes 1994). Here is a representative example involving a young woman who was sentenced to twenty-five years in prison for the murder of her common-law husband:

> I was first married when I was 17. It wasn't a good marriage, and Tom and I got divorced in a year. But I already had Bobby [her son] when we broke up.
>
> Me and Jim met up a month after I left Tom. Jim was no good. He was a drug dealer and a cokehead. I knew that when I moved in with him, but I did it anyhow.

Things were a little rough, really, from the beginning. He hit me a few times, and I would just take it. He was good to Bobby, so I thought it would all turn out all right.

One night, he got high and started to hit on me. He then hit Bobby and threw him across the room against the wall. Something just snapped in me. It was one thing for him to hit me. I wasn't going to let him beat up on Bobby. So I went into the bedroom and got his gun and shot him. He moved, and I shot him again.

No, I'm not sorry. I miss my son. He's staying with my parents until I get out. I just couldn't let him beat up on Bobby. Could I? (Holmes and Holmes 1994:20–21)

Murder of Children

Murder of children often occurs in the context of a pattern of abusive behavior. Angry parents lose control and kill a child (Daro 1995). Less often, children are killed by a sadistic pedophile (child molester) or by a parent with a major mental illness (for example, a parent with paranoid schizophrenia whose auditory hallucinations tell the parent to kill the children). For example:

- On June 20, 2001, Andrea Yates confessed to drowning her five young children, aged six months to seven years, in a bathtub at their Houston home. Yates pleaded not guilty by reason of insanity.
- In the fall of 1994 Susan Smith appeared on national television and pleaded for the return of her two missing sons, aged three and one. Smith claimed that her children had been kidnapped in Union, South Carolina, by an African American carjacker. Smith eventually confessed to murdering her children, who were found strapped into their car seats in the family car, which was in a local lake.
- In the early 1980s Genene Jones, a pediatric nurse, worked in a new clinic in Kerrville, Texas. She had also worked at Bexar County (Texas) Medical Center Hospital. Both facilities had experienced suspicious deaths involving children. Jones was eventually convicted of murdering and injuring child patients by injecting them with muscle-relaxing drugs.
- On May 19, 1983, Diane Downs shot and killed one of her three children and wounded the other two. The children were three, seven, and eight years of age. At the time the children were sleeping in a car in Willamette Valley, Oregon. Downs originally claimed that the chil-

dren were shot by a man who was standing in a gravel road and asked
Downs for help.

- On July 24, 1984, two Mormon fundamentalists, Ron and Dan Lafferty, stabbed to death their fifteen-month-old niece with a ten-inch
boning knife (they also murdered the child's mother, their sister-in-
law). Dan Lafferty told his niece, whose mother resisted the brothers'
fundamentalist form of Mormonism, "I'm not sure what this is all
about, but apparently it's God's will that you leave this world. Perhaps
we can talk about it later" (Maslin 2003).
- In June 2003 a Peekskill, New York, man, Willie Williams, was arrested
and charged with attempted murder, accused of tossing his ten-
month-old daughter out the seventh-floor window of her mother's
apartment. According to police, Williams had barged into his ex-
girlfriend's apartment in an effort to persuade her to get back together with him. The baby fell eighty feet, crashing through tree branches
before landing on the ground ("Father Accused of Murder Attempt"
2003).

Hate Group Murder

Some murders are committed in the name of hate. Groups such as the Ku
Klux Klan (KKK), Skinheads, and the Identity Church have been known
to target members of the gay community and members of particular racial,
ethnic, or religious groups. Here are several prominent examples:

- In October 1998 Matthew Shepard, a twenty-one-year-old gay college
student, was kidnapped, robbed, and tied to a fence for nearly eighteen hours in near-freezing temperatures in Laramie, Wyoming, by
Russell Henderson and Aaron McKinney. Shepard died five days after
being rescued from the fence and lapsing into a coma.
- In 1984 white supremacists targeted a Jewish radio host in Denver,
Alan Berg. Members of "The Order," a supremacist group that declared
war on the United States and sought to establish a white homeland in
the Pacific Northwest, were linked to the slaying of Berg outside his
home.
- On December 31, 1993, Jim Lotter and Marvin Thomas Nissen murdered Brandon Teena, Lisa Lambert, and Philip De Vine in a farmhouse
in Richardson County, Nebraska. These multiple murders occurred
one week after Lotter and Nissen forcibly removed Brandon's pants
and made Lana Tisdel, whom Brandon had been dating since moving

to Falls City from Lincoln three weeks earlier, look at Brandon's body, to prove to Tisdel that her boyfriend was "really a woman." Brandon was a female-bodied twenty-year-old who passed, to some extent, as a man, without hormonal or surgical intervention. Given the name "Teena Renae Brandon" at birth, Brandon used a number of different gender-neutral and masculine names.

- In 1998 three white men with links to white supremacist groups offered James Byrd Jr., a black man, a ride in Jasper, Texas. The men beat Byrd severely, chained him to their pickup truck, and dragged him down the road until he was decapitated and dismembered.

Mass Murder

Mass murder is typically defined as the killing of four or more people at one time at one place by use of a gun, arson, or bomb in order to satisfy personal desires related to power, profit, revenge, sex, loyalty, or control (Fox and Levin 1998). Notorious examples include

- Charles Whitman, who climbed the University of Texas Tower on August 1, 1966, with an arsenal and began shooting indiscriminately at people in and around the tower. During the siege Whitman shot forty-five people, eventually killing sixteen. The night before, Whitman had killed his wife and mother.
- Richard Speck, who forced his way into a house for student nurses in a Chicago suburb in 1966 by brandishing a knife and gun. Speck herded the women into a bedroom, made them lie down, and tied them up. In an adjoining bedroom Speck raped, stabbed, and strangled the women one by one. Speck slashed the throats of two and stabbed and strangled all his victims.
- Charles Manson and a number of his followers, known as "The Family," who moved onto a ranch in southern California in 1968. About a year later Manson instructed Charles Watson, Patricia Krenwinkel, Linda Kasabian, and Susan Atkins to get knives and a change of clothes. On August 9, 1969, the four members of Manson's group drove to the residence of Sharon Tate, the pregnant wife of the film director Roman Polanski, and brutally murdered Tate and her guests Jay Sebring, Voytek Frykowski, Abigail Folger, and Steven Parent. Manson's group inflicted 102 stab wounds and shot one victim. The following morning members of Manson's group murdered Leno and Rosemary LaBianca, neighbors of Tate and Polanski.

- Eric Harris and Dylan Klebold, two students who walked into Columbine High School on April 20, 1999, tossed homemade bombs throughout the school, and fired from a large arsenal. They killed twelve students and one teacher before committing suicide.

The typical mass murderer is a white male in his late twenties or thirties who targets strangers near work or home (Fox and Levin 1998). Although we have no contemporary evidence of an epidemic of mass murder, these incidents understandably generate great anxiety and attract widespread media attention.

Serial Murder

Serial murder is typically defined as the killing of three people over more than thirty days in order to satisfy personal desires related to power, profit, revenge, sex, loyalty, or control (Fox and Levin 1998). Examples include a nurse who poisons patients in his efforts to play God; a man with symptoms of paranoid schizophrenia who murders prostitutes to punish them for their "sins"; an armed robber who executes store clerks after taking money from them at gunpoint; a mother who methodically kills her children; and a member of a satanic cult who sacrifices human beings as an initiation ritual. Notorious serial murderers include

- John Allen Muhammad, found guilty in 2003 of committing a series of murders in the Washington, D.C., area. Evidence presented at trial showed that Muhammad participated in a twenty-three-day shooting spree and was linked to eleven sniper slayings and five other shootings.
- Gary Leon Ridgway, a truck painter from the state of Washington, who pleaded guilty in 2003 to strangling forty-eight young women in the Seattle area during the Green River killing spree in the 1980s and 1990s. Ridgway, the deadliest serial killer in U.S. history, informed the court that he buried most of the bodies in clusters.
- Ted Bundy—typically described as handsome, charming, personable, and articulate—who confessed to killing twenty-eight women during the 1970s. Among the victims were college-age women in Seattle, Washington; Salt Lake City, Utah; Aspen, Colorado; and Tallahassee, Florida.
- David Berkowitz, known as the "Son of Sam," who terrorized New York City in the mid-1970s, killing six people and wounding seven others. Berkowitz, a former postal employee, left a note at one of his

shooting sites stating: "I am a monster. I am Son of Sam." Berkowitz said he acted on orders from his neighbor, Sam Carr; the orders, Berkowitz said, were transmitted to him through Carr's dog, a black Labrador.

- Jeffrey Dahmer, who first murdered a hitchhiker whom he took home for drinks. When the hitchhiker tried to leave, Dahmer crushed his head with a barbell, strangled him, and dismembered and buried his body. This was followed by a series of bizarre incidents in the 1980s when Dahmer raped, murdered, and dismembered his victims. Police eventually found the dissected remains of eleven victims in Dahmer's apartment. He was eventually charged with fifteen counts of murder and received fifteen consecutive life sentences.

- Henry Lee Lucas, who spent most of his teenage years in and out of jail for a series of burglaries around Richmond, Virginia. In 1960 Lucas and his seventy-four-year-old mother drank at a bar and got into a fierce argument. The argument continued when they returned home; Lucas's mother struck him with a broom, and Lucas stabbed her to death with a knife. In June 1983, after a number of other arrests following his release from prison, Lucas confessed to murdering seventy-seven women in nineteen states. The list eventually grew to hundreds of victims whom Lucas claimed he molested, raped (some after their death), mutilated, strangled, and bludgeoned to death, although experts eventually concluded that many of Lucas's confessions were bogus.

- Martha Beck and Raymond Fernandez, known as the "Lonely Hearts Killers." Beck was Fernandez's lover and co-conspirator; in the late 1940s the couple were responsible for the murders of as many as seventeen women, mostly older, unmarried women and widows.

- John Wayne Gacy, who was a member of the Junior Chamber of Commerce in Des Plaines, Illinois; a performing clown at neighborhood children's parties; a precinct captain in the local Democratic Party organization; and the owner of his own contracting business. In the 1970s Gacy buried the bodies of twenty-eight teenage boys after he murdered them; he was convicted of killing thirty-three boys, most of them teenage prostitutes.

- In the mid-1980s Charles Ng murdered eleven people in California. Investigations produced evidence of torture, burning, mutilation, and murder. Ng was convicted of killing six men, three women, and two baby boys. The murders were part of a kidnapping and sex slavery plot that Ng organized with his accomplice, Leonard Lake. Police discovered more than fifty pounds of bone fragments from the victims. Soon after the body parts were found, Ng was arrested in Canada for shooting a security guard.

Like mass murderers, the typical serial murderer is a white male in his late twenties or thirties who targets strangers near work or home. However, unlike mass murderers, the typical serial murderer deliberately and methodically kills people over an extended period of time (Fox and Levin 1998).

The historical record suggests that serial murders have increased significantly since 1970 (Fox and Levin 1998). Most victims are white, female, and very young or very old (especially when there is a sexual element). Victims are more likely to be male or members of an ethnic minority in cases where the murders are motivated by profit or the elimination of homosexuals. In recent years serial murders have accounted for fewer than 1 percent of homicides (Fox and Levin 1999).

Terrorism

A number of murders are politically motivated and committed as a form of terrorism. On the domestic front examples include murders committed by political activists, religious fanatics, and anti-abortion extremists. Here are several prominent examples:

- In the 1970s members of the Symbionese Liberation Army (SLA), a radical terrorist group, were responsible for murdering Marcus Foster, the schools superintendent of Oakland, California, and a bank customer, Myrna Lee Opsahl, who was shot during a robbery at Crocker National Bank in Carmichael, California. The SLA was formed in the early 1970s to address issues of prison reform, race, and poverty.
- On June 18, 1993, Ted Kaczynski, who became known as the Unabomber, mailed two similar bombs; each was contained in a wooden box and packed in a padded envelope. One reached the geneticist Charles Epstein of the University of California, San Francisco, at his home. Epstein opened the package, which had a false return address, and the bomb exploded. Shrapnel ripped through Epstein's chest and face; the bomb ripped off three of Epstein's fingers and broke his arm. The second bomb was mailed to David Gelernter, a computer science professor at Yale University. The explosion destroyed part of Gelernter's right hand, the sight in one eye, and the hearing in one ear. All told,

Kaczynski mailed sixteen bombs that killed three people and wounded twenty-three. Kaczynski was a loner who claimed that his vengeful acts were part of his anti-technology campaign.

- On February 26, 1993, six people died when a terrorist attempted to blow up New York City's World Trade Center. A man who entered the United States on an Iraqi passport, Ramzi Yousef, eventually became a suspect in the case after he was linked to a 1995 plot to blow up eleven commercial aircraft. Yousef was an Islamic militant who was determined to destroy Israel and related American interests.
- On April 19, 1995, Timothy McVeigh, a man obsessed with survivalism and enraged by various U.S. government policies, detonated a bomb outside an Oklahoma City federal office building. As a result of McVeigh's bomb blast, 168 people died—including babies and grandparents.
- On September 11, 2001, armed terrorists hijacked four aircraft that eventually flew into New York City's World Trade Center, the Pentagon in Washington, D.C., and a field in Pennsylvania, killing more than three thousand people.

Sex-related Homicide

Murders that include a sexual component or element take various forms. They include necrophilia (having sex with a dead body), cannibalism, and mutilation. Often these cases include elements of fantasy, stalking, and sexual sadism (Holmes and Holmes 1994). This remarkably detailed first-person account by "Jose M." provides a glimpse inside the mind of a sexual sadist and is illustrative of the central role of fantasy, predation, stalking, preoccupation, contempt, and persistence in many sex-related homicides:

> Five hours. Five long wretched hours had passed. And, still I had not a damn thing to show for the time or the tankful of gas I'd burned up while cruising the highways surrounding my suburban hometown. Off to the west, I could see the sun was already beginning to drop behind the dirty-grey hills which lay several miles away. Soon it would be dark outside, and I'd have but little choice but to call it quits for the day. And the thought of this was so infuriating to me that I smashed my fist against the thinly padded surface of the dashboard of my car as if this eruption of pointed violence could somehow exorcise the raging frustration that was threatening to consume me from within. I was feeling threatened. I was feeling betrayed.

I felt as if some cruel and unseen power was toying with me, taunting me, deliberately making my life miserable by denying me what I both craved and deserved.

Yet, for all my resolve to crush and destroy, my shoulders were sagging from the weight of disappointment as I gazed off to the west again. Through the side window of my car, I saw that the sun was now completely below the hilly horizon, and I knew in my gut that this day's hunt was doomed to end in failure. It would only be a matter of minutes before twilight was blanketed by darkness. And, from the countless hunting excursions I'd made before this day, I knew all too well that nightfall's arrival had a maddening way of sweeping my desired prey off the highways, driving them indoors, keeping them impossibly beyond my reach.

Snarling with bitter frustration while switching on my car's headlights, I forced myself to swallow the fact that it was time to call off the hunt. To be sure, I was completely determined to resume my search on the highways tomorrow afternoon, just as soon as I could yank myself away from work. But, tonight, I'd have no use for the jagged-edged knife or the two lengths of rope which were tucked, still hidden, inside my jacket. Nor would I get to enjoy any of the novel punishments that I'd been so eager to try out on some low-life wench. Instead I'd be returning to my home completely alone. Empty-handed. Without the prize I was so desperately craving.

And then it happened. Just when I was counting the day a total loss, all of my nerve-endings bounced alive with excitement at what was being illuminated by the bright glare of my headlights. I could hardly believe what I was now seeing on the shoulder of the road some fifty yards in front of me. But there, at long last, I'd found what I'd been searching for throughout the entire afternoon: a lone hitchhiker. Yellow-haired and slender. Unmistakably young. Very definitely female. And there she stood, in the traditional beseeching pose, her thumb jutting toward the sky from the end of her outstretched arm.

Instantly, even before I was braking to slow my car's forward momentum, my decision was made: the small, solitary figure on the roadside was MINE. She didn't know it yet, and it would be perhaps awhile before the truth came crashing down upon her. But she now belonged to me. Plain and simple. She was my possession. My personal property. She was ALL MINE—to do with as I damn well pleased.

"Hi! My name is Becky," the girl stated brightly, after swinging open the passenger-side door and ducking her head inside. She was a pretty thing, stylishly dressed, probably no more than sixteen or seventeen years old. "Can you give me a lift as far as the Oxmoor Mall?"

I was pleasantly surprised by her stated destination. The mall she'd named was very close to where I lived, which would certainly make things a lot easier on me when it came to luring her to my house. "The Oxmoor Mall? Why, I live only a few blocks from there," I answered truthfully, smiling amiably as I spoke. "So I guess you found yourself the right taxi. Hop on inside, little lady! I'll take you all the way there."

Thanking me several times over as she settled into the seat beside me, the small blonde drew the passenger-door shut, and I slowly pulled my car back onto the highway. I'd given her no cause for any alarm; of course, she was completely oblivious to the fact that my hatred and contempt for her was already a rising storm beneath my outward show of friendliness. For, even as I was smiling at her bubbling words of gratitude, my brain was conducting a fast and furious trial inside the privacy of my skull—and SHE was the one and only defendant. I was judging her. And I was condemning her. I was damning this girl named Becky to a fate that would soon have her wishing she'd never been born.

Jose managed to persuade Becky to accompany him to his house so they could smoke marijuana together:

"Well, Becky, here we are," I announced cheerfully, slowing my car in front of my house and turning onto the driveway. By design, the electrically powered door to my two car garage was already wide open. Also by design, the small control box for the garage-door closing mechanism was tucked inside my jacket pocket, out of my passenger's view. Allowing my car to glide all the way inside the garage, I braked to a stop, then casually turned off the engine and my headlights.

Instantly, it was difficult to see anything beyond one another's shadowy outline. And, before she could suspect that anything was amiss by this sudden darkness, I was reaching inside my pocket and pressing the button on the control box. Noisily, my automatic garage door started clanking down beside us.

At the sound of the lowering door, the little blonde turned her face toward the rear and then back towards me. As I had no further need to respond to her questions and waste words on a continuing charade, I was silent. Instead, I lashed out my right arm with a hard, back-handed motion, plowing my balled up fist into her stomach. With a loud whooshing sound, the blow knocked all the air out of her lungs, and she doubled over to get her breath. Then, while she struggled to get her breathing muscles working again, I switched on my car's inside light and knelt on the seat beside her crumpled form, a yard-long piece of rope already in my hand. In my heart, I was the scourge of justice to this worthless tramp, so it bothered me not at all to see her clutching and clawing at her midsection in such obvious pain. Indeed, there was something very reassuring about the sight of her agony. It was a good feeling, a heady feeling, an arousing feeling of complete control. Spurred to action by this frame of mind, I grabbed her by the hair and yanked her up into a sitting position, snapping her head back over the top of my car seat. Quickly, then, my knife was against her throat, and her mouth opening wide in an effort to let out a scream. Inside of a scream, however, only a strangled gasp could escape past her lips.

"OK, pay attention slut. If I hear one more sound out of you, or if you make even one false move, you're gonna be dead real quick. And I mean exactly what I say. Do you get that loud and clear?"

As best she could with my hand still gripping her hair, my little captive nodded her head up and down just as I expected she would. I pulled out two lengthy pieces of cloth from beneath my seat, using them to cover her eyes and mouth. When they were tied securely, I let her sit unmolested for a few minutes while I smoked a cigarette. Finally when I finished my cigarette, I flicked off the inside light and pushed open the door of my car. After grabbing her by the arm, then, I pushed the bitch toward me, hauling her across my seat as I stepped onto the floor of my garage. Although she was whimpering and trembling very noticeably, she made no attempt to struggle as I lifted her up and helped her onto her feet.

Becky began to struggle with Jose. Jose put Becky over his shoulder and carried her into the house and into his bedroom.

Reaching my bedroom I dumped and locked her inside my closet for the moment, then hurried back to my living room where I peered nervously through the windows. All was quiet in front of my house. I knew in my gut that everything was going to be just fine.

And everything was ready for my little Miss Becky. Indeed, everything had been set-up and laid-out since mid-afternoon when my gut had loudly informed me that this was the day to take up the righteous hunt. Propped against one wall, there was a huge, full-length mirror, where the young wench would watch her own reflection as she stripped away by her own hand all the skin-tight harlot's clothing that she wore and showed off so proudly. And, snaking onto the mattress from the four corners of the bed, there were individual ropes, one for each wrist and ankle, which would stretch her out and hold her down while she received her just desserts.

Then, on a low wooden table next to my bed, there rested some of the tools that would assist in her punishment: an assorted collection of heavy leather belts; large pieces of rough grit sandpaper; a plastic box of jagged-tooth metal clips; a bare, scorching-hot light bulb attached to a small, handheld lamp; and, as an added twist, a small container of mace—the very same stuff that females so often loved to spray in the face of their male superiors.

Yes, all of this was ready and waiting for my little captive, and I was seething with anticipation, my temples pounding with excitement, as I pulled back the sliding bolt on the outside of my closet. Slowly, then, I started inching open the door, my fist raised to deliver still another blow to her stomach if she was stupid enough to resist me yet again. And when I saw that her legs were still extended flat upon the closet floor, I threw the door wide open, almost howling out loud from my eagerness to get my hands on the little bitch.

Suddenly, then, I froze where I stood, sensing immediately that something was terribly, terribly wrong. For, instead of reacting to the sound of my presence, the small blonde remained slumped over to one side, looking like a broken doll, her head sagging motionless against her breast. Her skin was an unnatural pasty-white color and several drops of blood stained the snug material on her thigh. She was perfectly still, much too still; her body exhibiting not even a twitch or a flicker of movement. Then, at last, I noticed the swelling and dark discoloration on the front of her neck, and I remembered the sickening crunching sound I had heard in my garage. And, almost at once, I realized that her throat had been crushed on my weight pile and she would never move another muscle on her own again. She was dead.

As the reality of this sank quickly into my brain, my mind just seemed to snap in two, and I exploded into a violent rage. Savagely, I yanked the whore out of my closet by her hair and threw her body onto my bed where I ripped away all her clothes in tattered shreds. Then everything took on the quality of a frenetic but disjointed dream as I was beating her with my fists this moment, whipping her with a leather strap the next, and then stomping her with my feet the minute after that. I was utterly beyond control, snarling like a rabid animal, attacking with all the fury of a madman. And, as I continued to batter the harlot's naked corpse, I became more and more enraged that she would not thrash in agony beneath my frenzied blows, that she would not fill my bedroom with the sound of anguished female screams. Yet I could not stop and face my demons of despair. So I hit and whipped her and kicked her again and again, as if I could somehow smash my way into the world of the dead and make her suffer still.

Once again I had been tricked and fallen victim to a harlot's treachery. So despite all the difficulties of a night-time hunt, I made up my mind to get back onto the highway without delay. The evening was still young, anything was possible.

The minutes passed until they tallied more than an hour. And, once again, I was smiling as I pulled my car onto my driveway for the second time that evening. Pressing gently on the brake pedal, I rolled to a stop inside my open garage, then nonchalantly switched off my ignition and headlights. Instantly, everything was very dark, and I reached inside my jacket to depress the button on a small, rectangular plastic box. Right on cue, my garage door began lowering automatically, and I felt a familiar twist of sudden movement from the passenger seat to my right.

"Hey, what are you doing?" cried a youthful feminine voice. And, just as this shrill voice went silent, my garage door slammed with a boom.

I had not returned empty handed. And the night indeed would be redeemed. (Holmes and Holmes 1994:151–56)

Children Who Murder

Many children who kill strike out against an abusive parent. Some children who kill do so as part of ritualistic rites or as an angry gesture directed against a group of schoolmates and staff. A disproportionate percentage of homicides occurs in the context of gang conflict (Maxson 1999). Prominent examples include

- Kipland Kinkel, then fifteen, who returned to his school in Springfield, Oregon, on May 21, 1997, shortly after having been expelled for carrying a gun. Kinkel walked into the school cafeteria with a semiautomatic rifle and started shooting. He killed one student and wounded eight others, one of whom later died. Following the shooting police went to Kinkel's home and discovered that he had murdered both his parents.
- Jamie Rouse, seventeen, who walked into the Richland School in Giles County, Tennessee, with a .22-caliber Remington Viper on November 15, 1995. Rouse shot and killed one teacher and a student who crossed Rouse's path as he aimed his weapon at the school's football coach.
- Barry Loukaitis, fourteen, who walked into his algebra class in his Moses Lake, Washington, school on February 2, 1996, with a number of concealed weapons, including two pistols, ammunition, and a rifle. Loukaitis began shooting and killed two students and a teacher.

- Luke Woodham, sixteen, who flew into a rage when his girlfriend broke up with him. The Pearl, Mississippi, youngster slashed and stabbed his mother on October 1, 1997, and then went to school with a rifle and pistol. Woodham killed his ex-girlfriend and another girl before wounding seven other students.
- Andrew Wurst, fourteen, who brought a gun to his eighth-grade graduation dance in Edinboro, Pennsylvania, on April 24, 1998, and killed a popular teacher. Wurst then began shooting into the crowd, wounding another teacher and two classmates.
- Michael Carneal, fourteen, who brought a gun to his school in Paducah, Kentucky, on December 1, 1997. He opened fire on a group of students in a prayer group, killing three girls and wounding five other students.

HOMICIDE TRENDS

The homicide rate in the United States has fluctuated dramatically for more than two hundred years. Unfortunately, reliable statistics have been available only since about 1900. Various historical records show that murder rates were relatively low during the nineteenth century (Bureau of Justice Statistics 2003; Lane 1997; Smith and Zahn 1999). Available evidence suggests that at the beginning of the twentieth century, the homicide rate was approximately six homicides per 100,000 citizens; the rate had increased to 9.5 per 100,000 by the 1930s (Zahn and McCall 1999). During the twentieth century the homicide rate formed a U-shaped line on the graph, with higher rates during the early and latter years of the century and with relatively low rates during the late 1940s and the 1950s.

Although the rate for murder and non-negligent manslaughter has fluctuated during recent decades—peaking in 1980 at 10.2 per 100,000—the rate in 2002 (5.6 per 100,000) was only slightly higher than the 1960 rate (5.1 per 100,000). The homicide rate doubled from the mid-1960s to the late 1970s. After declining somewhat in the mid-1980s, the homicide rate again increased significantly in the late 1980s and early 1990s. Since then the rate has dropped dramatically.

Homicide rates have varied significantly across regions in the United States. For example, in 2000 the homicide rate for the eastern south-central region (Alabama, Kentucky, Mississippi, and Tennessee) was 7.0 per 100,000, while the rate for New England (Connecticut, Maine, Massachusetts, New Hampshire, Rhode Island, and Vermont) was two-thirds lower at 2.3 per 100,000 (the overall rate for the United States was 5.5 per 100,000).

Blacks are disproportionately represented as both homicide victims and offenders. Blacks are six times more likely to be victimized, and about eight times more likely to commit a homicide, than are whites (based on rates per 100,000). Blacks constitute about 12 percent of the U.S. population but about 50 percent of homicide victims and more than half of those arrested for homicide (Bureau of Justice Statistics 2003; Lane 1997).

Males make up about three-fourths of homicide victims and nearly 90 percent of those who commit homicide—a pattern that has persisted since the Middle Ages (Lane 1997). Males are three times more likely than females to be victims of homicide and almost eight times more likely to commit homicide.

About one-third of murder victims and almost half of offenders are younger than twenty-five. The homicide victimization rate for fourteen-to seventeen-year-olds increased almost 150 percent between 1985 and 1993. Since the late 1970s those aged eighteen to twenty-four have experienced the highest homicide victimization rates.

The number of teenagers arrested for murder increased significantly in the late 1980s, while homicide rates for older age groups declined. Juveniles are especially likely to be involved in homicides with multiple perpetrators and homicides that are gang related. Most minors who commit murder are males who have a history of poor school performance and grew up in chaotic home and family environments (Heide 1999).

Young black males are a particularly high-risk group. Victimization and offending rates for this group increased significantly in the late 1980s and early 1990s, although they have declined somewhat since (Fox and Zawitz 2003).

The number of homicides of children younger than five has generally increased since the early 1980s, although with some fluctuation. The victimization rate for black children younger than five has been significantly higher than for white children (in 2000 the rate for black children was 7.8 per 100,000, whereas it was 2.2 per 100,000 for white children). Of all children younger than five who were murdered between 1976 and 2000, 31 percent were killed by their father, 30 percent by their mother, 23 percent by a male acquaintance, 7 percent by another relative, and 3 percent by a stranger. Most murdered children were male and were killed by a male.

Between 1976 and 2000 about 5 percent of murder victims were elderly (sixty-five or older). Elderly men were slightly more likely to be homicide victims than elderly women. Overall, the homicide rate for elderly victims has been declining. In 1976 there were 5.4 elderly victims per 100,000 elderly; by 2000 the rate had dropped dramatically, to 1.9 per 100,000. Elderly people are significantly more likely to be murdered during the commission of a felony offense than are people in other age groups. For example, between 1976 and 2000, 26 percent of forty-year-old murder victims were killed during the commission of a felony; the comparable figure for sixty-five-year-old murder victims is about 43 percent, and about 64 percent for eighty-five-year-olds.

The percentage of homicides committed by spouses declined toward the end of the twentieth century (Browne, Williams, and Dutton 1999). In 1974 a little more than 12 percent of homicides involved spousal killing (including common-law relationships), and 23 percent of homicides involved family members. By 1994 the rates had dropped dramatically, with only 5 percent of homicides involving spousal killings and 12 percent involving family members.

Female murder victims are much more likely than male victims to be killed by an intimate. In recent years about one-third of female homicide victims, and 4 percent of male homicide victims, were killed by an intimate. Most assailants in these cases were spouses, and the weapon was most likely to be a gun. In murders involving intimate partners, women are twice as likely to be killed by men as men are to be killed by women (Browne, Williams, and Dutton 1999). The number of men killed by intimates (spouses, ex-spouses, boyfriends, girlfriends) declined significantly (by 68 percent) between 1976 and 2000. Rates of homicide among friends and acquaintances have also dropped significantly (Lane 1997).

The phenomenon of multiple homicides—cases involving serial and mass murder—is unique. Relatively few homicides involve multiple victims, but the percentage of homicides involving multiple victims has increased gradually since the 1980s, from just less than 3 percent of all homicides in 1976 to 4.1 percent in 2000. In 2000, 3 percent of homicides involved two victims, 0.5 percent involved three victims, 0.1 percent involved four victims, and 0.1 percent involved five or more victims (Fox and Zawitz 2002). Young offenders commit a disproportionate percentage of homicides involving multiple victims and offenders. In 2000, homicides involving multiple offenders represented 31 percent of homicides committed by offenders aged fourteen to seventeen, 25 percent of homicides committed by offenders aged eighteen to twenty-four, and 11 percent of homicides committed by offenders who were twenty-five and older.

The historical record shows clearly that murders in the United States increasingly involve strangers rather than spouses, partners, and family members. This is due in part to the increased number of homicides associated with drug trafficking and other drug-related crimes that involve strangers (such as robberies and burglaries committed by people under the influence, in order to obtain goods and money for drugs) (Fox and Zawitz 2002). Scholars have suggested a number of complex, interacting factors that account for the general decline in the nation's homicide rate and the diverse patterns among various demographic groups (Blumstein and Rosenfeld 1998; Lane 1997; Parker and Cartmill 1998; Sorenson and Berk 2001). They include

- Changes in police tactics and strategies, for example, the aggressive use of stop-and-frisk, community policing
- Stricter gun-control policies and procedures
- Assertive gang mediation programs
- More job opportunities during periods of economic expansion, which result in less violent crime involving guns and other dangerous weapons
- Increased incarceration (more people sentenced to prison and for longer terms) of serious offenders
- Aggressive drug control and enforcement
- Changes in alcohol consumption, which correlates with homicide rates

RAPE AND SEXUAL ASSAULT

Unfortunately, rape is as old as human existence. The word *rape* is derived from the Latin *rapere*, which means to steal, seize, or carry away (Warner 1980). Fortunately, many attitudes about rape have changed over time. Although we still have a long way to go, as a society we have moved some distance from blaming the victim, which was evident as far back as 500 B.C.E., when Herodotus, the Greek historian, observed that "the abduction of young women was not a lawful act, but it made no sense to make a fuss about it after the event" (Warner 1980:1).

Rape has been especially prominent during wars. According to legend, many Trojan women were raped by the victors at Troy. In 1453, the year that Constantinople fell, "the city's women and young girls were repeatedly and unmercifully raped by Ottoman troops numbering from 70,000 to 250,000. In more recent times, the 1937 fall of Nanking to the Japanese army resulted in a wholesale rape of its women—a sorry event that became known worldwide as the 'rape of Nanking'" (Warner 1980:2).

Rape also takes many forms. Many rapes involve individuals who have had a relationship with each other (so-called marital, partner, acquaintance, or date rape), whereas others involve complete strangers. Rape can also involve the brutal exploitation of young children who are victimized by highly organized international sex-trafficking rings (Landesman 2004). In recent years both scholars and mental health professionals have begun paying serious attention to male-on-male rape (Scarce 2001; Williams 2001).

The incidence of rape and sexual assault is notoriously difficult to measure. According to Russell and Bolen (2000), rape is the most under-reported violent crime in the United States. The first national survey to assess the prevalence of rape (Kilpatrick, Edmunds, and Seymour 1992) found that only 16 percent of victims of completed rape reported the assault to police (Russell and Bolen 2000). Russell's 1984 survey found that only 9.5 percent of all rape victims made police reports. According to Nelson, a therapist with extensive experience in working with sexual assault victims, about two-thirds of the women in his study "would absolutely not report this fact to an unknown interviewer" (1980:10). Interviews with victims reveal a number of reasons why they are reluctant to report these assaults to police (Russell 1975; Russell and Bolen 2000):

1. Victims are concerned about their family members' knowing they had been raped.
2. Victims are concerned that people will blame them for the attack.
3. Victims are concerned about nonrelatives' knowing about the rape.
4. Victims are concerned about having their names broadcast or published by the news media.
5. Many rape survivors anticipate sexist and demeaning treatment by police.
6. Many fear being retraumatized by going through the investigation and trial.
7. Many consider their rape to be a private matter and want to keep it that way.
8. Many find it too embarrassing to contemplate having to talk explicitly and repeatedly about the sexual details of their rape experience to police and court officials.
9. Many believe that no purpose will be served by reporting the rape because they have no faith in how the justice system deals with this crime and because victims anticipate a negative outcome.
10. Some fear retribution by the rapist and his friends; other victims fear their partner will seek retribution on their behalf.

11. Some victims want to try to forget the experience as soon as possible and not prolong the agony by a long, drawn-out trial.
12. Some choose not to report the rape for political reasons. For example, because of a sense of loyalty or guilt or fear of being "guilt-tripped" by other members of their ethnic community, minority women may be unwilling to report attackers who belong to their ethnic group.
13. Minority women who are raped by white men may opt not to report because they anticipate no justice from what these women regard as racist law enforcement and criminal justice systems.
14. Politically progressive middle-class white women may be unwilling to report minority men for the same reason.

Nonetheless, the incidence of forcible rape reported to the police has increased significantly. According to the FBI's Uniform Crime Reports (FBI 2003), the number of rapes known to the police per 100,000 was 9.6 in 1960, peaked in 1992 at 42.8, and declined some, to 32.0, in 2000. However, the National Crime Victimization Survey (Bureau of Justice Statistics 2003a) reports that the rape rate per 1,000 people aged twelve and older declined dramatically, from 2.5 in 1973 to 0.6 in 2001 (or 250 per 100,000 and 60 per 100,000, respectively). These conflicting trends suggest that the actual incidence of rape may have declined but that those who are victimized have become more willing to report the offense to police.

Most rape victims are aged twelve to twenty-four, with the highest rate of victimization for those aged sixteen to nineteen. The National Incident-based Reporting System (NIBRS)—which gathered data from twelve states—shows that between 1991 and 1996 approximately two-thirds of sexual assault victims were juveniles (younger than eighteen), about one-third (34 percent) were younger than twelve, and about 1 in 7 (14 percent) was younger than six (Bureau of Justice Statistics 2004).

Blacks and whites are victimized at approximately the same rate; however, residents of very low-income households (less than $7,500 per year) are victimized at a much higher rate than members of higher-income households. Women are seven times more likely than men to be raped or sexually assaulted.

Not surprisingly, rapists are a diverse group. Some use physical force and some rely primarily on threats. Some only rape their victims, and others commit rape in conjunction with other offenses, such as robbery, burglary, kidnapping, assault with a deadly weapon, and child abuse.

Rapists cover the age spectrum and come from all ethnic and cultural groups. As a group rapists tend to have relatively low levels of education and income. Many have children. According to one comprehensive assessment of various major studies of rapists,

The profile of the rapist is similar to that of a felon involved in crimes against persons or property. He is a young, poor male; probably belongs to an ethnic minority; and is likely to have used alcohol or drugs just prior to his crime. He has a history of previous criminal activity and may well merit the diagnostic label of antisocial personality, but he is unlikely to suffer from a psychotic disorder. He is distinct from other sex offenders . . . primarily because of his violent tendencies. (Wolfe and Baker 1980:275–76)

Diverse first-person accounts by rape victims provide a compelling glimpse into victims' profound sense of vulnerability and violation. The first commentary is by Stephanie Booth, who was raped during the summer before her senior year in high school by a man who sneaked up behind her as she was walking home alone after a party. Booth's (2001) self-blame and self-doubt, and the insensitive responses of others, are typical of many rape victims' experience:

It was almost midnight, but I never thought twice about walking at night, even in downtown Santa Fe; I knew the area like the back of my hand. I was behind the old Woolworth when I heard footsteps. Before I could turn around, I felt hands grabbing my hips.

"Shhh," someone whispered into my ear.

For a second I felt really relieved—maybe Drew [Stephanie's boyfriend, who was flirting with other girls during the party] wasn't such a jerk after all. But the next thing I knew, I was on my back in the middle of the alley. Someone was on top of me, pinning me down by the shoulders, jamming his knee between my legs. I couldn't see his face clearly in the dark, but he had on a white button-down shirt with the sleeves rolled up—that's the thing I saw and remembered the most.

I kicked and screamed and clawed at him, but he was so heavy on top of me that I couldn't move.

"Shhh," he kept telling me. "Shhh."

I kept screaming anyway, but no one heard me. He lifted my dress and pulled down my underwear. Then I heard him unbuckle his belt.

I don't know how long it was before he climbed off me. It felt like hours. He stood up and said, "Not bad." When I heard his voice, I thought, It's Marco [a man Stephanie met at the party].

I dragged myself up and stumbled into the street. Every part of me ached, and I was bleeding. Then I started screaming again as though I'd never stop.

The manager of a hotel heard me and helped me inside. A police officer came and drove me to the emergency room. I was crying and shaking, saying, "I'm so sorry!" to everyone. I was sure all of this was my fault: I shouldn't have worn that dress. I shouldn't have been walking alone.

"You should be able to walk down the street at any time and be safe," the rape crisis counselor at the hospital said. "No one deserves what you've been through."

Then why did I feel like such a slut? I'd never felt more humiliated in my life.

When my parents arrived, I couldn't look my dad in the eye. Drew showed up, too, and he was crying harder than I was, which made me feel even worse.

I was in the emergency room for hours. They did a "rape kit," sticking cotton swabs under my fingernails and pulling hair out of my head and my pubic area for evidence. My ripped, bloody clothes were put in a plastic bag for the police.

After the doctor examined me, I filled out a police report. My parents had gone to get the car, and Drew put his arm around me while I wrote down what had happened. But when I mentioned Marco, he told me to stop and take a deep breath: Wasn't it possible that I was really freaked out and looking for someone to blame?

I didn't know what or who to believe.

"It's over with," Drew said. "You're going to be OK. That's the important thing. Just don't think about it."

I didn't trust myself enough to press charges, so I let it go.

For weeks afterward, I was so depressed. I couldn't go to work, and I didn't want to talk to my friends. Every guy, whether I knew him or not, seemed like a threat. Even though it was summer, I hid beneath baggy jeans and sweatshirts.

The physical part of the rape was horrible, but the emotional agony was worse. Each time I had a nightmare about it, I woke up soaked in sweat. And I was so mad at myself—why couldn't I remember what happened? (121–22)

Marjorie Preston's (2001) reflections about being raped by a man who broke into her home in the middle of the night provide an all-too-common example of the ways in which rape can lead traumatized victims to cope by self-medicating:

I kissed my five-year-old daughter and waved good-bye as she walked toward the airport terminal, hand-in-hand with her father. They were off to Florida on vacation, and I looked forward to a few days alone. . . . A couple of hours later, I thought I was having a nightmare. I couldn't breathe, and began to thrash around, struggling to wake. Then, I felt gloved hands pressing hard on my eyes and mouth. A stranger stood over me in the dark, and I heard a man's soft voice at my ear. "Where's the money?" Though his hands covered my mouth, inside I was already screaming. *Oh no. Not this.* I had no money, but I told him he could take my car. "I don't want your car," he said. "Turn over."

That's when I panicked. "I can't," I said. "I'm too afraid. Please don't make me." But he was merciless. In the same soft voice, the stranger ordered me to do as he said, warning that if I saw his face, he would kill me. "I have a knife," he said.

Now I know how I'm going to die, I thought. *Tonight I'm going to be murdered in my bed.* I wondered who would find me. *And, oh God, who will tell my child?*

My attacker twisted my face into the mattress, and instinctively, I started talking about my little girl. "She's on vacation. She's coming home in a few days. I need to be here for her. She's only five." *Maybe he won't kill me if I can make him know me.*

"I won't hurt you," he said, as he started to rape me. Face down on the bed, I strained to catch a glimpse of him from the corner of my eye. *Remember everything*, I told myself. *If I live, I will be able to tell.*

I immediately called my parents, but there was no answer, so I dialed the police. Within minutes, half a dozen squad cars pulled into the driveway. Briefly, I told them what had happened, and they drove me to the hospital. I cried just once, remembering that my five-year-old often crept into the bed where I had just been raped. *Thank God she wasn't home*, I thought. . . .

At first, friends and family overwhelmed me with offers of help, but I refused them all. I felt oddly euphoric; I was alive, and impressed at how well I was handling this.

In reality, my emotions stopped functioning the night I was raped. Shock enabled me to think, and kept me from becoming hysterical. It may

have saved my life. But that sense of dissociation lingered, keeping me totally out of touch with my feelings. In fact, when newspapers carried stories
about the "brutal rape," I felt as if I were reading about someone else. . . .

For months afterward, sleep was difficult. I would bolt out of bed in the
middle of the night, heart racing, certain someone was in the room with
me. Tranquilizers kept the anxiety at bay; so did food. I would do anything
to divert my racing thoughts. Soon I added alcohol to the mix to help me
sleep. Between overeating and drinking too much, I gained sixty-seven
pounds in less than a year. It was strange to look in the mirror and see
myself so puffy, so haggard. I now realize I had made myself as unattractive
as possible to stave off any man's attention. If I was ugly, I would be safe.
(125–26)

Several research studies suggest that somewhere between 5 and 10 percent of all *reported* rapes in any given year involve male victims; the actual
incidence no doubt is higher, given evidence that male rape survivors are
much less likely to report their victimization than are female survivors
(Scarce 2001). Here is a summary of key research findings (Scarce 2001):

- A 1982 study of a sample of rape victims in South Carolina found that
  5.7 percent were male.
- Seven percent of the males in the Los Angeles Epidemiologic Catchment Area Project, conducted in 1987, reported having been sexually
  assaulted at least once as an adult.
- Of the 528 clients seen at the San Francisco Rape Treatment Center
  in 1990, 9.8 percent were male.
- In 1992 the Sexual Assault Center in Hartford, Connecticut, logged
  400 calls from men out of a total of 4,058 (9.9 percent).
- In 1993 the director of the Orange County Rape Crisis Center in
  North Carolina reported that 7 percent of the 147 victims served by
  her agency were men.
- In 1994 the Ohio Coalition on Sexual Assault polled rape crisis organizations in Ohio and found that 7 percent of the clients served were
  males.
- Approximately 10 percent of the rape survivors seen each year at a
  major hospital (Beth Israel in New York) are males (average number of
  survivors per year is 250).

Fred Pelka (1995), a male survivor of rape, offers rarely reported first-
person details of this phenomenon:

The man who raped me had a remarkable self-assurance which could only have come from practice. He picked me up just outside Cleveland, heading east in a van filled with construction equipment. That early morning in May I'd already spent a sleepless 24 hours trying to hitchhike from Oxford, Mississippi to Buffalo, New York, so it felt good when I was offered a ride through the western fringe of Pennsylvania. First, though, the driver told me he needed to stop along the way, to pick up some building supplies. We drove to a country club undergoing renovation, where I hung out with his co-workers while he signed for several boxes of equipment which we carried back to his van. Getting back onto the turnpike he told me about one more stop he had to make. . . .

The second building seemed deserted. We went up a flight of stairs, down a corridor into a side room. I looked around for the equipment he'd mentioned, and noticed him locking the door behind us. He slugged me before I could react, forced me down with his hands around my throat. As I began to lose consciousness I heard him say, "If you scream, if you make one wrong move, I'll kill you." The police told me later that the man who raped me was a suspect in the rapes of at least six other young men. During the assault his mood swung from vicious, when he promised to strangle me or break my neck, to self-pity, when he wept because we were both among "the wounded ones." In that enormous calm that comes after the acceptance of death, I wondered who would find my body. . . .

"I have a special place," the man who raped me said after a long while. "It's out in the country, where we can make all the noise we want." It seemed obvious what would happen to me once we arrived at "his special place," but I knew there was no hope for my survival as long as we stayed in that room. So I agreed to go with him to "the country." I promised not to try to escape. It is perhaps an indication of his fragile hold on reality that he believed me.

We walked back to his van and drove away. I waited until I saw some people, then jumped as we slowed to make a turn, rolling as I hit the pavement. I ran into the nearest building—a restaurant—just as patrons were finishing their lunch. Conversation stopped, and I was confronted by a roomful of people, forks raised in mid-bite, staring.

"I think you'd better call the police," I told the waitress. This was all I could say, placing my hands flat on the counter between us to control their trembling. She poured me a cup of black coffee. And then the police arrived.

The two detectives assigned to my case conformed to the good cop/bad cop archetype. The good cop told me how upset he'd seen "girls" become after being raped. "But you're a man, this shouldn't bother you." Later on he told me that the best thing to do would be to pull up my pants "and forget it ever happened." The bad cop asked me why my hair was so long, what was I doing hitchhiking at seven o'clock in the morning? Why were my clothes so dirty? Did I do drugs? Was I a troublemaker? . . .

Because I gave them such detailed information—the country club, the name painted on the side of his van—the detectives were able to locate my assailant not too many hours after I was brought into their precinct. The good cop asked, after I identified the rapist, whether I wanted to press charges. He explained how I'd have to return to Ohio to appear before a grand jury, and then return again for the trial, how the newspapers would publish my name, how little chance there was of a conviction.

"He says you seduced him," the good cop said. "So it's your word against his."

The bad cop glared at me when I told them there was no way I wanted any of this to be made public. "You mean," he fumed, "I wasted my whole afternoon on this shit?" Standing in front of me with an expression of disgust, he asked, "How do you think this makes me feel?"

By then it was getting dark. I hitchhiked the remaining 200 miles home, studying every movement of every man who offered me a ride. I arrived at my apartment after midnight, walking the last 10 miles. (250–53)

Another form of rape that is much more common than many realize is marital rape (Harmes 1999). According to Finkelhor and Yilo (1995):

The lack of public awareness about the reality of marital rape can be ascribed largely to the secrecy surrounding the problem, a secrecy maintained by most parties to the problem—victims, abusers, and the public at large. Victims are ashamed. Abusers help to keep them quiet and intimidated through threats, emotional blackmail, and a kind of "brainwashing" that makes the victims feel that they are to blame. The rest of us feel awkward, uncomfortable, and helpless to do anything, so we choose not to ask and not to hear.

Many women who have been sexually assaulted by their husbands do not see themselves as having been raped. They tend to view the assault as part of a marital conflict for which they are to blame, wondering if their own inadequacies as wives and partners are the root of the problem and believing their own sexual problems provoke their husbands. That their husbands are violent is taken by many to be a judgment on themselves: a judgment that they could not maintain a normal marriage or please their partners enough. A marital rape is part of a personal shame that they do not want others to know. (153)

Finkelhor and Yilo (1995) present a compelling description of a marital rape victim:

[Gretchen's husband] would often beat her and then would want to take her to bed. "I was too afraid to say no. I was afraid I'd get another beating." Sometimes she tried to push him away, but he just persisted until she relented. It got to the point where she was impossibly tense whenever he came near her. At the beginning of the relationship the violence was the worst part, but as the relationship went on, it was the forced sex and the sexual sadism that became the worst. . . . "He must have got some satisfaction from hurting me. There wasn't a time when sex with him wasn't violent or painful."

He beat her up and forced her to have sex with him two days before their son was born, and then again two days after. The doctor and nurse wanted to turn him over to the police, but she talked them out of it. "I had just had a baby and I didn't want to raise him by myself." One time she asked her family doctor what was wrong with her husband. "The only thing wrong with him is that he is a sex maniac," the doctor told her. "He needs to have his sexual satisfaction."

"He was possessed," she said in her interview with us, "really possessed. He had this idea that he wanted to pull the insides out of me." Once when he did this he began to hurt her so badly that she kicked him away with her feet. As he pulled away, his fist ripped her vagina, and she started to bleed "like somebody had turned the water on."

A doctor was called, but when he proved unable to stop the bleeding, she was sent to the hospital. As the doctor prepared to sew up the five-to-six-centimeter wound, the husband hit him for touching her genitals ("Nasty as he was, he was jealous, too"). Four blood transfusions later, she recovered, but the doctor told her she had been very, very lucky. Unfortunately, the doctor neither asked about the cause of the injury nor reported it to the police. (155)

CHILD SEXUAL MOLESTATION AND RAPE

As with some other heinous crimes, it is difficult to generate a precise estimate of the incidence of child sexual abuse and child rape. A key source of data is the National Incidence Studies of Child Abuse and Neglect

(NIS; Sedlak and Broadhurst 1996). The NIS is a congressionally mandated effort to collect data periodically on reported and unreported child abuse in the United States. The first NIS was conducted in 1979 and 1980, and the most recent NIS was conducted in 1993. The 1993 NIS was based on counts of cases obtained from a nationally representative sample of 42 counties and 842 agencies. It includes statistics from public child welfare agencies responsible for child abuse investigations and law enforcement agencies, as well as data from interviews with a group of mandated reporters (such as doctors, educators, child care providers, and mental health professionals). The cases include children who were seen by professionals who did not report their cases to child welfare authorities, youngsters whose cases were "screened out" by child welfare authorities without investigation, and children whose cases were investigated by child protective service agencies (Russell and Bolen 2000; Sedlak and Broadhurst 1996).

For purposes of the NIS, the sexual abuse of a child had to be "nonaccidental and avoidable" and was "perpetrated or permitted by a parent [or parent substitute such as a foster parent or step-parent] or caretaker" (Sedlak and Broadhurst 1996:2–9). The NIS distinguishes among three types of child sexual abuse:

- Intrusion: Evidence of oral, anal, or genital penile penetration or anal or genital digital or other penetration.
- Molestation with genital contact: Acts during which some form of actual genital contact had occurred, but there was no specific sign of intrusion.
- Other or unknown sexual abuse: This category was used for unspecified acts not known to have involved actual genital contact (e.g., fondling of breasts or buttocks, exposure) and for allegations concerning inadequate or inappropriate supervision of a child's voluntary sexual activities.

The 1993 NIS reports an estimated 300,200 sexually abused children, of whom 198,732 were female. The estimated incidence rate for female victims of child sexual abuse was 6.8 per 1,000, compared to 2.3 per 1,000 males (Russell and Bolen 2000; Sedlak and Broadhurst 1996).

For a number of years researchers have been concerned about the relatively narrow definition of child sexual abuse used in the NIS—abuse perpetrated by a child's parent, parent substitute, or caretaker. Several studies have found that only 5 to 7 percent of cases of child sexual abuse were perpetrated by a parent and that approximately 70 percent of child sexual abuse cases occurred outside the family (Russell 1983; Russell and Bolen 2000).[4] Russell and Bolen (2000) report that a number of other rigorous studies, using different methodological approaches, provide wide-ranging estimates of the incidence of child sexual abuse.

- Russell surveyed a probability sample of 930 women in San Francisco and found that significant numbers of women had been sexually abused as children (cited in Russell and Bolen 2000). Here is a summary of the percentage of women who answered each question affirmatively:

1. Before you turned 14, were you ever upset by anyone exposing their genitals? 27 percent
2. Did anyone ever try or succeed in having any kind of sexual intercourse with you against your wishes before you turned 14? 9 percent
3. In those years, did anyone ever try or succeed in getting you to touch their genitals against your wishes (besides anyone you've already mentioned)? 4.5 percent
4. Did anyone ever try or succeed in touching your breasts or genitals against your wishes before you turned 14 (besides anyone you've already mentioned)? 19 percent
5. Before you turned 14, did anyone ever feel you, grab you, or kiss you in a way you felt was sexually threatening (besides anyone you've already mentioned)? 14 percent

Russell found that 16 percent of the 930 women in the sample reported at least one experience of incestuous abuse—defined as any kind of exploitative sexual contact or attempted sexual contact that occurred between relatives, no matter how distant the relationship—before the victim turned eighteen. Almost one-third of the sample (31 percent) reported at least one experience of sexual abuse by a nonrelative before the victim turned eighteen.

- Kercher and McShane (1984) surveyed a random sample of two thousand adult Texas residents about their victimization as children. Kercher and McShane defined child sexual abuse as contacts or interactions between a child and an adult when the child is being used for the sexual stimulation of the perpetrator or another person. Child sexual abuse included "the obscene or pornographic photographing, filming or depiction of children for commercial or personal purposes, or the rape, molestation (fondling), incest, prostitution or other such forms of sexual exploitation of children under circumstances which indicate that the child's health or welfare is harmed or threatened thereby" (497). Their results show that 11 percent of the female respondents disclosed having been victims of sexual abuse in childhood.

• Wyatt (1985) used a different approach in her survey of 248 women in Los Angeles County. Her sample included roughly equal numbers of African American and white respondents aged eighteen to thirty-six. For Wyatt child sexual abuse included contacts of a sexual nature, "ranging from those involving non-body contact such as solicitation to engage in sexual behavior and exhibitionism, to those involving body contact such as fondling, intercourse and oral sex" (510). Wyatt did not find any significant differences in prevalence rates between the two ethnic groups. Wyatt found that 62 percent of her total sample reported at least one incident of sexual abuse before the age of eighteen; 21 percent of respondents reported at least one experience of incestuous abuse, and 32 percent reported at least one experience of extrafamilial child sexual abuse.

• Kilpatrick et al. (1985) surveyed 2,004 adult women in Charleston County, South Carolina. Fifty-five respondents (2.7 percent) reported having been victims of completed child molestation, and 37 women (1.8 percent) reported having been victims of attempted child molestation.

• In their survey of 1,645 women in Los Angeles, Siegel et al. (1987) found that 6.8 percent had been sexually abused before the women were sixteen. Women in the sample responded to the question "In your lifetime, has anyone ever tried to pressure or force you to have sexual contact? By sexual contact I mean their touching your sexual parts, your touching their sexual parts, or sexual intercourse."

• Lewis conducted a national survey of adult Americans, designed to determine the prevalence of child sexual abuse. The sample included 2,625 adults aged eighteen and older within the United States, 1,481 (56 percent) of whom were women. Slightly more than one-fourth of the women (27 percent) disclosed at least one experience of child sexual abuse (sexual intercourse, fondling, taking nude photographs, oral sex, sodomy, and so on). According to Russell and Bolen's (2000) secondary analysis of these results, 8 percent of the women respondents reported having been victimized by rape or attempted rape in childhood.

• Murphy (1991) surveyed 777 adult women in Minnesota about their victimization. Eighteen percent of the sample had been sexually abused before age eighteen. Child sexual abuse was defined as an adult's exposing himself to the child; an adult's touching or fondling the breasts or sexual parts of the child's body; having to touch an adult's body in a sexual way;

an adult's sexually attacking the child or forcing the child to have sexual intercourse; an adult's taking nude photographs of the child or performing a sexual act in the child's presence; and experiencing oral or anal sex with an adult.

• As part of the National Comorbidity Survey, Kessler et al. (1995) surveyed 3,065 women concerning their victimization as children. About 1 in 8 (12.3 percent) reported having been sexually abused.

• In 1995 the Gallup Organization interviewed a national sample of more than six hundred mothers and mother substitutes. As part of a more comprehensive interview on the subject of disciplining children, respondents were asked two key questions related to their own victimization: (1) "Before the age of 18, were you personally ever touched in a sexual way by an adult or other child, when you did not want to be touched that way, or were you ever forced to touch an adult or older child in a sexual way—including anyone who was a member of your family, or anyone outside your family?" (2) "Before the age of 18, were you ever forced to have sex by an adult or older child—including anyone who was a member of your family, or anyone outside your family?" Thirty percent of the mothers reported at least one experience of childhood sexual abuse before they were eighteen (Moore, Gallup, and Schussel 1995).

What this collection of studies shows, sadly, is that many children are victims of various forms of sexual abuse. A number of major studies have focused explicitly on the severest form of child sexual abuse—rape:

• Russell's (1983) survey of 930 women in San Francisco found that 6.6 percent of respondents reported that they were forcibly raped (penile penetration) as children. Nearly 1 in 7 respondents (13.9 percent) was a victim of attempted penile penetration. Using a broader definition of rape for female children and adolescents that includes unforced acts of oral, anal, and penile-vaginal penetration, the prevalence rate for child rape was 20.6 percent (cited in Russell and Bolen 2000).

• Analysis of data from the Los Angeles Times Poll, which included a national probability sample of women, found that 13.8 percent of respondents were victims of child rape (Finkelhor et al. 1990, cited in Russell and Bolen 2000).

• Analysis of data from a national sample of 4,008 women found that 8.5 percent were forcibly raped as children. Twenty-nine percent of all rapes perpetrated against these women—whether they were adults or children—occurred when the respondents were younger than eleven, and nearly one-third (32 percent) occurred when victims were aged eleven to seventeen (Kilpatrick et al. 1992, cited in Saunders et al. 1999).

• The National Survey of Family Growth documented a prevalence rate for completed forcible child rape of 11.8 percent. Approximately 6 percent of the 10,847 women respondents reported that they were forced to have intercourse before they were fifteen (Abma et al. 1997; Russell and Bolen 2000).

• The 1995 Gallup Organization survey of a national sample of more than six hundred mothers found that 12 percent of respondents said they had been victims of completed child rape (Moore, Gallup, and Schussel 1995).

• Russell and Bolen's (2000) secondary analysis of data, obtained from the National Violence Against Women Survey (Tjaden and Thoennes 1998), suggests a 9.5 percent prevalence rate for completed and/or attempted forcible rape of respondents when they were children (younger than eighteen). The prevalence rate for children younger than eleven was 3.8 percent.

AGGRAVATED ASSAULT

FBI data show that arrests for aggravated assault have increased dramatically, from a rate of 90.3 per 100,000 in 1971 to 165.5 per 100,000 in 2002 (FBI 2003). However, according to the National Crime Victimization Survey, reports of aggravated assault have declined from 12.5 per 1,000 in 1973 to 5.3 in 2001 (or 1,250 per 100,000 and 530 per 100,000, respectively). More specifically, rates declined between the mid-1970s and the mid-1980s, leveled off until about 1990, increased between 1990 and 1993, and then declined between 1994 and today. That is, according to these data, the number of reports has declined, but the arrest rate has increased.

Data from the National Crime Victimization Survey (Rennison and Rand 2003) show that males are much more likely to be the victim of an aggravated assault (6.5 per 1,000 in 2001) than females (4.2 per 1,000). Blacks are more likely to be victimized (8.1 per 1,000) than whites (5.1 per 1,000) or other races (2.6 per 1,000). General population data show that people aged sixteen to nineteen are at greatest risk of being victimized (12.3 per 1,000); the elderly, including those sixty-five and older, are the least likely to be victimized (0.4 per 1,000) (FBI 2003). Overall, in 2001 the aggravated assault victimization rate was 5.3 per 1,000; incidents involving personal injury occurred at the rate of 1.7 per 1,000, and incidents involving threats with a weapon occurred at the rate of 3.6 per 1,000 (Rennison 2002).

Offenders commit aggravated assaults for a wide range of reasons. As the cases that follow illustrate, assaults may occur as acts of revenge (for example, in the context of domestic disputes or between hostile neighbors), while under the influence of drugs or alcohol, or while an offender is committing another crime (for example, when an offender assaults an uncooperative victim during a robbery).[5]

• Alvan L. and Belinda L. had lived together for nearly three years. The couple met when they worked at a local jewelry factory; they started living together after Belinda became pregnant. One evening Alvan started screaming at Belinda after she returned to their apartment from having dinner with a friend. Alvan accused Belinda of having an affair with a co-worker. During their shouting match Alvan grabbed Belinda by the neck, threw her onto the living room sofa, punched her in the face, and began to strangle her. Neighbors heard Belinda screaming and called the police. Belinda lost consciousness and was rushed to the hospital with severe head injuries.

• Natalie S., forty-two, lived with her eighty-year-old mother, Alma V. Natalie had divorced her husband six years earlier and moved in with her mother. Natalie and Alma often argued. One afternoon Natalie, who was alcoholic, returned to their apartment inebriated after spending several hours drinking at a nearby bar. Alma began to chastise Natalie for drinking too much. Natalie flew into a rage and pushed her mother into the kitchen table with considerable force. Alma fell, broke her hip, and fractured her skull.

• Jeremy L. was a heroin addict. He cruised a suburban neighborhood on his stolen motor scooter, looking for a house to break into so he could steal goods, sell them, and buy drugs. Jeremy settled on a ranch house that looked unoccupied and was nestled in a cul-de-sac. He entered the house through a den window and began to ransack drawers, looking for jewelry. As he was about to leave, one of the homeowners walked through the front door and confronted Jeremy. Jeremy panicked, grabbed a fireplace utensil, and smashed it against the homeowner's head before fleeing.

ROBBERY

FBI data show that the number of robbery arrests has declined over time, from a rate of 65.4 per 100,000 in 1960 to 37.7 per 100,000 in 2002 (FBI 2003). Robbery rates increased between 1978 and 1981, declined up to 1985, then rose until 1994, declined until 1997, and have leveled off since. Data from the National Crime Victimization Survey (Rennison and

Rand 2003) suggest that the incidence of robbery of individuals aged twelve and older has declined from 6.7 per 1,000 in 1973 to 2.8 in 2001. Blacks are somewhat more likely to be robbed (3.6 per 1,000) than whites (2.6 per 1,000) and members of other races (2.4 per 1,000). Males are much more likely to be robbed (3.8 per 1,000) than females (1.7 per 1,000). Adolescents aged sixteen to nineteen have the highest rate of victimization (6.4 per 1,000); those aged fifty and older have the lowest (approximately 1.2 per 1,000).

Offenders commit robberies for various reasons. As the cases that follow illustrate, some robberies occur because addicts need money to pay for drugs or because offenders are in desperate need of money to pay off a debt or to pay the rent. Some offenders commit robberies for no reason other than greed, that is, to obtain money or valuables to enhance the quality of their lives.

- Lawrence M., a heroin addict, was on probation after his conviction on shoplifting charges. As a condition of probation Lawrence was required to attend drug counseling and a methadone treatment program. Lawrence M. relapsed and desperately needed heroin. One afternoon he robbed a businesswoman as she walked to the parking garage near her office building. He stole the woman's pocketbook, gold necklace, and gold bracelet.
- Marissa D. was recently reunited with her two children, who had been living in foster care. A family court judge had placed the children after Marissa was convicted of possessing and selling drugs. For months Marissa participated in a drug treatment program in an effort to regain custody of her children. About five months after the family was reunited, Marissa's landlord evicted her for nonpayment of rent. She feared that she would again lose custody of her children if she did not have a permanent residence. In desperation she robbed a local convenience store, using a handgun, to get cash to pay her landlord. The convenience store clerk recognized Marissa and contacted the police.
- Evan P., who owned a fitness club, liked the fast life. He "needed" to eat in the fanciest restaurants, have the latest car, and wear the finest clothes. About two years after he opened the fitness club, city inspectors closed it down after Evan fell behind on his property taxes and failed to install mandated fire protection equipment. Evan tried to no avail to negotiate an agreement with the city that would allow him to continue operating his business. Shortly thereafter Evan fell behind in his car and home mortgage payments. In a fit of desperation he robbed a local bank.

FIRST-DEGREE ARSON

The number of arsons that involve incendiary fires or fires of suspicious origin has declined significantly, from 9.0 per 100,000 in 1979 to 5.9 per 100,000 in 2000. Nonetheless, arson is the second leading cause of death by fire in the United States, second only to smoking that leads to fire (for example, smoking in bed, falling asleep, and inadvertently setting a mattress on fire). According to the National Fire Protection Association (Karter 2001), in 2000 the United States had 75,000 incendiary fires and 29,500 fires of suspicious origin. Fire investigators refer to a fire as an "incendiary fire" if they have solid evidence that it was arson—a can of gasoline, the torching mechanism used, and so on. A fire of "suspicious origin" is just that—not enough evidence to prove it was arson but enough to suspect strongly that it was. The number of arson-related deaths has dropped only modestly in recent years, from 635 in 1977 to 505 in 2000. Most arsons are committed by relatively young people; nearly three-fifths of such fires were set by individuals younger than twenty-one. According to the National Fire Protection Association (2003),

- Arson killed more than five hundred Americans in 2000, an increase of 36.5 percent from 1999.
- About 25 percent of all fires are arson.
- In 2000 fire officials found that about seventy-five thousand structure fires were arson or suspected they were arson.
- Incendiary or suspicious structure fires resulted in $1.34 billion in property damage (15.7 percent of all structure property loss).
- Vehicle fires of incendiary or suspicious origin numbered 46,500 and accounted for $186 million in property damage.

People commit arson for various reasons. As these cases illustrate, some acts of arson are acts of revenge, whereas others are motivated by profit. In some instances the arsonist sets a fire so that he can perform heroic, life-saving feats for victims.

- Marvin N. had worked at an automobile shop for nearly seven years. He recently had gotten into several heated arguments with the owner's son, Gary S., who had just stepped into a key supervisory position. Gary fired Marvin, and asked him for his set of office keys, after he allegedly conspired to turn a number of employees against Gary. That night, just before midnight, someone sprinkled gasoline around the perimeter of the automobile shop and set it on fire. The shop was a total loss. About three weeks later Marvin was arrested and confessed to the arson charge in exchange for a reduced sentence.

• Lionel P. owned a thriving dry-cleaning business; he was also a serious gambler. He spent many hours each week at a local casino, mostly playing blackjack. After one particularly bad stretch, Lionel P. owed about $213,000 to a loan shark. Lionel P. quickly ran out of options; he could no longer borrow money from credible financial institutions or generous family members. Eventually, he hired a local teenager to set fire to the dry-cleaning business. Lionel P. planned to use the insurance proceeds to pay off his gambling debts.

• Arnold H., thirty-nine, was fascinated by fires, fire fighters, and fire trucks. His IQ was about 65 (mild retardation), and he would often listen to his police scanner to find the locations of active fires. When possible, Arnold would stand near the fire site and watch the fire fighters attempt to extinguish the flames. One Saturday night Arnold started a fire in a four-unit tenement near his parents' house. Soon after the fire started, Arnold ran up to the house and screamed for its occupants to leave as quickly as possible. He then ran into one of the first-floor apartments and escorted two young children and their dog out of the building. For two days Arnold was heralded as a hero and was interviewed by newspaper, radio, and television reporters. However, several days after the fire Arnold was named as a suspect, based primarily on the eyewitness accounts of two neighborhood residents who had seen Arnold run from the back entrance of the building shortly before it went up in flames.

Heinous crimes come in all shapes and sizes. By definition, all heinous crimes are serious. In recent years, especially since the early 1990s, when violent crime peaked, the number of violent crimes has declined. Nonetheless, heinous crime rates are far too high and continue to generate widespread anxiety and fear among the general public.

In this chapter I have defined the various types of heinous crimes, provided an overview of pertinent statistics and trends, and illustrated key heinous crimes. In the next chapter I discuss why people commit heinous crimes—what criminologists refer to as etiological theory. This will set the stage for the subsequent discussion of meaningful ways for a society to respond to heinous crimes.

2

HEINOUS CRIME: CAUSES AND CASES

Why people commit heinous crimes defies simple explanation. Rather, based on decades of research and experience, we are able to identify a series of factors that, independently and in concert, help us to understand why people commit heinous crimes. Such understanding is essential in order for us to fashion thoughtful, principled, and just responses to heinous crime.

AN OVERVIEW OF ETIOLOGICAL THEORY

Theories of crime causation—known as etiological theories—have evolved and matured since their origin in the mideighteenth century.[1] These theories have ranged from narrowly focused speculation about the influence of genetic and biochemical factors on criminal behavior to broad analyses of the structural implications of market economies.

In general, theories of crime causation fall into three groups. The first includes theories that focus on the role of the "free will" that some individuals exercise when they decide to commit crimes. From this perspective, generally known as the classical point of view, criminals make conscious choices to commit heinous crimes; thus prevention and treatment programs, public policy, and judicial responses should assume that people have the capacity and inclination to make deliberate, rational choices about whether to engage in criminal conduct. Put simply, classical theorists argue that criminal conduct reflects offenders' free will, which is motivated by their self-centered, hedonistic pursuit of pleasure. According to the classical view, criminals commit murder, rape, aggravated assault, child molestation, robbery, and arson because of the pleasurable sensations and personal gains that they associate with these offenses. From this perspective, these heinous acts are the product of purposeful, conscious, and rational choices that take into consideration the tradeoffs involved in pleasurable consequences and the various risks involved in the commission of heinous crimes, such as physical injury, legal expenses, court fines, and imprisonment. Hence, the classical view regards heinous crime as the product of a cost-benefit calculus by the offender.

The earliest serious writings on the classical perspective began with Cesare Beccaria's publication of *On Crime and Punishments* (1764). Early adherents of classical theory included the well-known nineteenth-century British philosopher Jeremy Bentham (1748–1832), who argued that human nature leads people to act in a way that produces the greatest ratio of good to evil (the so-called utilitarian perspective).

The second prominent school of thought approaches etiological issues from a fundamentally different vantage point. From this perspective, generally known as the positivist point of view, people commit heinous crimes as a result of a variety of factors that are entirely or largely beyond their personal control. Typical positivist theories assert that a variety of environmental, geographic, economic, psychological, cultural, and biological factors cause crime. For example, in the nineteenth century, Cesare Lombroso argued in *The Criminal Man* (1876, 1911) that criminals have distinguishing physical stigmata, or characteristics, in the form of unique facial features, cheekbones, arches, palm lines, and so on. Also in the nineteenth century, Karl Marx prefigured the economic theory of crime, which claims that capitalism creates inequality, poverty, and forms of social conflict that lead to crime (for a prototypical application of Marxist concepts to the analysis of crime, see Willem Bonger, *Criminality and Economic Conditions* [1910]). During this same general period Charles Darwin, in *On the Origin of Species* (1859), introduced theories of evolution and natural selection that provided the conceptual foundation for biological positivism, the belief that factors such as genetics, body type, and biochemistry cause criminal behavior. Other noteworthy positivist views include the claims of Robert Dugdale (1877) and Henry Goddard (1912) about the hereditary nature of criminality based on their analyses of generations of criminals in the notorious Jukes and Kallikak families; the twentieth-century hypotheses of Ernst Kretschmer (1926) and Sheldon and Eleanor Glueck (1956) about the correlation between distinct body types and personality traits of criminals; and the conclusions of Charles Goring (1913) about the prominence of feeblemindedness among criminals.

A wide range of twentieth-century sociological theories of crime—which are largely positivistic in nature—have also been highly influential. Among the best-known and most-cited perspectives are the so-called anomie theories, which focus on the breakdown (or lack) of social norms that constrain criminal behavior (Durkheim 1951, 1964). The concept of anomie provided a conceptual anchor for a number of prominent theories, including Robert Merton's (1957) "strain theory," according to which crime is a by-product of society's failure to provide everyone with the means to attain the material goods to which they aspire; Richard Cloward and Lloyd Ohlin's (1960) "differential opportunity" theory, which emphasizes offenders' selective use of "illegitimate opportunity structures" to get what they want (social status, goods, and so on) because these items either are or seem to be unattainable through more legitimate avenues; and Albert Cohen's (1955) "subculture theory," which focuses on the reactions of lower social class members to middle-class values and aspirations.

Other prominent sociological theories include social process theories, labeling theories, and radical theories. Social process theories view criminal behavior as a product of learned behavior, typically learned through cultural norms (Hagan 1990). Prominent social process theories include Robert Park's (1952) emphasis on "natural areas," or subcommunities, that produce crime and Ernest Burgess's (1925) discussion of geographic "zones of transition" that breed crime; Clifford Shaw and Henry McKay's (1942) "social disorganization theory," which was based on the authors' extensive use of maps and arrest statistics to find the ecological patterns associated with crime; Edwin Sutherland's (1947) "differential association theory," which argues that individuals who have extensive contact with people who engage in deviant behavior are themselves more likely to engage in criminal conduct because of their opportunity to learn these behaviors; and Walter Miller's (1958) "focal concerns theory," which identifies a number of supposed preoccupations in lower-class cultures: trouble, toughness, smartness, excitement, fate, and autonomy.

Labeling theory emerged in the 1960s, based on the argument that individuals engage in criminal behavior in large part because the broader society has labeled them as deviant. That is, many crimes are not inherently deviant; rather, the broader society has labeled them as such and, in so doing, exacerbates criminal conduct. Key assumptions of labeling theory are that no act is inherently criminal in nature; those in positions of authority (for example, legislators and administrators) define what is and is not criminal; the act of being caught sets the labeling process in motion; certain demographic traits (such as age, social class, gender, race/ethnicity) increase the likelihood of one's being labeled criminal; and the labeling process strengthens offenders' identification as criminal as well as their "rejection of the rejectors" (Hagan 1990:192; see also Becker 1963, 1964; Lemert 1951; Schrag 1971; Schur 1969, 1971; Tannenbaum 1938).

Perhaps the best-known labeling theory is based on Edwin Lemert's (1967) distinction between "primary deviance" and "secondary deviance." *Primary deviance* refers to the initial offense itself, such as molesting a child, assaulting a domestic partner, or robbing a storeowner. *Secondary deviance* entails the formation of a deviant or criminal identity as a result of being caught by the police, prosecuted, convicted, incarcerated, and otherwise processed as a deviant. According to labeling theory, this new identity greatly increases the likelihood that the individual will continue to engage in criminal activity (a form of self-fulfilling prophecy).

In contrast, radical theory—sometimes known as Marxist theory— is rooted in the belief that capitalism and the forces of free-market economies create the conditions for criminal behavior. Richard Quinney (1970, 1974, 1977, 1979) and William Chambliss (1975) argue forceful- ly that in capitalist nations the criminal law is an instrument of the privi- leged elite ruling class, and the elite use it to maintain social order by con- trolling and oppressing those who are poor and otherwise subordinate (the proletariat). According to Anthony Platt (1974), a noted radical theorist, criminologists have become conservative handmaidens of state repression.

The third major group of theories incorporates elements of the clas- sical and positivist perspectives. From this perspective—which has been dubbed the neoclassical view, the mixed view, and soft determinism— crime is best understood as the product of, to varying degrees and in dif- ferent proportions, both individual choice and structural or environmental circumstances that are largely or entirely beyond the control of the indi- vidual. A prototypical example of this perspective is David Matza's (1964) "drift theory." Matza argues that while outside forces determine human behavior to some extent, individuals nonetheless have the capac- ity to exercise some degree of free will. Matza argues that offenders tend to drift between criminal and conventional behavior and rationalize (or, to use Matza's term, *neutralize*) their conduct by blaming it on their toxic home life or communities, denying that their actions have harmed their victims, condemning people in positions of authority as corrupt, and so on.

Other prominent examples of the mixed view include so-called social control theories. Social control theories typically focus on the influence of social institutions and norms as mechanisms that contain crime. Walter

Reckless (1961), for example, advanced the so-called containment theory, arguing that crime is the result of flawed external conditions (for example, poverty, chaotic neighborhoods and families, unemployment) and internal conditions (for example, poor self-concept and impulse control). Travis Hirschi (1969), in his discussion of his "social bond theory," stresses the importance of social connections among individuals and family, friends, schools, employers, neighbors, and religious institutions as mechanisms that enhance the ability of an individual to engage in law-abiding behavior and avoid criminal behavior.

THE CAUSES OF HEINOUS CRIME: AN OVERVIEW OF TYPOLOGIES

Criminologists have drawn on these diverse etiological perspectives to generate various conceptually based typologies of criminal behavior (see, for example, Barkan 2000; Bernard, Vold, and Snipes 2002; Crutchfield, Kubrin, and Bridges 2000; Gottfredson and Hirschi 1990; Reid 1999; Schmalleger 2001; Sheley 2000; Siegel 2000; Wilson and Petersilia 2002). These typologies, which are an effort to summarize patterns of criminal behavior, are of two types. The first group focuses on different causal, or etiological, theories, to explain why people commit crimes by exploring the relevance of, for example, psychological, biological, economic, political, community, and familial factors. The second group focuses on different types or categories of offenders, based on the patterns of their criminal activities and behaviors. Gibbons (1982), for example, distinguishes among a wide variety of "criminal role careers," such as professional thieves, embezzlers, white-collar criminals, naive check forgers, semiprofessional property offenders, violent sex offenders, amateur shoplifters, addicts, and so on. Clinard and Quinney (1973; also see Clinard, Quinney, and Wildeman 1994) differentiate groups by types of criminal behavior: violent personal crime, occasional property crime, occupational crime, corporate crime, political crime, public order crime (victimless crimes such as prostitution and public drunkenness), conventional crime, organized crime, and professional crime. Glaser (1978) also classifies offenders according to types of crime: predatory crime, illegal performance offenses (vagrancy, disorderly conduct), illegal selling offenses (drug selling, prostitution), illegal consumption offenses, and illegal status offenses. Abrahamsen (1960) compares and contrasts "acute criminals" (including situational, associational, and accidental offenders) and "chronic offenders" (including neurotic, psychopathic, and psychotic offenders), whereas Schafer (1976) classifies offenders based on their "life trends," for example, occasional, professional, abnormal, and habitual criminals.

A number of scholars have constructed typologies focused explicitly on specific heinous crimes, especially murder, rape, and arson. For example, Holmes and Holmes (1994) place murderers in eight conceptual categories:

- Depressive type: These offenders often conclude that life is hopeless and not worth living. They do not manifest psychotic symptoms. Typically, they respond to their hopelessness by killing loved ones and then committing suicide.
- Mysoped: This category includes the sadistic child murderer who experiences sexual gratification in conjunction with the homicide. It is not unusual for these offenders to perform sexual acts on children before and after the murder.
- Sexual killer: These offenders are often serial killers. They commit acts of sexual violence along with the murder.
- Psychotic killer: These offenders typically hear voices and commands (auditory hallucinations) that tell them to kill.
- Psychopathic killer: These killers do not experience remorse, sorrow, shame, or empathy after they murder someone. These offenders tend to be preoccupied with their own feelings and needs.
- Organic or brain disorders: In some instances evidence of brain damage, brain trauma, and organic symptoms may explain offenders' propensity to murder.
- Mentally retarded: These killers have low IQs and may not fully grasp the seriousness of their homicidal behavior.
- Professional hit killers: These killers murder others for economic, political, or ideological reasons.

Holmes and Holmes (1994) also focus more narrowly on specific subtypes of murder. For example, they classify mass murderers into four groups:

- The disciple: The disciple killer follows the dictates of a charismatic leader. Examples include members of the Manson family and followers of Jim Jones at Jonestown, Guyana.
- The family annihilator: This murderer—often the senior male in the family, who has a history of alcohol abuse and depression—kills an entire family at one time. Typically, this killer is filled with despair and does not want anyone in the family to survive (Dietz 1986).

- The pseudocommando: This murderer is preoccupied with weaponry, such as assault rifles, machine guns, and hand grenades. These killers often stockpile weapons in their home and feel a need to teach the world a lesson, for example, because of its moral or political failings (Dietz 1986).
- The disgruntled employee: These offenders are usually distressed about having been fired from their jobs or placed on medical leave for psychiatric reasons.
- The set-and-run killer: Unlike mass murderers who commit suicide, these offenders set the stage for a mass murder and then plan to escape unharmed. They may set a bomb with a timing device or poison food or medicine that will be consumed by others at a later time (Dietz 1986).

Prominent typologies of serial murderers, who kill people over an extended period of time rather than at one moment in time, take a different approach. Holmes and DeBurger (1988), for example, classify serial murderers according to four groups:

- Visionary: The visionary serial killer is impelled to murder because he has heard voices or seen visions demanding that he kill a certain person or category of people. Some perceive the voice or vision to be that of a demon; others may perceive the voice as coming from God.
- Mission: The mission serial killer has a conscious goal in his life to eliminate a certain identifiable group of people. He does not hear voices or see visions. He has a self-imposed duty to rid the world of a group of people who are "undesirable" or "unworthy" to live with other human beings.
- Hedonistic: The hedonistic serial killer kills simply for the thrill of it, because he enjoys it. The thrill becomes an end in itself. The lust murderer can be viewed as a subcategory of this type because of the sexual enjoyment experienced in the homicidal act. Anthropophagy (cannibalism), dismemberment, necrophilia, and other forms of sexual aberration are prevalent in this form of serial killing.
- Power/control: The power or control serial killer receives gratification from the complete control of the victim. This type of murderer experiences pleasure and excitement not from sexual acts carried out on the victim but from his belief that he has the power to do whatever he wishes to another human being, who is completely helpless to stop him.

In contrast, Fox and Levin's (1999) prominent typology places serial killers in three broad groups, each with two subgroups:

- Thrill: Most serial killings are motivated by thrill. Thrill-based serial killings involve sexual sadism (where the offender sexually assaults the victim) or dominance (where the offender feels the need to exercise power and control; one example is the killing vulnerable or frail patients by health care staff).
- Mission: The serial murder is committed in the name of some cause. These offenders may be reformist (where the offender wants to rid the world of filth and evil, such as by killing prostitutes, gay men, Jews, ethnic minorities, or homeless individuals) or visionary (offenders who believe that they hear the voice of the devil or God instructing them to murder).
- Expedience: These serial killers are motivated by profit or some sort of self-protection. They may be profit oriented (they kill to gain access to insurance proceeds or social security checks, for example) or protection oriented (the killer uses murder to cover up criminal activity, such as a robbery).

Fox and Levin (1998) conducted a comprehensive review of typologies of both serial and mass murderers and constructed a five-category typology of the motives that drive "multiple murderers":

- Power: Power and dominance are key to most serial killings and a substantial number of mass killings (for example, multiple homicides committed by health care professionals, pseudocommando killers in battle fatigues, and mission-oriented killers such as the Unabomber).
- Revenge: Revenge against specific individuals (for example, estranged lovers, family members, or employers), particular groups of people (for example, church or synagogue worshipers, peace demonstrators at a rally, students), or society at large motivates a significant number of multiple murderers. In some instances the revenge is directed against people who are not known to the murderer personally but who are somehow affiliated with an enemy—what is known as "murder by proxy" (Frazier and Carr 1974).
- Loyalty: A twisted determination to save loved ones from further torment and misery motivates some multiple murderers. For example, a father-husband may kill his family in order to protect them from

impending financial ruin stemming from his unemployment or to protect them from the emotional turmoil resulting from a failed marriage—a form of "suicide by proxy," for example, murdering the close friend or relative of one's enemy (Frazier and Carr 1974).

- Profit: Some multiple murders are motivated by self-protection, for example, to eliminate evidence associated with another crime (such as an armed robbery) or to facilitate access to victims' assets (bank accounts, retirement benefits).
- Terror: Some multiple murders are the direct result of politically motivated, ideologically driven acts of terror. Terrorism that leads to multiple murders is usually designed to send a strong message regarding some cause. Some terrorist acts are carried out by true crusaders who are politically motivated, whereas others are carried out by members of organized crime or people with major psychiatric disorders and delusions (Hacker 1976).

Several scholars have also constructed typologies of etiological factors associated with rape. For example, Scully and Marolla (1995) interviewed a large sample of convicted, incarcerated rapists and identified six major etiological factors:

- Revenge and punishment: Some rapists vent their anger toward women by raping them—a form of "collective liability." According to the concept of collective liability, the rapist's victim is a substitute for the woman against whom he wants revenge. Rapists often talk about using rape "to get even" with their wives or partners.
- An "added bonus": In some instances offenders who commit a burglary or robbery decide to sexually assault their victims as an afterthought (sometimes the reverse is true as well).
- Sexual access: Although rape is often less about sex and more about male violence, aggression, and power, sometimes the rapist's goal is explicitly sexual in nature.
- Impersonal sex and power: Some rapists prefer to have sex with a partner who is a total stranger and to whom they have no personal commitment. This kind of anonymous assault provides the rapist with an opportunity to control and dominate.
- Recreation and adventure: This form of rape is most often found in the context of gang activity, for example, when a gang abducts a hitchhiker or pedestrian in order to rape that person, or a gang member invites other gang members to rape his date ("gang date" rape).

Looking beyond motives per se, Russell's (1984) typology focuses on a wide range of etiological factors associated with rape:

- Biological factors: Some rapists appear to have biological attributes and inherited genetic traits that predispose them to sexual aggression (Thornhill and Palmer 2000).
- Childhood experiences of sexual abuse: Professionals believe that victims of childhood sexual abuse are at increased risk of committing sex offenses as adults. Children who are victimized may grow up believing that victimizing others is acceptable. Also, the adult rapist's behavior may be a product of built-up aggression from earlier victimization.
- Exposure to mass media that encourage rape: Many professionals believe that steady exposure to sexually provocative movies, television shows, and advertisements encourages sexual aggression.
- Exposure to pornography: Similarly, many professionals believe that exposure to sexually explicit images—especially those that portray sexual abuse, exploitation, and victimization—exacerbates sexual aggression and rape.

Finally, it is useful to examine typologies of arsonists as another prominent example of scholars' attempt to construct taxonomies of heinous crimes and to better understand key etiological factors. For example, associates of the FBI's National Center for the Analysis of Violent Crime examined arson-related research literature, various existing typologies (Douglas et al. 1997; also see White 1996), and actual arson cases, and interviewed arsonists throughout the United States. Their comprehensive typology includes six major categories of arson motives:

- Vandalism-motivated arson: Malicious or mischievous fire setting that results in damage to property. One of the most common targets is a school or school property and educational facilities. Vandals also frequently target abandoned structures and flammable vegetation.
- Excitement-motivated arson: Offenders motivated by excitement include seekers of thrills, attention, recognition, and sexual gratification (the stereotypical arsonist who sets fires for sexual gratification is rare). Some fire fighters set fires (for example, in an occupied apartment house at night) so they can engage in the suppression effort, and some security guards have set fires to relieve boredom and gain recognition.
- Revenge-motivated arson: Revenge-motivated fires are set in retaliation for some injustice, real or imagined, perceived by the offender. Often

revenge is an element of other motives. The four major subgroups are personal revenge (setting a fire to retaliate for a personal grievance); societal retaliation (setting a fire to "get back" at an allegedly unjust society that has wronged the arsonist); institutional retaliation (setting a fire to retaliate against governmental, educational, military, medical, religious, or other institutions); and group retaliation (setting a fire to strike out against a religious, racial, ethnic, or other group that the arsonist opposes).

- Crime concealment–motivated arson: In these instances arson is the secondary criminal activity. The fire is set to cover up another crime, such as murder or burglary, or to eliminate evidence left at the crime scene. Other examples include fires set to destroy business records to conceal embezzlement.
- Profit-motivated arson: Arsonists in this category hope to profit from their fire setting by obtaining insurance payments, dissolving unprofitable businesses, destroying inventory, clearing a parcel of land, or creating employment opportunities (for example, a construction worker who wants to rebuild an apartment complex he destroyed, or an unemployed laborer seeking employment as a forest fire fighter or as a logger to salvage burned timber).
- Extremist-motivated arson: Arsonists may set fires in support of social, political, or religious causes. Examples of targets include abortion clinics, slaughterhouses, animal laboratories, fur farms, and furrier outlets.

THE TYPOLOGY OF CRIMINAL CIRCUMSTANCES

In an effort to synthesize and draw on the diverse array of existing typologies of crime in general and heinous crime in particular—all of which have considerable merit and have contributed to criminal justice professionals' understanding of offenders' behavior and criminal careers—I offer a broad typology that classifies heinous offenders on the basis of the *circumstances* that led to their crimes (Reamer 2003a). This "typology of criminal circumstances" incorporates what we have learned about three key dimensions of crime and criminal behavior: the causes of crime, the diversity of types of crime, and various types of criminal careers and patterns during the offenders' lives.[2] I have developed a seven-category typology of the circumstances that lead to diverse heinous crimes. What follows is a brief overview of the typology's major categories, with a series of case illustrations involving heinous crimes. I will draw on these case illustrations in my discussion in subsequent chapters of possible responses to offenders who commit heinous crimes.

Crimes of Desperation

Many heinous crimes are committed by people who are desperate or who believe that they are living in desperate circumstances. These are people who conclude that they have run out of options and end up committing a heinous crime in their attempt to resolve their seemingly untenable predicament. The term *desperate* means "reckless or dangerous because of despair or urgency," "having an urgent need, desire," "leaving little or no hope," and "undertaken out of despair or as a last resort" (*Random House Webster's College Dictionary* 1991).

Some heinous crimes of desperation are committed in the context of acute crises, where offenders thrash around for a quick way out of what are, or at least appear to be, desperate circumstances. For example, a heroin addict who is in desperate need of money for drugs may hold up a convenience store; he panics when a customer confronts him, and he shoots the customer impulsively in response to the threat.

In contrast, other heinous crimes of desperation may be the product of more chronic, cumulative pressure. A man who is informed by an organized crime figure that he must pay off his large loan "in the near future" if he wants to protect his children from serious harm may spend weeks arranging to commit arson or arrange a hit as a way to raise badly needed cash.

Many heinous crimes of desperation have a financial stimulus. These offenses are committed in an effort to fix a money-related problem, for example, obtain cash to pay the living expenses for one's family or to pay off a large gambling debt. However, other heinous crimes of desperation have little or nothing to do with money and much more to do with interpersonal conflict, for example, vicious assaults that arise out of a desperate attempt to resolve an intense, overwhelming family or domestic dispute.

FINANCIAL DESPERATION

Many heinous crimes are committed by people who believe that they are in dire financial straits. Many such offenses are a direct attempt to obtain money for a financial bailout. In some instances the heinous crime is not a direct attempt to obtain money but is committed in an effort to resolve a serious problem related to money, for example, arranging to murder a creditor who is sending threatening messages about repaying an overdue loan.

Case 2.1   Alfred B. was released from prison after serving his full eighteen-month sentence for breaking and entering. Alfred was a heroin addict who had never received substance abuse treatment. He refused to participate in the prison-sponsored drug treatment program and, as a result, was denied parole. Upon his release Alfred moved into an apartment with his brother, who also had a history of substance abuse problems. Within several weeks of his release from prison, Alfred relapsed and resumed his heroin use. In a desperate attempt to obtain quick cash to buy heroin, Alfred walked into a convenience store, threatened the clerk with a loaded handgun, and demanded money. The clerk panicked and hesitated in opening the cash register drawer. Alfred leaned over the counter to intimidate the clerk, the clerk pushed Alfred, and Alfred shot the clerk with his handgun. The clerk died while in emergency surgery.

Case 2.2   Carlos L. had borrowed about $17,000 from a local loan shark. Carlos had a very poor credit history and thus was not able to borrow money from conventional sources. He felt in desperate need of the money to pay off his gambling debts.

The loan shark contacted Carlos almost daily, pressuring him to repay the money, plus interest. Carlos believed that he had run out of options and impulsively decided to rob a bank. He put on a ski mask and borrowed a handgun from a friend. Carlos, who had never committed a violent crime, walked into a branch bank, ordered the customers to lie down, and threatened a bank teller. One customer sneaked up behind Carlos and tried to wrest the gun from him. Carlos shot the customer in the head, killing him instantly.

Case 2.3   Barry J. had invested heavily in the real estate market. Within ten years he had purchased a number of multifamily dwellings in low-income neighborhoods. He also owned two small businesses, an automobile repair shop and a chain of pizza shops.

The local economy became quite weak, and Barry was having difficulty meeting his financial obligations, especially the mortgage payments on his own newly constructed home and on a vacation home that he had purchased. Sales at Barry's businesses had dropped dramatically, and he was having difficulty finding tenants for several rental units. Barry received a demand notice from his mortgage holder, who threatened to foreclose on his new home.

In desperation Barry contacted an old acquaintance who had links to organized crime. Barry arranged to have one of his pizza shops destroyed by arson. Unbeknown to the arsonist, the pizza shop and an adjacent apartment shared a common wall. On the day of the fire the apartment's tenant was home, sick in bed. The fire destroyed both the pizza shop and the apartment, killing the tenant.

WHITE-COLLAR FINANCIAL DESPERATION

People in white-collar jobs and occupations commit a significant number of financial crimes, motivated by a sense of desperation more than unadulterated greed. Typically, these white-collar criminals have jobs that provide them with relatively easy access to enormous sums of money, which they feel compelled to take to resolve a pressing financial problem (Shover 1998; Weisburd, Waring, and Chayet 1995).

Case 2.4   Marsha R. lived with her seventy-four-year-old mother and worked as a bookkeeper at a small company that supplies oil to heat homes and businesses. She had worked at the company for almost twenty years and considered herself part of the owners' extended family.

Marsha had never married and spent a great deal of her time shopping and playing bingo. Along the way she accumulated nearly $35,000 in credit card debt and began embezzling funds from the oil company. Because she was a bookkeeper, she was able to manipulate several accounts in order to siphon off money for her personal use. Eventually, the company's accountant noticed a significant drop-off in revenue and encouraged the owners to conduct a thorough audit. The audit uncovered Marsha's embezzlement of more than $110,000. As a result, the company's creditors sued for nonpayment, the company's owners incurred enormous legal fees, and the owners had to file for bankruptcy.

Case 2.5   Evan A. was a judge on the state's superior court. He had been on the bench for twenty-four years, presiding over civil and criminal court cases. Over time, his personal lifestyle became more and more lavish and extravagant. He and his wife joined an exclusive country club, purchased two expensive automobiles, and began traveling extensively. Evan did not disclose to his wife that they were experiencing serious cash-flow problems.

Evan was approached by a local attorney who was about to try a multimillion-dollar malpractice case before Evan. During their lunchtime meeting the attorney, who was aware of the judge's financial predicament, slipped him a sealed envelope containing $10,000. The attorney, who was under investigation himself for illegal activity, was cooperating with law enforcement officials when he attempted to bribe the judge.

Case 2.6   Melvin S. was a physician who treated many automobile accident victims. Melvin often collaborated with lawyers who represented accident victims and sued other drivers for damages. For a number of years one particular lawyer referred many clients to Melvin for treatment; the lawyer and Melvin had a tacit agreement that Melvin would consistently exaggerate the number of these patients' office visits and inflate invoices that would be included in the legal claim filed in court. Melvin had agreed to the arrangement after he suffered significant stock market losses and a bitter divorce and property settlement with his ex-wife. He and the lawyer agreed to split the profits from their fraudulent activity. Over the years they split hundreds of thousands of dollars.

Eventually, the lawyer was indicted on unrelated charges and agreed to testify against Melvin in exchange for a lighter prison sentence. Melvin was eventually convicted.

CRIMES OF FEAR: DESPERATE PERSONAL CIRCUMSTANCES

Some heinous crimes are committed by people who are desperately afraid for reasons that are not financial. Their fear may be rooted in anxiety about legal repercussions and risks, the potential loss of a marriage or other intimate relationship, or loss of a job. This fear leads some people to commit very serious crimes.

Case 2.7   Lyle K. was a town councilman generally regarded as a rising star. Like his mother, Lyle became a council member at a young age. He quickly rose through the ranks and seemed destined to assume a leadership position on the council.

One evening, after a town council meeting, Lyle stopped at a nearby restaurant, had several drinks, and began driving home. His blood alcohol level was 0.20, nearly three times the legal limit. Lyle drove through a red light and slammed into a pedestrian, causing fatal injuries. Lyle was so afraid of the public humiliation and legal consequences that he did not stop to help the victim or notify the police. The following morning Lyle was arrested on a manslaughter charge of causing a death while driving under the influence.

Case 2.8   Daniel S. was having an extramarital affair with a co-worker, Mary Ann K., at the catering firm where he had been employed for nearly six years. For some time Daniel had been having marital problems and found solace in his relationship with Mary Ann.

For a number of months Mary Ann had been pressuring Daniel to leave his wife and move in with her. She threatened to break off the affair if Daniel would not commit himself to the relationship. Daniel could not bear the thought of losing Mary Ann but did not feel ready to leave his wife. He became so distraught that he decided that the only way out of his predicament—the only way to preserve his relationship with Mary Ann—was to murder his wife.

Case 2.9   Barry M. was hitchhiking home one afternoon after finishing his classes at the local community college. A driver in a late-model sports car offered Barry a ride. The driver, Alan F., was a part-time athletics coach at the community college.

After chatting some during their brief ride together, Alan gave Barry his telephone number and encouraged Barry to contact him. Barry and Alan got together the following week for dinner. After dinner Alan invited Barry to his apartment to watch a nationally televised basketball play-off game. During the game Alan made sexual advances toward Barry. Barry reacted angrily and began fighting off Alan's advances. During the scuffle Barry strangled Alan to death.

Crimes of Greed, Exploitation, and Opportunism

There is no doubt that some people commit heinous crimes because of factors over which they have little, if any, control. As I will explore shortly, some individuals with major mental illness—such as schizophrenia or other psychotic disorders—commit heinous crimes and have little ability to control their behavior.

Some individuals, however, commit heinous crimes with explicit intent, motivated by self-centered greed, exploitation, and opportunism. The definition of *greed* in the *Random House Webster's College Dictionary* (1991) is "excessive or rapacious desire, especially for wealth and possessions; avarice; covetousness." Exploitation is "the use or manipulation of another person for one's own advantage," and opportunism is "the policy or practice, as in politics or business, of adapting actions, decisions, etc., to expediency or effectiveness without regard to principles or consequences." Individuals whose heinous crimes are motivated by greed, exploitation, and opportunism have set their sights on something they want—valuable property, money, sex—and they are determined to get it, no matter the cost to victims. Often these individuals have little ability to empathize with their victims, at least not at the time they commit their crimes.

I have met many offenders whose heinous crimes are a function of such greed, exploitation, or opportunism; they manifest symptoms of what are typically labeled antisocial personality disorder and narcissistic personality disorder (American Psychiatric Association 2000). According to widely accepted psychiatric criteria, the essential feature of antisocial personality disorder is a "pervasive pattern of disregard for, and violation of, the rights of others that begins in childhood or early adolescence and continues into adulthood" (American Psychiatric Association 2000:701–3). Typical behaviors include manipulation, deception, lying, destroying property, and stealing. Individuals diagnosed with antisocial personality disorder show little remorse for the harmful consequences of their behavior.

Offenders who manifest symptoms of narcissistic personality disorder often display a profound need for admiration and have a grandiose sense of their own importance. They often overestimate their abilities, act pretentiously, inflate and boast about their accomplishments, and are preoccupied with their own pursuit of success, power, domination, superiority, and brilliance (American Psychiatric Association 2000:714–15). Narcissistic offenders also have difficulty empathizing with the harmful consequences of their behavior.

Many heinous crimes that are motivated by greed, exploitation, and opportunism are financial in nature; some are committed by people associated with organized crime. Other heinous crimes are committed by gang members or take the form of sexual exploitation.

FINANCIAL CRIMES

Not surprisingly, a significant percentage of crimes motivated by greed, exploitation, and opportunism are financial in nature (Hagan 1990). In contrast to financial crimes of desperation—where offenders conclude that their dire financial circumstances can be resolved only by the commission of a serious crime—financial crimes of greed, exploitation, and opportunism are motivated by offenders' more basic, primitive, and hedonistic pursuit of pleasure (Block and Geis 1970; Edelhertz 1970).

Case 2.10 Theo N. was fired from his job as the night-shift manager at a large furniture warehouse. According to his supervisor, Theo had missed work too many times. Theo deeply resented being fired. He was especially angry that his loss of income limited his ability to buy nice clothes, eat in upscale restaurants, and attend professional sporting events.

Theo was determined to sustain his lifestyle. He plotted with his roommate to set up a bogus storefront where he planned to "sell" expensive jewelry. Theo and his roommate rented commercial space and arranged for several jewelry salesmen to bring their lines to the storefront to discuss a wholesale purchase. Theo and his roommate robbed each salesman at gunpoint and stole all the jewelry, the total value of which was $215,000.

Case 2.11 Malcolm G. owned a popular restaurant. After twenty-three years in the business Malcolm grew weary of the early mornings, late nights, and unrelenting personnel challenges. He fantasized about retirement but knew that he could not afford to stop working without making a major adjustment in his lifestyle.

One evening Malcolm was complaining about his plight to a close friend. The friend told Malcolm that he knew of a ticket out of misery: arson. The friend and

---

Malcolm orchestrated a sophisticated arson plan that destroyed the restaurant. Eventually, the friend was arrested on an unrelated income tax evasion case and disclosed his, and Malcolm's, involvement in the arson in an effort to negotiate a reduced sentence.

Case 2.12 Pat M. dropped out of school at sixteen. He spent most of his time hanging out on the streets with friends. On occasion Pat worked odd jobs for extra cash. Most of his cash came from selling cocaine in the neighborhood. Pat had been arrested several times for possessing drugs, assaults, and shoplifting.

One afternoon one of Pat's friends told him that he knew of a way that Pat could earn a lot of money very quickly. Pat learned that a local businessman was eager to find someone to seriously injure his wife's lover. Pat and his friend agreed to do the job in exchange for $5,000. They assaulted the man one evening as he was about to enter his home. Pat and his friend knocked the man out by hitting him on the head with a tire iron and then pummeling him with their fists. The man lost the sight in one eye and suffered permanent brain damage.

ORGANIZED CRIME

Organized crime figures have been responsible for heinous crimes as far back as the colonial period. By the early twentieth century organized crime was heavily involved in various gangland slayings and other heinous crimes associated with drug trafficking, firearms smuggling, money laundering, gambling, labor racketeering, loan-sharking, prostitution, kidnapping, and robbery (Jacobs and Panarella 1998). Contemporary organized crime has moved far beyond gangsters of Italian and Sicilian descent to include other ethnic groups (such as Jamaicans, African Americans, Russians, Chinese, Chicanos, and Mexicans) and nontraditional groups such as the Pagans and Hell's Angels (Abadinsky 1989; Albanese 1989; Bequai 1979).

Case 2.13 For several years Donnie A. was groomed by a local organized crime family to take over its drug-trafficking business. At a relatively young age, Donnie was released from a correctional facility for young adult offenders and went on to supervise a large-scale, and very profitable, heroin and cocaine operation. He and his colleagues obtained the drugs from several overseas connections that smuggled the drugs into the United States through several ports.

Donnie was arrested during a sting operation conducted at a major international airport through which the drugs regularly were being smuggled; undercover narcotics agents posed as baggage handlers and truck drivers. While awaiting trial on various drug-related charges, Donnie murdered a man he believed had worked as a police informant and leaked information about Donnie's drug dealings.

Case 2.14 Angela U. dated and eventually married Jose R., who was heavily involved in a large burglary and robbery ring that operated in New England. Angela did not have a significant criminal record, but over time she became more and more involved in the ring's activities. On several occasions she coordinated telephone communications among ringleaders and supplied them with information about potential victims (addresses, location of jewelry and other valuables, and so on).

At Jose's request Angela agreed to drive a car that a group of accomplices used in their robbery of a jewelry company employee who was on her way to make a large bank deposit. The robbers abandoned the scheme in midheist when they heard police sirens in the distance. Angela realized that the jewelry company employee had seen her face and the car; she drove her car right into the employee. The employee survived the crash but ended up in a persistent vegetative state.

Case 2.15 Darwin J. was a correctional officer at a county jail. When he was off duty, he spent considerable amounts of time playing blackjack at a nearby casino, betting on major sports events (mostly college and professional basketball and football games) and using cocaine. Darwin also earned money by helping a small group of organized crime members process bets.

Darwin accumulated considerable gambling debts; he owed nearly $23,000 to one of his organized crime connections, Marvin O. When Marvin realized that Darwin could not pay off his debt, Marvin recruited Darwin to smuggle large quantities of heroin and cocaine into the county jail. Darwin was arrested when an inmate decided to cooperate with a state police team that was investigating drug activity in the jail.

GANG EXPLOITATION

Street gangs, which are composed principally of male youths, account for a significant portion of heinous crime (Klein 1998). Conflict between rival gangs often leads to aggravated assaults and other serious offenses, such as rape and murder (Spergel 1995).

Case 2.16 Saravane S. was raised in the United States by his Laotian parents, who emigrated from Laos in the late 1970s. Saravane's family settled in a mediumsize industrial city in New England. During his teenage years Saravane joined a Laotian street gang. The gang became involved in drug activities and home invasions. One day Saravane and three other gang members drove about thirty-five miles to a nearby city to rob the home of a wealthy Laotian family. The gang members had detailed information about large sums of cash and valuable jewelry in the home. After they broke in, Saravane and the other gang members threatened the family members with guns, bound all of them—including two elderly family members and a teenager—with duct tape, and robbed the family of its possessions.

Case 2.17   When he was seventeen, Theo L. joined an urban street gang, the Low Boyz. The Low Boyz gang was well known to the police; many Low Boyz members had been arrested on drug trafficking, assault, and loitering charges.

Late one night Theo and several gang members left a nightclub, where they had been drinking, and headed downtown to a strip club. At the strip club the gang members continued to drink. At closing time Theo and the other gang members pulled out handguns and robbed patrons of their wallets. One patron resisted. Theo shot and killed him.

Case 2.18   Floyd G., twenty-two, was a member of the Fourteenth Street Gang, which had a long-standing feud with the rival Posse Disciples Gang. Members of the two gangs encountered each other in a local park. Various members exchanged words and a vicious fight broke out. Lavoy K., a member of the Fourteenth Street Gang, grabbed the girlfriend of a member of the Posse Disciples Gang and forced her into his car. Lavoy drove the woman to an acquaintance's apartment, where he and Floyd raped her.

SEXUAL EXPLOITATION

Some sex offenders have diagnosable disorders that explain their crimes—paraphilias such as exhibitionism, voyeurism, and pedophilia (American Psychiatric Association 2000). Other sex offenders simply take advantage of victims, knowing full well that their actions are exploitative, manipulative, and opportunistic (Paludi 1999; Searles and Berger 1995; Williams 2001). Their behavior does not rise to the level of a sex-related disorder in the strict sense of the term.

Case 2.19   Barry T. married for the first time when he was thirty-six. He worked at a car dealership and married a woman he met at work. At the time Barry's wife, Maria, had a fourteen-year-old daughter, Andrea.

About a year after their marriage, Barry and Maria began having difficulty getting along. Both struggled with alcohol abuse and argued frequently. One night Maria left their apartment to stay with her mother after an argument. Barry walked into Andrea's bedroom as she was getting ready for bed. He sat next to the girl on her bed and told her that he really needed to talk. After several minutes Barry began stroking Andrea's hair and back and began fondling her. Andrea resisted, but Barry insisted that he would not hurt her. Andrea was afraid to fight with Barry, who told her that he could teach her what it is like "to be a woman." Barry had Andrea perform oral sex and had intercourse with her. Their sexual contact continued for almost four months, until Maria ended her relationship with Barry.

Case 2.20 Stan E. was a junior at a state university and lived in a fraternity house. One Saturday evening the fraternity cosponsored a party with a sorority. Stan spent the evening talking with a sorority member, Donna H. Both drank several beers and shots of tequila with six other partiers who had gone up to Stan's room.

By 1:30 A.M. only Stan and Donna remained in his room. The two listened to music and engaged in foreplay on Stan's bed. Stan invited Donna to spend the night, but she said she would rather go back to her sorority house and asked Stan to escort her. Stan tried to convince Donna to spend the night with him but to no avail. He became increasingly frustrated and accused Donna of leading him on. He began stroking Donna, who became increasingly upset. Several minutes later Stan raped her.

Case 2.21 Hank S. was a twenty-one-year-old seminarian who had taken a leave of absence after his mother died. Hank spent considerable time in Internet chat rooms. Eventually, Hank "met" a sixteen-year-old on line, Stephen R.; both lived near the same seaside town.

During one of their on-line conversations, Hank told Stephen that he was a photographer who was in the middle of major "shoot" for a national men's magazine. Hank said that he needed to replace a young male model for a number of photos and asked Stephen whether he would like to stop by a major hotel the following afternoon to audition. Stephen went to the hotel and met Hank in Suite 223. Hank explained that he needed to make some adjustments in his equipment and offered Stephen an alcoholic drink. About a half-hour and several drinks later Hank asked Stephen to pose nude. Stephen hesitated, but Hank persisted. After taking a number of photographs of Stephen, Hank raped him in the suite's bedroom.

Crimes of Rage

Surges of rage precipitate many heinous crimes. Intense conflict, fueled by anger and hostility, can erupt in vicious forms, leading to serious injury or death. A significant percentage of crimes of rage occur between family members and acquaintances, such as neighbors and co-workers. Other heinous crimes of rage occur between total strangers.

FAMILY AND RELATIONSHIP VIOLENCE

Not surprisingly, a significant percentage of heinous crimes of rage involve family members (spouses, parents, children) and intimate partners (Finkelhor and Yilo 1985; Gelles 1998; Gelles and Straus 1987; National Center on Elder Abuse 1998; Russell 1984; Tatara 1995). Living under the same roof, where opportunities for conflict thrive, sometimes provides a toxic incubator for domestic violence. In a recent case that received widespread publicity, Clara Harris, a dentist, was found guilty of murdering her adulterous husband by running over him repeatedly with her Mercedes-Benz while the victim's daughter (Dr. Harris's stepdaughter) was riding in the car as a passenger. According to the *New York Times,* the victim's daughter testified and "vividly described her stepmother's fury as she sought out her husband" (Madigan 2003:2).

Case 2.22   Yolanda F., sixteen, lived with her grandmother. Yolanda never knew her father, and her mother was in a residential drug treatment program.

Yolanda's grandmother, Bessie, was very concerned about her granddaughter's relationship with a twenty-seven-year-old man, Devin. Bessie lectured Yolanda about how risky it was for her to be involved with an older man.

One afternoon Bessie got into a fierce argument with Yolanda and Devin while the three were standing in the kitchen. Bessie ordered Devin to leave her apartment. During the argument Yolanda impulsively grabbed an iron frying pan and slammed it repeatedly against her grandmother's head. Yolanda also threw a toaster oven at her grandmother's head. Bessie fell to the floor, lost consciousness, and later died. Yolanda panicked, called the police, and reported that a Hispanic man broke into the home and attacked her grandmother. Yolanda later confessed and was tried in criminal court as an adult.

Case 2.23   Larry K. was estranged from his common-law wife, Penney. The couple had lived together for twenty-one years. Their fourteen-year-old daughter lived at home and their nineteen-year-old son was in the army.

Larry and Penney fought incessantly. They argued about finances and child rearing, and each accused the other of infidelity. One night, after their daughter went to a friend's home for a sleepover and Penney had gone to bed, Larry went to the family's garage, grabbed a machete, tiptoed into the bedroom where Penney was sleeping, and attacked her viciously. Penney survived Larry's assault with the machete but sustained severe injuries to her face, neck, and left arm. She suffered permanent nerve damage, lost partial use of her left arm, and had difficulty seeing out of her left eye.

Case 2.24   Frankie D. had been married to Bernadette D. for almost seven years. Her sixteen-year-old son from her first marriage, Dale, lived with the couple. Dale had dropped out of high school and had developed a substance abuse problem. Dale worked only sporadically and did not pay for rent or food.

Frankie and Dale had always had difficulty getting along. According to Frankie, Dale always resented his mother's decision to divorce his father and remarry. Frankie and Dale argued constantly; their disagreements often erupted into shouting matches.

On one occasion Frankie threatened to throw Dale out of the house when Frankie accused Dale of stealing money from his wallet. The two exchanged punches. During the fight Frankie lost control, pinned Dale to the floor, and strangled him to death.

SOCIAL VIOLENCE

Some heinous crimes of rage involve individuals who have no family connection—friends and neighbors, for example. Relationships between social acquaintances sometimes sour and trigger rage-filled violence.

Case 2.25   Warren C. was evicted from his single-room-occupancy hotel room when he was unable to pay the weekly rent. Warren was a Vietnam veteran who lived on disability income.

After his eviction he visited a local soup kitchen for meals. There Warren met a volunteer, Doris K., and spent considerable time talking with her about his life. Doris eventually offered Warren the opportunity to live in a spare room in her home until he was able to find more permanent housing.

After several weeks of this arrangement Doris became frustrated with Warren's volatile temper and lack of personal hygiene. Doris told him that he would have to leave her home by the end of the week. The two argued; Warren flew into a rage, raped Doris, and beat her with his fists. Doris suffered several broken ribs, a broken jaw, and lacerations. Warren also beat Doris's two dogs, killing one and severely injuring the other.

Case 2.26   Milton L. lived with Evelyn S. for nearly two years. Their relationship was filled with conflict from the start. Most of their arguments concerned Milton's alcohol use; Evelyn often accused Milton of drinking excessively and mistreating her.

Evelyn decided to leave Milton. One afternoon she packed her belongings, wrote Milton a long note, and left their apartment. That night Milton returned to the apartment, read Evelyn's letter, and started fuming. He was convinced that their next door neighbor, Nancy, had encouraged Evelyn to leave and knew where she was. Milton confronted Nancy, who denied any involvement in the situation. He smashed the windshield on Nancy's car, flooded the basement of her home with a garden hose, carved the word *betrayed!* on Nancy's front door, and destroyed furniture on her porch.

Case 2.27   Gary M., was thirty-one and lived with his parents. He had dropped out of high school and had difficulty maintaining a steady job.

For several years Gary and his parents were involved in a feud with a neighbor. Originally, Gary's parents accused the neighbor of building a new driveway that extended into property owned by Gary's parents without permission. Since then the neighbors had argued repeatedly about a series of issues.

One weekend afternoon Gary and the neighbor were outside and began arguing about how best to control a large amount of standing water that extended across the line between their properties. Gary accused the neighbor of failing to properly grade his property when the driveway was built, and the neighbor accused Gary's family of creating all kinds of legal trouble. The argument escalated; Gary went into his family's garage, retrieved a handgun from a tool box, and shot and killed the man.

WORKPLACE VIOLENCE

Sadly, we have become all too familiar with violent crimes committed in workplaces by disgruntled employees and customers. While some of these heinous offenses are carefully planned acts of vengeance, others are much more spontaneous acts of rage triggered by adverse employment decisions (abrupt terminations, for example) or infuriating customer service (Beck and Harrison 2001; National Institute 1996).

Case 2.28   Harris O. had worked as the manager of a fast-food restaurant for about six years. During the last five months the district manager had received a series of complaints from employees about Harris's behavior. According to the employees, Harris often used abusive language, belittled them in front of customers, and made sexist and racist remarks. The district manager, Barton I., met with Harris twice to discuss the complaints and implement a course of corrective action.

Despite these steps, Barton continued to receive complaints about Harris and decided to fire him. When Barton told Harris that he was being terminated, Harris flew into a tirade and accused Barton and a number of employees of conspiring against him. Harris began arguing with Barton, leaped across the table in the conference room where they were meeting, pushed Barton hard against the wall, and started beating Barton. Harris wrapped his hands around Barton's neck and strangled him. Barton survived the attack but suffered brain damage.

Case 2.29 Manuel L. bought a new car from a local automobile dealer. After driving his new car for two weeks, Manuel noticed that the car's transmission was not working properly. Manuel took the car back to the dealer, whose service department attempted to fix the problem. Several days later Manuel returned to the dealer, complaining that the problem had not been fixed. Once again the service department attempted to fix the problem, but Manuel complained soon thereafter that the problem persisted and was worsening.

Manuel made an appointment with the dealer's general manager and insisted on receiving a new car. The general manager explained that he could not simply replace the car and attempted to convince Manuel that the service department would continue working on the car until it was properly repaired. Manuel became enraged and stormed out of the general manager's office, retrieved a handgun from his glove compartment, returned to the general manager's office, and shot the man to death.

Case 2.30 Ira P. operated a printing press at a large commercial printer. Ira made no secret of his being gay.

Two of Ira's co-workers were homophobic and frequently made snide remarks about gay people within Ira's earshot. Occasionally, these two co-workers would taunt Ira about his sexual orientation.

Over time Ira became more and more frustrated with the harassment, although he never shared his frustration and anger with anyone at work. One afternoon, when the co-workers' harassment was unusually intense, Ira lost control, grabbed a large metal stake that was lying near the printing press, and stabbed one of the two co-workers to death. The second co-worker fled.

STRANGER RAGE

Although most heinous crimes of rage involve family members and acquaintances, some involve complete strangers whose paths happen to cross. These unfortunate encounters usually occur in public settings, such as highways, restaurants, and sporting events (Brewer 2000; Callahan 1997; Dukes et al. 2001; Ellison et al. 1995; Rathbone and Huckabee 1999).

Case 2.31 Merrill S. pulled onto the highway and headed home after visiting his mother, who had just moved into a nursing home. About five minutes after he entered the highway, a car with a teenage driver and three teenage passengers began to tailgate Merrill's vehicle. Merrill motioned for the driver to pass. The car with the teenagers pulled alongside Merrill's car, and all the passengers leaned out the windows, made obscene gestures toward Merrill, and began screaming at him. Merrill blew his horn and returned the obscene gesture. For several minutes the two cars jockeyed for position on the highway.

Eventually, Merrill slowed down as he neared his exit. The driver of the other car followed Merrill off the exit ramp and gently rear-ended his car at the end of the ramp. Merrill jumped out of his car and began screaming at the teenage driver and passengers. When the teenagers got out of their car and began to approach Merrill, Merrill reached beneath the seat of his car, grabbed a handgun, and shot each of the teenagers. All the teenagers were wounded; one died.

Case 2.32 Anthony Y. was shopping at a large discount department store on a crowded Saturday afternoon. Only two checkout lines were open, and customers were growing increasingly impatient.

A customer in front of Anthony began yelling at the checkout clerk to hurry up. The checkout clerk admonished the rude customer for his behavior and told him that she was working as quickly as possible; the two continued to exchange heated words. A store security guard walked over and began to escort the customer from the store. The customer resisted, and Anthony stepped in to try to help the security guard. During the brief fracas the unruly customer grabbed a baseball bat from a nearby shopping cart and began swinging furiously. The bat struck Anthony in the head, fracturing his skill, jaw, and eye socket. Anthony suffered permanent nerve and brain damage and lost the sight in his right eye.

Case 2.33 Josefina A. and Marcia D. were inmates in the women's division of the state prison. Both were awaiting trial—Josefina on drug charges and Marcia on breaking-and-entering charges. The two had never met before.

One morning, as the two were moving slowly in the chow line to pick up their breakfast trays, Josefina heard Marcia make a racist remark about Hispanics to another inmate. Josefina, who was born and raised in Colombia, became very upset and told Marcia to "keep your mouth shut." The two began arguing and pushing each other. Before the correctional officers could intervene, Josefina pulled a homemade prison knife (a "shiv") out of her sock and stabbed Marcia in the chest. Marcia's heart was punctured, and she was rushed to the hospital, where she died.

Crimes of Revenge and Retribution

Heinous crimes of rage are impulsive, spontaneous, and committed with virtually no premeditation. They are truly crimes of passion arising out of spontaneous emotional combustion.

In contrast, heinous crimes of revenge and retribution are the products of plotting and deliberation (Bradford 1982; Marks 1988; McCullough et al. 2001; Pettiway 1987; Seton 2001; Stuckless and Goranson 1994; Terris and Jones 1982; Vidmar 2001). Offenders are determined to get revenge and spend time thinking through how best to do it—physically, psychologically, or financially. Victims may be injured physically, tortured emotionally, or ruined financially. Revenge is "to exact punishment or expiation for wrong on behalf of, especially in a vindictive spirit." Retribution is "requital according to merits or desert, especially for evil" (*Random House* 1991).

FAMILY AND RELATIONSHIP REVENGE AND RETRIBUTION

As with crimes of rage, most heinous crimes of revenge and retribution occur among people who know one another. Consistent contact among people who have sustained relationships increases the likelihood of conflict. While most conflict among family members and acquaintances is resolved without catastrophic consequences, some conflict leads to deep-seated resentment and wish for vengeance (Abrams and Robinson 2002; Sheridan and Davies 2001).

Case 2.34 Oliver Y. lived with Mary Lou L. for three years. The couple had an on-again, off-again relationship, although recently they had talked seriously about getting married.

One afternoon Oliver overheard Mary Lou talking with a friend on the telephone. Mary Lou did not realize that Oliver was in the apartment at the time. She told the friend that she had been having an affair and just found out that she was pregnant with her lover's child. The child was conceived during a time when Mary Lou and Oliver were separated.

Oliver was furious. He felt angry and betrayed but decided not to confront Mary Lou immediately. Oliver took time to plot his revenge. One Saturday evening Oliver told Mary Lou that he had a special surprise planned for her. Oliver drove her to a seaside town and told her that he wanted to tell her something special at a lovely spot by the water's edge. Near sunset, Oliver walked with Mary Lou to a ledge overlooking the ocean and pushed her over the ledge. She and her unborn baby died when she landed on rocks hundreds of feet beneath the ledge.

Case 2.35 Becky and Sal M. had been married for twelve years. According to Becky, Sal had abused her physically and emotionally for years. After much consultation with her therapist, Becky decided to leave the marriage. Sal screamed and fumed when Becky told him of her plans, yelling that "you'll be sorry," and stormed out of the house.

Sal spent the night at the home of one of his best friends, where he stayed up all night stewing about his marital collapse and plotting revenge. The next day Sal canceled the couple's accounts with the gas and electric company, the telephone company, and the cable television company in an effort to harass Becky. He also closed their primary bank account. That night Sal left several threatening messages on Becky's car windshield and slashed her tires. Two days later Sal arranged with a well-known crime figure to set fire to Becky's house while she was at work. Unbeknown to Sal, Becky had asked her brother to stay with her for protection after she received Sal's threatening messages. Becky's brother was asleep in the house at the time of the arson and died in the fire.

Case 2.36 Ted E. was living with Bertha N. and her fifteen-year-old daughter, Lawanda. Ted and Bertha had met at a summer cookout and eventually became intimately involved. Ted moved into Bertha's home.

After living together for more than a year, serious issues emerged in Ted and Bertha's relationship. Both struggled with alcohol abuse and often fought while under the influence. After one bitter argument Bertha stormed out of the house and screamed at Ted that he had better make plans to move. Bertha did not return for days.

Ted's resentment of Bertha grew and grew. He could not believe that she would simply walk out, leaving Lawanda in his care. Ted decided that the ultimate form of revenge would be to become sexually involved with Bertha's daughter. One night during Bertha's absence Ted climbed into Lawanda's bed and raped her.

ACQUAINTANCE REVENGE AND RETRIBUTION

As with family members and intimate partners, regular, sustained contact among friends and social acquaintances also provides increased opportunity for conflict. Unresolved conflict among these parties occasionally leads to intense anger and resentment that culminates in planned vengeance.

Case 2.37 Darryl P., seventeen, was a member of a juvenile gang. The gang caused most of its mayhem by stealing cars, robbing downtown pedestrians, and shoplifting.

One of the gang's newest and youngest members, Lon T., was arrested by the police in connection with an armed robbery. While being interrogated by police, Lon confessed to a number of robberies and automobile thefts and supplied the names of his accomplices. Darryl and several other gang members were arrested.

All the defendants made bail pending trial. Darryl and two other defendants met to discuss how they should deal with Lon's betrayal. One night Darryl and his colleagues intercepted Lon as he was getting out of his car at his home, forced him into Darryl's car, drove to a large bridge about thirty minutes away, and pushed Lon off the bridge into the water. Lon fell to his death.

Case 2.38 Jose S. and Marlin K. were actively involved in the illegal drug trade. The pair sold cocaine and heroin to a number of steady customers in their midsize city.

Jose and Marlin discovered that one of their suppliers, Alex B., had sold them a large quantity of cocaine that was diluted with lactose, significantly diminishing its street value. Jose and Marlin arranged to meet Alex in the parking lot behind a popular movie theater, ostensibly to discuss another drug buy. Alex climbed into Jose's car, and Jose quickly drove off to a secluded area adjacent to a state park. When Alex began to panic at the change in plans, Marlin tied a rope around his neck in order to restrain him. When the car arrived at the state park, Marlin held onto Alex's neck with the rope, while Jose pulled out a large hunting knife and severed Alex's hands. Marlin shoved Alex out of the car and Jose drove off. On their way back to town, a state police officer pulled Jose's car over for speeding. When the officer smelled marijuana, he asked Jose and Alex to step away from the car so that he could search the vehicle. The state police officer found Alex's severed hands inside a gym bag on the backseat of the car.

Case 2.39 Ronald B. became friendly with the owner of an escort service, Harris L., and eventually joined the business. The escort service provided prostitutes to men. Over time Ronald also became close friends with Harris's girlfriend, Lynne N.

Lynne disclosed to Ronald that Harris had been abusing her. For several months Lynne and Ronald talked about her conflict-filled relationship with Harris. Lynne spoke at length about how she loved and hated Harris.

Early one morning Lynne knocked on Ronald's apartment door and stumbled in. Her cheek was scratched and bruised. Lynne told Ronald that Harris had become upset with her about "something silly—the amount I was spending at the shopping mall" and "he just lost it and started beating me."

Without telling Lynne of his plan, that night Ronald resolved to "teach Harris a lesson." Ronald called Harris and told him he needed to meet with him to discuss a new business idea. Ronald went to Harris's apartment and told Harris that before they discussed the business-related issue, Ronald needed to discuss a problem involving Lynne. Ronald told Harris that he never should have mistreated Lynne, pulled out a handgun, and shot Harris at short range. Ronald left Harris's apartment and let him bleed to death.

CO-WORKER REVENGE AND RETRIBUTION

Many heinous crimes committed in workplace settings are impulsive, spontaneous acts. However, many result from much more deliberate, planned, and calculated revenge and retribution (Beck and Harrison 2001; Biess and Tripp 1996; Bies, Tripp, and Kramer 1997; Douglas and Martinko 2001; Kim and Smith 1993; National Institute 1996).

Case 2.40 Florence I. was employed by a heating and air-conditioning company for sixteen years. Growing up, Florence was the best friend of the daughter of the business's owner, David O. David hired Florence as a bookkeeper shortly after she graduated from the local community college.

Florence had a falling out in her relationship with David's daughter, Meredith. Meredith had accused Florence of flirting with her husband. Soon thereafter Florence sensed that David was much more critical of her work and was less flexible with her work schedule.

Over time Florence became more and more resentful of David and Meredith. Rather than look for another job, Florence began embezzling money from the company's accounts. Florence got the money by creating fraudulent invoices, writing checks to bogus companies, and cashing the checks herself. The fraudulent activity lasted about eighteen months; by the time she was caught, Florence had stolen nearly $120,000. While she awaited trial, Florence arranged to have Meredith's car firebombed.

Case 2.41 Donald S. worked for seven years at a computer software company. Over time Donald's supervisors became more and more concerned about the quality of his work. He was often late for work and had difficulty completing assignments on time. Several co-workers had been complaining that Donald was becoming more and more irritable and contentious.

At the end of one workday Donald's immediate supervisor informed him that he was being fired. Donald was incensed and demanded to know on what grounds he was being terminated. The supervisor explained the company's concerns and insisted that Donald clean out his desk and turn in his supplies and office keys by 5:00 P.M. the following day. Donald complied. During the next week Donald spent hours plotting his revenge. Two weeks later he drove to the office building in the early morning and parked near the front entrance. He waited for the company president to arrive for work. When the president left his car and began walking into the building, Donald got out of his car, walked up to the president from behind, and shot him in the back of the head.

Case 2.42 Allan L. and Derk R. were co-managers of a warehouse owned by a national chain of home improvement stores. For several years the two got along well; they often went bowling and sailing together, and their families socialized.

For more than a year both Allan and Derk aspired to be regional manager of the home improvement company, although neither had discussed his goal with the other for fear of ruining the friendship. A senior company administrator, who was Derk's cousin, confided in Derk that Allan had sent company officials two memoranda listing problems with Derk's work performance. Both Derk and his cousin were convinced that Allan was trying to sabotage Derk's opportunity for promotion.

Derk confronted Allan, who denied sending the memoranda. Later that week Derk poisoned a thermos of Allan's coffee with a toxic amount of digoxin, a drug that controls or slows an irregular heartbeat. Allan died six days later.

AUTHORITY FIGURE REVENGE AND RETRIBUTION

People who are in positions of authority—such as judges, teachers, supervisors, parole officials, prosecutors, and parents—are sometimes targets of intense anger and vengeance. Offenders who feel wrongly prosecuted and convicted, employees who feel wrongly sanctioned or terminated, students who believe they have received unfair grades, and children who feel persecuted by their parents sometimes seek revenge and retribution.

Case 2.43   The leader of a white supremacist group, Matt Hale, was arrested on charges that he tried to have a federal judge, Joan Humphrey Lefkow, murdered. Hale was head of the World Church of the Creator. The judge had been presiding over a trademark infringement lawsuit and had ordered the church to stop using the church's name because it infringed on the rights of an Oregon organization (O'Connor 2003).

Case 2.44   On March 20, 1996, brothers Lyle and Erik Menendez were convicted of first-degree murder for shooting their parents to death with a shotgun in 1989. The brothers admitted during trial that they killed their parents, Kitty and Jose Menendez, but claimed that they did so in response to years of being subjected to psychological and sexual abuse ("Menendez Brothers Escape Death Sentence" 1996).

Case 2.45   Luke B. was a student at a community college. He had originally attended a four-year college with the dream of becoming a doctor, but he was placed on academic probation after his freshman year and decided to transfer to the community college.

Luke struggled in his organic chemistry course at the community college; he received a D+ on the final and a C- for the course. He made an appointment with his instructor in an effort to negotiate a higher grade. The instructor reviewed Luke's work and decided not to change the final grade. Luke stormed out of the office, muttering threats under his breath.

Two days later Luke staked himself outside the instructor's office. When the instructor arrived, Luke asked him whether they could chat for a few minutes. The instructor agreed, opened his office door, and invited Luke inside. Luke pulled handgun out of his backpack and shot and killed the instructor.

Crimes of Frolic

Heinous crimes sometimes occur without any sinister intention. What starts out as mere mischief sometimes ends in mayhem. Often these circumstances involve youthful perpetrators who start out only to have a good time—usually a *very* good time that is fueled by alcohol, drugs, and fast cars. Crimes of frolic—"playful behavior or action; prank," according to the *Random House Webster's College Dictionary* (1991)—usually occur in groups, where perpetrators encourage each other's mischief and pressure each other to engage in risk-taking behavior (Asch 1951; Campbell 1980; Festinger, Schachter, and Bach 1950; Friedkin and Cook 1990; Janis 1972; Sherif and Sherif 1964). Too often frolic ends in tragedy. There are several types of crimes of frolic.

THRILL-SEEKING ENTERTAINMENT

Heinous crime sometimes arises out of seemingly innocent attempts by a group of people to have fun. Young men who gather to push the recreational envelope are a particularly high-risk group (Amir 1971; Carpenter and Hollander 1982; Maxwell 2002; Porter and Alison 2001; Warr 1993), although young women are not exempt (witness, for example, the notorious case involving thirty-one students at Glenbrook North High School in Illinois who were expelled after videotaped evidence showed that they had struck girls in the junior class and pelted them with pig intestines, urine, and excrement [Black and Huppke 2003]).

Case 2.46 Four young men—Darry L., Eddie Z., Al R., and Marc P.—spent much of their social time together. One Saturday afternoon they gathered at Eddie's apartment and decided to go to the woods adjacent to the apartment building to shoot rifles loaded with BB pellets. After about a half hour Al noticed three adolescents hiking through the woods. Al convinced his friends that it would be fun to use the teens for target practice. The four young men hid behind trees and began shooting at the teens. One teen was struck in the eye by a BB pellet and blinded.

Case 2.47 Bert S., Barry N., and Leon K. were lounging around Leon's apartment, complaining of boredom. They had been watching television for hours. All three young men were unemployed; Barry and Leon were on probation (for cocaine possession and shoplifting, respectively).

Bert suggested that the three look for a car to "borrow" for an entertaining joyride. The three strolled through a downtown neighborhood that housed several college dormitories. Bert noticed a young couple getting out of a Jeep and approached the driver, a young man, and ordered him to hand over the keys. The driver resisted and began wrestling with Bert. Barry and Leon came to Bert's aid and forced the couple back into the Jeep. Bert got into the driver's seat and drove off. He drove aimlessly for about fifteen minutes, afraid to release the couple, who, he thought, would go directly to the police. Bert ended up driving to an abandoned drive-in theater.

At the theater's parking lot Bert, Barry, and Leon ordered the couple to get out of the car. They tied up the young man and placed him in the backseat of the Jeep. They dragged the young woman to the nearby woods, raped her, and shot her with a handgun. When they returned to the Jeep, Leon shot the young man as well and left him to die.

Case 2.48 Malcolm L. and Arnie C. had been friends since high school. Both had dropped out of high school; Malcolm worked at a local gas station, and Arnie was unemployed.

Arnie had always fantasized about being a fire fighter. He loved going to major fires and watching fire fighters in action. As a child Arnie would occasionally set small fires and pretend to be a heroic fire fighter.

One winter afternoon Arnie convinced Malcolm to accompany him to an abandoned warehouse to set it afire: "Wait 'til you see this thing go up! It'll be awesome," Arnie said.

Arnie started the fire with some combustible material that he found on the first floor of the abandoned building. Within minutes the building was burning out of control. Fire fighters arrived and spent hours putting out the fire. During their inspection of the damage, fire investigators found the bodies of six homeless people—four men and two women—who apparently had been living in the building to escape the ravages of winter weather and were killed in the fire.

FROLIC UNDER THE INFLUENCE

Many heinous crimes of frolic are fueled by alcohol and other drugs. What begins as relatively innocent tomfoolery can quickly escalate into vicious misconduct when the culprits also indulge in alcohol and drugs, which inhibit impulse control and impair judgment.

Case 2.49 Earl W. and Kirk L. met as juveniles when both were residents of a state-sponsored group home. Both young men had lived in a series of foster homes and group residences after their respective parents' rights were terminated because of neglect and abuse. The two now shared an apartment.

Earl and Kirk often sat around the apartment and drank beer and alcohol. One day—at about 1:00 A.M.—after the two were quite inebriated, Earl told Kirk he was hungry and wanted to head out to the twenty-four-hour convenience store for some food. The two walked around the block, headed into the convenience store, and gathered some bread, deli meats, and cookies. At the cash register the men discovered that they had neglected to bring money with them. Earl pulled a handgun out of his jacket and playfully told the clerk that it might be a good idea to let the pair have the food for free. The cashier panicked and started screaming. Earl told her to calm down, but that didn't work. The cashier began to run out of the store, yelling for the police. Earl was afraid that the police would arrive and find out that he was on probation; without thinking, Earl shot the clerk in the back, killing her.

Case 2.50   Four teenagers—Paul C., Brandt L., Benjie K., and Cindy D.—skipped school and went to Brandt's home to drink and smoke blunts (cigars laced with marijuana and cocaine). After about two hours of drinking and smoking, Paul suggested that Cindy perform a striptease for the three boys. After some pressuring, Cindy relented and performed on top of a coffee table. Paul then suggested that the three boys have sex with Cindy. Cindy protested, but the three young men raped her.

Case 2.51   Lester J. and Anthony S. were diehard sports fans. They often went to professional basketball and football games together.

Lester and Anthony managed to get tickets for a football play-off game. Sitting near them was a small group of fans who had driven a couple of hundred miles to support the opposing team. Throughout the game Lester and Anthony exchanged reasonably good-natured barbs with the rival group of fans. Toward the end of the game, however, after Lester and Anthony had drunk a great deal of beer, the exchanges became more tense and hostile. As Lester and Anthony's team began to fall behind in the waning minutes of the game, a visiting fan made a taunting remark. Lester climbed over several rows of seats and began pummeling the rival fan. A fight ensued, and Lester ended up banging the fan's head repeatedly against the metal railing adjacent to his seat. The victim suffered a brain hemorrhage and permanent brain damage.

Crimes of Addiction

Overwhelming empirical evidence shows that a substantial percentage of heinous crime is committed by people who struggle with addictions, including substance abuse and pathological gambling (Ball et al. 1982; Ditton 1999; Goldstein 1985; Goldstein, Brownstein, and Ryan 1992;

Greenfeld 1998; Harrison and Gfroerer 1992; MacCoun and Reuter 1998; Mumola 1998, 1999). These include heinous crimes committed while under the influence of drugs (especially narcotics) and crimes committed to obtain money for drugs or to pay off gambling debts (Blaszczynski and Silove 1995; Blume 1995; Custer and Milt 1985; Dickerson and Baron 2000; National Research Council 1999; Shaffer et al. 1989; Volberg 1994).

SUBSTANCE ABUSE

Substance abuse and heinous crimes intersect in two principal ways. First, some heinous crimes are committed by addicts who are under the influence of drugs or alcohol. Narcotics, alcohol, and other substances can lead otherwise nonviolent people to commit remarkably violent acts and may exacerbate the tendencies of individuals who are prone to violence. A significant number of murders, aggravated assaults, and armed robberies are committed by people whose judgment is severely impaired by drugs or alcohol. Second, many heinous crimes are committed by addicts who are desperate for money or valuable property to enable them to purchase drugs to feed their addiction (Ball et al. 1982; Goldstein 1985; Goldstein, Brownstein, and Ryan 1992; Greenfeld 1998; Harrison and Gfroerer 1992; MacCoun and Reuter 1998; Mumola 1998, 1999).

Case 2.52 Dean E. was a heroin addict. He had been imprisoned twice for drug manufacturing and selling and was recently released after serving his full sentence. Dean was being supervised by a probation officer and was enrolled in an outpatient drug treatment program. He returned to his job with a landscape contractor.

About four months after his release from prison, Dean relapsed on heroin. This occurred not long after Dean learned that his twenty-year-old daughter had committed suicide. Dean was soon fired from his job due to his erratic behavior and was desperate for money to buy heroin. One evening Dean walked into an upscale restaurant, held a gun to the head of the cashier, and demanded money from the cash drawer. The restaurant's maitre d' walked in and confronted Dean. Dean shoved his shoulder into the maitre d' and the gun went off accidentally, killing the maitre d'.

Case 2.53 Colleen O. was a cocaine addict. She left a friend's party under the influence and began driving home. She ran a red light and broadsided an oncoming car driven by a young mother who had her twin infants in the backseat. The twins were killed instantly; their mother lingered in the hospital in a persistent vegetative state and died six weeks after the accident.

Case 2.54   Antonia L. was a hospital nurse who took a leave of absence after a freak accident at home in which she severely injured her back. Antonia's doctor prescribed Vicodin, a powerful pain medication derived from opium. Over time Antonia became addicted to the Vicodin and began snorting it.

Antonia returned to work and got a job at a nursing home. To feed her addiction she began stealing a liquid opioid, Oxyfast, from three elderly residents who were suffering from cancer-related pain. In an effort to conceal her theft Antonia replaced the residents' pain medication with water and food coloring to match the medication's original color.

PATHOLOGICAL GAMBLING

Not surprisingly, the proliferation of legalized gambling has caused an increase in gambling-related crime. The relatively small percentage of gamblers who have a pathological addiction are responsible for a number of heinous crimes committed to obtain money for gambling or to pay off gambling debts (Blaszczynski and Silove 1995; Blume 1995; Custer and Milt 1985; Dickerson and Baron 2000; National Research Council 1999; Shaffer et al. 1989; Volberg 1994).

Case 2.55   Tim M. was a police officer who had been on the force for three years. About a year after he joined the force, he began gambling at a nearby casino. Tim preferred blackjack and craps.

Over time Tim spent more and more time gambling. At first he convinced himself that his gambling was under control. Soon it became clear that Tim was addicted and in over his head. His recent losses totaled $67,000—nearly all his savings.

One night, while at work, Tim was dispatched to the scene of a robbery of an exclusive jewelry store. During his search of the premises he stumbled across an open case of diamonds that the thieves apparently dropped. He glanced around and saw that no other officers or detectives were in the room with him. Tim slipped several diamonds, worth a total of about $90,000, into his pocket. Tim reasoned that the jeweler's insurance company would cover the loss, and Tim would be able to cover his substantial gambling debts.

Case 2.56   Howard G. was a young lawyer. In college Howard started placing bets on professional sports—primarily basketball, baseball, and football. Howard's bets got larger and larger as he enjoyed professional success as a real estate attorney.

About five years after he started practicing law, Howard became addicted to sports betting. In a typical weekend Howard bet more than $10,000 on various games. During one particularly bad spell Howard was $130,000 in debt. In desperation he wrote himself checks on the escrow accounts of several clients in order to cover his gambling losses. Howard also lied to two clients about the size of the settlements that he had negotiated on their behalf in real estate–related lawsuits. Howard pocketed $87,000 that should have gone to these two clients.

Case 2.57   Karen R. was the office manager for a large independent supermarket. Her duties involved managing payroll, invoices, and daily bank deposits.

Karen had become addicted to casino gambling. She started out by playing bingo and eventually became addicted to slot machines and roulette. She had lost so much money gambling that she was at risk of losing her house and car. Karen had received a foreclosure notice from the bank after failing to make a number of mortgage payments, and she bounced several checks that she had sent to her credit union for her automobile loan.

In her job at the supermarket Karen processed large amounts of cash. She started skimming cash in relatively small amounts, but over time the amounts increased. The supermarket's accountant noticed a cash-flow problem when she conducted a routine audit and notified the market's owners. Karen was indicted on charges of embezzling more than $140,000 during a two-year period. The market's owner never recovered the lost money and had to spend considerable sums on attorneys to negotiate settlements with the Internal Revenue Service concerning unpaid taxes.

Crimes of Mental Illness

Some perpetrators of heinous crimes intend their offenses and understand the actual and potential consequences. Consistent with classical theories of etiology and crime causation, some offenders are able to control their actions but, for a variety of reasons, choose not to.

Clearly, other perpetrators have no, or very little, understanding of their behavior and are able to exercise no, or very little, control over it. Consistent with positivist theories of crime causation and etiology, these perpetrators' behavior is a function of circumstances over which they have little, if any, control. Often this lack of control results from the offender's bona fide mental illness or mental retardation (Ditton 1999; Guy et al. 1985; Powell, Holt, and Fondacaro 1997; Steadman et al. 1989; Teplin 1990). Recent studies suggest that 7 percent of federal prison inmates are mentally ill; 16 percent of inmates in state prisons, local jails, or on probation report a mental condition or have stayed overnight in a psychiatric hospital, unit, or treatment program; and 20 percent of violent offenders manifest symptoms of mental illness (Ditton 1999).

PSYCHOTIC DISORDERS

Some heinous crimes are committed by people who are in the midst of a psychotic episode or have a chronic history of psychosis. The term *psychotic* usually refers to the presence of delusions (severely distorted thinking or cognition) or prominent hallucinations (for example, hearing voices that issue commands to commit crimes).

Schizophrenia is a common psychotic disorder found among heinous offenders who have a major mental illness. Schizophrenia entails some combination of delusions, hallucinations, disorganized speech (incoherence), and grossly disorganized or catatonic behavior involving significant psychomotor disturbance (such as excessive motor activity). Some people with schizophrenia may also manifest symptoms of paranoia (for example, persecutory delusions where an offender assaults or kills someone whom he or she imagines is "out to get" him or her), disorganized speech and behavior, and flat or inappropriate affect (American Psychiatric Association 2000).

Case 2.58 Charles Z. was diagnosed with schizophrenia when he was seventeen. Charles had been hospitalized on a number of occasions but was able to manage in the community when stabilized on psychotropic medication. He lived with his parents in a suburb adjacent to a large city.

Over a period of time Charles became sexually involved with four young boys in the community. Charles lured them to an abandoned clubhouse close to his home and sexually abused them. During a three-month period, three of the boys disappeared and were reported missing. Charles eventually became a suspect, and for several weeks undercover police followed him closely. The dismembered bodies of the three missing boys were found in plastic garbage bags hidden in a closet at the abandoned clubhouse.

Case 2.59 Sam E. lived about three blocks from a small women's college. He had been diagnosed with paranoid schizophrenia when he was twenty-one. He had spent nearly four years in state prison on a variety of drug-related charges and sex offenses. Since his most recent release from prison, Sam had been receiving outpatient services (mental health and substance abuse counseling) at a local community mental health center.

Sam's symptoms worsened, and he stopped going to the community mental health center for counseling and medication. He became more and more paranoid and began to hear voices that told him he needed to hurt women at the college in order to protect himself from harm. Sam believed that God sent him personal commands through the temperature displayed on the outdoor thermometer at his home. During a two-month period Sam abducted and raped three students at the college. Two managed to escape, and one was never found.

Case 2.60   Joy H. began to manifest psychotic symptoms when she was twelve. She lived with her parents until she was twenty and became pregnant. Joy received services from the local community mental health center, lived in a supervised apartment, and was reasonably stable while on psychotropic medication. She maintained a relationship with her son's father.

During a routine visit at Joy's apartment, a visiting pediatric nurse noticed tears in the baby's anus. The baby displayed various distress symptoms, suggesting that he may have been sexually abused. Evidence presented at trial showed that Joy, whose psychotic symptoms were florid when she was arrested, had been performing oral sex on her son and held her son down while the baby's father sodomized him.

MOOD DISORDERS

Some perpetrators of heinous crimes suffer from serious disturbances of their mood, usually in the form of major depression or bipolar disorder. Along with other symptoms related to changes in diet, sleep, and sexual activity, major depression typically entails a sustained period of some combination of severely depressed mood most of the day, nearly every day; markedly diminished interest or pleasure in all, or almost all, activities during most of the day; psychomotor agitation or retardation; feelings of worthlessness or excessive or inappropriate guilt nearly every day; diminished ability to think or concentrate, or indecisiveness; and recurrent thoughts of death, recurrent suicidal ideation, or suicide attempts (American Psychiatric Association 2000; Mondimore 1995).

Bipolar disorder typically entails some combination of depressive episodes and manic episodes. A manic episode involves an abnormally and persistently elevated, expansive, and irritable mood during a significant period of time, with symptoms such as grandiosity, reduced need for sleep, increased talkativeness, racing thoughts, distractibility, increased activity, and excessive pleasure seeking (American Psychiatric Association 2000).

Case 2.61   Scott N. was a well-known plastic surgeon. Unbeknown to his wife, Sally, Scott had been having an affair with a colleague. At one point Scott's mistress, Laura D., threatened to tell Scott's wife about the affair unless he left the marriage and moved in with Laura.

During this time Scott was also being treated by a psychiatrist for severe depression. For several days during a one-week period Scott was feeling profoundly depressed and contemplated suicide. He failed to show up for office appointments and stopped communicating with Laura and Sally.

One afternoon Scott wrote out a suicide note, drove over to Laura's home, shot her in the head with a handgun, and then killed himself.

Case 2.62   Sean R. was a nurse in a clinic that provided services to patients with HIV-AIDS. For years he had coped with symptoms of bipolar disorder that were usually managed well with psychotropic medication, although recently Sean's mood swings were worsening.

One afternoon Sean was driving home from work and stopped at a service station that he often patronized. Another customer had parked his car at an odd angle and in such a way that Sean was not able to pull his car next to the gas pump. When the customer left the service station's office, Sean lost his temper and began berating the customer. The customer responded in kind, and the two threatened to harm each other. Sean retreated to his car where he kept a handgun in the glove compartment. He grabbed the gun and threatened his adversary, who dared Sean to shoot him. Sean pulled the trigger and killed the other customer. Evidence presented at trial showed that for more than two months Sean had not been taking the psychotropic medication prescribed for his bipolar disorder.

Case 2.63   Edgar C. was a psychologist employed at a state psychiatric hospital. He worked primarily with patients diagnosed with schizophrenia.

One patient sent a letter to Edgar's supervisor complaining that Edgar was making sexual advances toward him and proselytizing about his religious beliefs. The supervisor told Edgar about the letter and assumed that it reflected the patient's chronic psychiatric condition. The patient continued to write similar letters to hospital administrators. Each letter was filled with details about alleged sexual advances and proselytizing.

One afternoon a nurse supervisor was leaving the hospital when she noticed that the psychologist was kneeling outside the main entrance. She approached him and discovered that he was delusional and hallucinating. The nurse supervisor ushered the psychologist into the hospital and notified the chief psychiatrist. The psychiatrist examined the psychologist and concluded that he was in the midst of a manic episode with psychotic features.

Once he was stabilized, the psychologist disclosed that for years he had been treated for bipolar disorder but had stopped taking his medication. The psychologist also confessed that he had made sexual advances toward the patient and had fondled him on several occasions. The psychologist blamed his behavior on his untreated bipolar disorder.

PARAPHILIAS

Some of the most heinous crimes in recorded history have been committed by offenders who have had diagnosed, or diagnosable, paraphilias. Paraphilias involve "recurrent, intense sexually arousing fantasies, sexual urges, or behaviors generally involving 1) nonhuman objects, 2) the suffering or humiliation of oneself or one's partner, or 3) children or other nonconsenting persons" (American Psychiatric Association 2000:566).

Pedophilia is the most prominent paraphilia found among perpetrators of heinous crimes. Pedophilia involves sexual activity with a prepubescent child (generally thirteen or younger). Pedophiles usually report an attraction to children within a particular age range. Some offenders prefer males, some prefer females, and some have no preference (Feierman 1990; Quinsey 1998; Schwartz and Cellini 1995, 1997, 1999).

Pedophiles engage in a variety of behaviors; they may limit themselves to undressing a child and only looking, or they may expose themselves, masturbate in the child's presence, fondle the child, perform fellatio or cunnilingus on the child, or penetrate the child's mouth, vagina, or anus with their fingers, foreign objects, or penis.

Case 2.64 Jason O. was a supervisor in the county child welfare department. He was primarily responsible for administering the county's mental health program for low-income children with major psychiatric needs.

One afternoon the county sheriff's department received a telephone call from the manager of a local motel. The motel manager told the police that he suspected that a child was being sexually abused in a motel room. The manager explained that the man who accompanied a young boy behaved suspiciously when he registered and that he heard screams coming from the motel room, which was close to the registration desk.

The sheriff obtained a search warrant and found Jason in the motel room engaged in sexual activity with the boy. The two were surrounded by sexual paraphernalia and cocaine. Jason was charged with child molestation. Later investigation revealed that the boy was in the legal custody of the child welfare department when the sexual abuse occurred.

Case 2.65 Danny T., twelve, was having considerable difficulty in school. His parents met with the school's vice principal and social worker. Everyone was mystified by the relatively sudden decline in Danny's schoolwork. After several conversations and interviews with Danny, he finally told his parents that their priest has been fondling him after choir practice on Thursday evenings. Danny also reported that the priest had recruited Danny to perform fellatio on him. The priest was arrested and negotiated a reduced sentence in exchange for his guilty plea. Danny's family agreed to the plea bargain to avoid having Danny testify in court.

Case 2.66 Keith A. worked as a technician at a veterinarian's office. He was primarily responsible for greeting customers and their pets and caring for pets postoperatively. Keith sometimes worked the overnight shift.

One night, at about 11:00 P.M., Keith soaked a large piece of gauze with Halothane, an anesthetic agent, walked up quietly behind the only other technician on duty, Michelle S., and placed the gauze over her mouth and nose. After she lost consciousness, Keith undressed her, put on her underwear, and masturbated. Keith then fondled Michelle and inserted his fingers in her vagina and anus. Keith was discovered when one of the clinic's veterinarians paid an unexpected visit to check on the status of a vulnerable dog.

MENTAL RETARDATION

A relatively small percentage of heinous crimes are committed by people who qualify for a formal diagnosis of mental retardation. These perpetrators are often known as "naive offenders" because of their limited cognitive capacity.

The diagnosis of mental retardation applies when an individual has an intelligence quotient (IQ) of approximately 70 or less, as measured by standardized tests such as Wechsler Intelligence Scales and the Stanford-Binet (American Psychiatric Association 2000; Beirne-Smith, Patton, and Ittenbach 2001). Individuals with mental retardation who commit heinous crimes typically manifest deficits or impairments related to basic communication, self-care, social and interpersonal skills, self-direction, health, and safety.

Case 2.67 Adam M., twenty-four, had an IQ of 60. Since his preteen years he had been fascinated by fires. Adam also had a history of fondling young children.

As a juvenile Adam had been arrested six times on arson charges; as an adult Adam had been arrested twelve times. His most recent arrest was for setting fire to a small apartment building in his neighborhood. Just before he set the fire, Adam fondled a ten-year-old boy who lived in the building.

Case 2.68 As a child Ira D. was always in special education classes. His family always considered him slow, but it was not until Ira was in the sixth grade that school personnel concluded that he had mental retardation.

Ira was expelled from his middle school because he repeatedly exposed himself to male students. On one occasion Ira fondled a male student in the boys' restroom and performed fellatio on him.

As an adult Ira lived in a supervised group home. He was arrested for sodomizing one of the other group home residents.

Case 2.69 Brenda G., thirty-one, had the cognitive capacity of a ten-year-old. Brenda lived in a group home for women with mental retardation.

One evening Brenda got into an intense argument with another group home resident, Thalia R. The argument began when the two disagreed about which television station to watch on the set in the living room. Brenda started screaming at Thalia, who responded by pushing Brenda. Brenda ran into the kitchen, grabbed shears that were on the counter for trimming the property's bushes, and stabbed Thalia in the chest.

DISSOCIATIVE DISORDERS

Another small percentage of perpetrators of heinous crimes manifest symptoms of so-called dissociative disorders, which entails "a disruption in the usually integrated functions of consciousness, memory, identity, or perception" (American Psychiatric Association 2000:519). Some offenders have problems with basic memory (dissociative amnesia); sudden and unexpected travel away from home or work, accompanied by an inability to recall one's past and confusion about personal identity or the assumption of a new identity (dissociative fugue); a persistent or recurring feeling of being detached from one's mental processes or body (depersonalization disorder); and the presence of two or more distinct identities or personality states that recurrently take control of one's behavior, accompanied by an inability to recall important personal information that is too extensive to be explained by ordinary forgetfulness (dissociative identity disorder, formerly known as multiple personality disorder) (American Psychiatric Association 2000; Kluft and Fine 1993; Piper 1996; Ross 1996).

Case 2.70 Leon F. ran his own computer consulting business. He had contracts with a number of small retail store owners to provide technical assistance with their computers. Leon preferred running his own small business; he had always had difficulty working in larger settings.

Leon had been severely abused as a young child by his mother's live-in boyfriend; the boyfriend was an alcoholic who often beat Leon when he wet his bed, did not clean up his toys, or made a mess during meals. Leon had received counseling off and on but not in recent years.

One afternoon Leon got on a Greyhound bus, traveled to a city about 180 miles away, got off the bus, and began walking the streets near a college campus. He walked through a wooded park connecting two sections of the campus, accosted a female student, dragged her to a small shelter, and raped her. Soon after, Leon was arrested, based on a tip provided police by an eyewitness. When Leon was questioned by the police, he could not recall his name or details about his departure from his home.

Case 2.71   Jeffrey E., thirty-nine, was sexually abused as a child by several neighborhood children. The brutal abuse occurred over several months and involved sodomy, fellatio, masturbation, and fondling.

As an adult Jeffrey had difficulty sustaining friendships and intimate relationships. In his early twenties he began to manifest symptoms of dissociative disorder; he occasionally assumed different identities and names. His personalities had different accents, histories, family members, and occupations.

One night Jeffrey was arrested on child molestation charges. Police came to his apartment after receiving a telephone call from a neighbor who suspected that Jeffrey was molesting children. When he answered the door, Jeffrey identified himself as "Gregory" and claimed, sincerely and earnestly, that he was not Jeffrey E. and did not know Jeffrey E.

Case 2.72   Marion T., forty-one, had been hospitalized in psychiatric units a number of times during her adolescent and young adult years. Her symptoms typically involved some kind of dissociation, where Marion seemed unable to remember her name or recognize family members.

In recent years Marion lived with an older sister in a large apartment complex. She was unable to work because of her psychiatric challenges and received disability income.

One afternoon Marion got into an argument with a neighbor, with whom Marion was quite friendly and sometimes socialized, when both wanted to use the one available washing machine in the apartment building's laundry room. According to the neighbor, who was later interviewed by detectives, Marion began calling her by someone else's name and referred to herself by an unfamiliar name. The neighbor reported that the argument escalated and that Marion stabbed her repeatedly with a screwdriver that a repair person had left on top of a washing machine.

Heinous crimes and criminals are complicated. Diverse etiological theories and conceptually based typologies have enriched our collective understanding of the attributes of offenders and the reasons why they commit crimes. The typology of criminal circumstances will be particularly helpful as I explore such appropriate responses to heinous crimes as punishment, incarceration for public safety, rehabilitation and treatment, and restorative justice.

3

RETRIBUTION AND REVENGE

What heinous crimes have in common is that they are shocking. These cases, more than any other crimes, lead to newspaper headlines, television and radio news reports, and Internet bulletins that invariably make us shake our heads, go weak in the knees, feel faint, and cry.

These are also the cases that boil our blood and make us seethe with vengeful rage. Reports that a man slit the throat of a sleeping four-year-old, that a toddler was raped by his mother's boyfriend, an elderly couple died in a fire-for-profit, a nurse was kidnapped as she left the hospital and then was raped and murdered by her assailant, that a priest sodomized a young parishioner, and a man pushed his lover off a bridge to her death take our breath away. In countless conversations around the dinner table, office water cooler, hairdresser's waiting room, and in the psychotherapist's office, ordinary human beings with commonsense instincts yearn to understand what defies comprehension and yearn for revenge and punishment. It is a basic, perhaps even primordial, response to the most cruel, inhumane offenses one can imagine.

REVENGE AND RETRIBUTION: THE CONCEPTS

Why is it that human beings sometimes feel a compelling need for revenge? Our instinctive wish to punish people who commit heinous acts reflects what is known in philosophical circles as the retributivist view of justice (Ezorsky 1972; von Hirsch 1998). According to Michael S. Moore, "Retribution is the view that punishment is justified by the moral culpability of those who receive it. A retributivist punishes because, and only because, the offender deserves it" (1995:94). As the sixteenth-century Dutch jurist Hugo Grotius said, punishment is "the infliction of an ill suffered for an ill done" (cited in Bean 1981:4).

Retribution carries out the expressive function of punishment (Feinberg 1965); condemnation of the offender provides the broader society with an opportunity to "restore the moral balance disturbed by crime" (Ezorsky 1972:xvii). According to Ezorsky, "for all retributivists punishment has moral worth independently of any further desirable effects. *Ceteris paribus,* the world is better, morally speaking, when the vicious suffer. Thus it is not surprising that retributivism is sometimes characterized as the vindictive theory of punishment" (1972:xviii).

For strict retributivists what matters is that punishment be exacted for the sake of punishment. Whether the punishment prevents future crime by rehabilitating or deterring offenders is entirely or largely irrelevant.[1] Punishment restores balance or equilibrium in the relationship between the offender—who took unfair advantage of others—and the broader culture (Dagger 1995). As Morris (1972) observes,

> A person who violates the rules has something others have—the benefits of the system—but by renouncing what others have assumed, the burdens of self-restraint, he has acquired an unfair advantage. Matters are not even until this advantage is in some way erased. Another way of putting it is that he owes something to others, for he has something that does not rightfully belong to him. Justice—that is punishing such individuals—restores the equilibrium of benefits and burdens by taking from the individual what he owes, that is exacting the debt. (117)

Proponents of retribution tend to use four key arguments to justify their belief that punishment is an appropriate response to heinous crime: revenge, condemnation, deontological theories, and just deserts (Tunick 1992; von Hirsh 1998).

Revenge

For many the wish for vengeance and retribution is rooted in hateful feelings directed at the heinous offender—a common and understandable response to odious conduct. As Murphy (1995) observes,

> I have come to the conclusion that most of us *do* accept, as a matter of common sense, the appropriateness of hatred and revenge in some circumstances—specifically when these responses are exhibited by victims of serious

wrongdoing and are directed against those who have wronged them. . . . Although most people pay a kind of general Sunday school lip service to the idea that even these hatreds are evil, their more casual conversations and practices will often fly in the face of these pious clichés. (134–35)

Victims of heinous crimes, and those who merely hear the gory details recounted in media reports and casual conversations, often feel unmitigated hatred toward the offenders. It is only human to abhor, detest, and revile the perpetrator of heinous crime. As the vindictive Achilles says in the *Iliad* with respect to getting even with Agamemnon: "Not if his gifts outnumbered the sea sands or all the dust grains in the world could Agamemnon ever appease me—not till he pays me back full measure, pain for pain, dishonor for dishonor" (IX:383–86, cited in Murphy 1995:132). The nineteenth-century jurist James Fitzjames Stephen also articulates this sentiment succinctly in his 1883 publication, *A History of the Criminal Law in England*: "I think it highly desirable that criminals should be hated, and that punishments inflicted upon them should be so contrived as to give expression to that hatred, and to justify it so far as the public provisions of means for expressing and gratifying a healthy natural sentiment can justify and encourage it" (cited in Bean 1981:21).

I have heard many crime victims speak venomously about the offenders who harmed them. Often the victims' words drip with an intense, pressured anger that permeates their passionate wish for retribution and revenge:[2]

He better hope he never bumps into me in a dark alleyway—I'd kill the bastard. I wake up every morning feeling angry. I never used to be like that. This guy is scum. I probably shouldn't tell you about the things I'd like to do to him. He should suffer the way my poor kid has suffered. If there's any justice in the world, he will.

Father of a young child who was molested by the inmate

I can't tell you how much I'd like to give him a taste of his own medicine so he can feel what it's like to have his head split open by a baseball bat. Do you have any idea what it's like to be attacked like that? I hope it never happens to anyone you know. Please don't let him out—let him sit here and think about what he did to me. He deserves this—and worse.

Victim of domestic violence

I lay in bed at night fantasizing about how I could torture him, to pay him back for what he's done to me. He's ruined my life and he should pay. Before all this happened, I used to enjoy being with people, trusting people.

Ever since the rape I haven't been able to trust anyone. I know it doesn't really make sense, but that's the fact. Maybe someone in prison will assault him the way he assaulted me. I can only hope.

Rape survivor

She has ruined us, you know. For years we treated her like a daughter and what does she do? She ruins us financially by stealing from us, right from under our noses. We've had to declare bankruptcy because of her. Bankruptcy! I want her to sit here and suffer for the next four years. We're suffering; she should suffer too.

Victim of embezzlement

Condemnation

Many people feel a need to do more than seek retribution against offenders who commit heinous crimes; after all, retribution reflects an individual's *private* desire for revenge. In addition, many people feel compelled to publicly condemn the offender. As Thomas Carlyle, the early-nineteenth-century English essayist and historian, observed: "Revenge, my friends, revenge and the natural hatred of scoundrels, and the ineradicable tendency to *revancher* oneself upon them, and pay them what they have merited; this is forever intrinsically a correct, and even a divine feeling in the mind of every man" (cited in Blanshard 1968:70).

Condemnation entails several key elements. First, it includes a public statement that the offender has injured victims, including the broader society whose rules the offender violated (Feinberg 1965). Second, condemnation entails a deliberate effort to shame the offender. According to this view, "we do not punish to deter, incapacitate, reform, or satisfy a private desire for vengeance; rather, punishment is justified as an expression of society's condemnation of the offensive act" (Tunick 1992:90; also see Cullen, Fisher, and Applegate 2000). It is not unusual for victims of heinous crimes to yearn for public condemnation as a supplement to their more personal wish for revenge:

Remember the old stockades they used to use when people committed crimes? I'd like to put him in one of those out in the middle of town. I'd like to see him sit there and bake in the sun while people march by and stare. I'll lead the tours!

Victim of a home invasion

You know what I'd like to do? I'd like to take her to nursing homes and force her to tell her story to residents there. Can you imagine how that would make her feel? She should feel ashamed of herself.

Daughter of nursing home resident whose pain
medication was stolen by an employee

Here's what I want: I want his picture plastered all over town, on television, on the Internet. I want everyone to know that he's a child molester. I don't want him to be able to hide anywhere. I want him to feel like people are staring at him, wherever he goes.

Mother of child molestation victim

Deontological Theories

In classic moral philosophy deontology (from the Greek *deontos*, "of the obligatory") is the view that certain actions (such as telling the truth or keeping promises) are inherently right (or wrong), without regard for their consequences. The deontological view is typically contrasted with the tele-ological (or consequentialist) view that the moral rightness of any action is determined by the desirability or goodness of its consequences. With regard to punishment a deontologist would argue that retribution is inherently right, simply because the offender has engaged in wrongdoing. A teleologist, however, would feel compelled to justify retribution and punishment based on its consequences, for example, the extent to which retribution and pun-ishment deter future crime, rehabilitate the offender, save the public money, and so on (Hancock 1974; Reamer 1989, 1990). That is, retribution and punishment must be imposed as a means to an end. As Tunick observes, "Where retributivism is seen as a deontological theory that is mutually exclusive of teleological theories, the retributivist insists that we punish, not for any consequences, such as to deter future crimes, or to reform or incapacitate the criminal, but, rather, for the sake of punishing, because punishing is in itself just or right—regardless of the good it may yield" (1992:95). Immanuel Kant is typically regarded as the quintessential de-ontologist, particularly with respect to punishment. Among the earliest classic commentaries on the retributive functions of punishment are Kant's nineteenth-century observations in *The Philosophy of Law:*

> Juridical punishment can never be administered merely as a means for pro-moting another good, either with regard to the criminal himself or to civil

society, but must in all cases be imposed only because the individual on whom it is inflicted has committed a crime. For one man ought never to be dealt with merely as a means subservient to the purpose of another, nor be mixed up with the subjects of real right. Against such treatment his inborn personality has a right to protect him, even although he may be condemned to lose his civil personality. He must first be found guilty and punishable, before there can be any thought of drawing from his punishment any benefit for himself or his fellow-citizens. (1887, cited in Ezorsky 1972:103–4)

The standard deontological view of retribution—as exemplified by Kant—clearly rests on an assumption that the offender is guilty as charged and should be held accountable. Viewed strictly, this suggests that offenders who have so-called diminished capacity—for example, as a function of their mental illness or mental retardation—should not be condemned or punished retributively. Here the central legal and moral concept of *mens rea*—or criminal intent—is relevant (Hart 1968). In the narrow legal sense *mens rea* is

a guilty mind; the mental state accompanying a forbidden act. For an act to constitute a criminal offense, the act usually must be illegal and accompanied by a requisite mental state. Criminal offenses are usually defined with reference to one of four recognized criminal states of mind that accompanies the actor's conduct: (1) intentionally; (2) knowingly; (3) recklessly; and (4) grossly (criminally) negligent. (Gifis 1991:296)

Therefore, when we respond retributively to heinous crimes, it is important for us to consider the extent to which the offender truly intended his crime and did so understanding the recklessness and likely effect of his actions. Offenders who lack *mens rea* do not warrant punishment and condemnation in the strictest sense of these terms (Hart 1968). According to McCloskey (1965),

Our moral conscience suggests that a punishment, to be just, must be merited by the committing of an offence. It follows from this that punishment, to be justly administered, must involve care in determining whether the offending person is really a responsible agent. And it implies that the punishment must not be excessive. It must not exceed what is appropriate to the crime. (cited in Ezorsky 1972:121)

The eminent British philosopher of jurisprudence H. L. A. Hart (1968) argues in his classic essay, *Punishment and Responsibility*, that four types of responsibility are relevant in discussions of the extent to which an offender should be punished:

- Role responsibility: People sometimes assume specific duties and responsibilities in life. Thus parents have a duty to care for their children. Physically abusing and neglecting one's children constitute a violation of one's role responsibility. A priest has a duty to minister to parishioners. A priest who sexually molests a child who is a member of the church choir violates his role responsibility.
- Causal responsibility: To say that an accused individual is responsible for a heinous crime is to say that a causal connection exists between the individual's conduct and the tragic consequences (what lawyers call proximate cause). In the narrow legal sense a court must have sufficient forensic evidence (as opposed to only circumstantial evidence) to demonstrate that the accused did, in fact, rape the victim, start the fire that killed a building's tenants, molest the child, or fire the gun that killed the victim.
- Legal liability responsibility: Individuals accused of committing heinous crimes may be legally liable if evidence exists that they were not, for example, psychiatrically impaired, immature (younger than the age of majority), or coerced. The law has strict criteria and rules for establishing whether one is legally responsible and therefore should be made to suffer or pay compensation to victims.
- Capacity responsibility: To conclude that an accused individual is responsible for committing a heinous crime, the state must show that he or she had the ability (or capacity) to understand what legal rules or ethical standards require, to reason and deliberate about these requirements, and to control his or her conduct.

No discussion about the nature of offenders' responsibility and culpability would be complete without some mention of the classic free will–determinism debate. On one side of the debate are those who argue that human beings—in this case, criminals—are willful actors who actively shape their destinies by making choices freely based on their personal preferences, wishes, and desires. On the other side are those who claim that human behavior is largely or entirely determined by a series of antecedent events and factors, such that any given "choice" or behavior is a mere byproduct of other factors, be they psychological, environmental, familial, physical, economic, or biological (Reamer 1983, 1993).

The free will–determinism debate has ancient philosophical roots. Empedocles and Heraclitus, for example, are early sources of pre-Socratic thought on the meaning of determinism in nature and the idea of natural law. In the fourth century B.C.E., the Stoics, the Greek school of philosophy founded by Zeno, gave prominence to ideas concerning determinism—especially the influence of divine will.

The origins of modern international debate about free will and determinism ordinarily trace to the work of the eighteenth-century French astronomer and mathematician Pierre Simon de Laplace. Laplace's assertions about determinism in the world as we know it depended heavily on the scientific theory of particle mechanics, according to which a knowledge of the mechanical state of all particles at some particular time, together with a knowledge of all other forces acting in nature at that instant, would enable one to discover all future and past states of the world. With this information one could, in principle, discover not only all future and past mechanical states in the world but all others as well, such as electromagnetic, chemical, and psychological.

According to determinism, then, we can trace problems such as heinous crime to historical antecedents that have led progressively to the offender's current difficulties and misconduct. The responsibility for the behavior of murderers, arsonists, rapists, child molesters, and armed robbers is not their own; rather, it resides in the occurrence and consequences of earlier events. Heinous offenders are not to be blamed for their unfortunate circumstances. It may *appear*, of course, that offenders are engaged in rational, independent choices to commit heinous crimes, but this, after all, is only an illusion, according to hard-core determinists. The modern philosopher John Hospers (1966) describes this view well in his essay "What Means This Freedom?"

> The position, then, is this: if we can overcome the effects of early environment, the ability to do so is itself a product of the early environment. We did not give ourselves this ability; and if we lack it we cannot be blamed for not having it. Sometimes, to be sure, moral exhortation brings out an ability that is there but not being used, and in this lies its occasional utility; but very often its use is pointless, because the ability is not there. The only thing that can overcome a desire, as Spinoza said, is a stronger contrary desire; and many times there simply is no wherewithal for producing a stronger contrary desire. Those of us who have the wherewithal are lucky. (40)

Proponents of the free-will school of thought, alternatively, deny that our thoughts, emotions, and behaviors—*criminals'* thoughts, emotions, and behaviors—are always a function of earlier circumstances over which we have little or no control. Free-will adherents rarely claim that no events are determined or that all events are truly random occurrences. Rather, they claim that some events—criminal acts—result from the exercise of free will or deliberate choice and that individuals do in fact have the capacity to behave independent of earlier circumstances and determinants, although to varying degrees.

My experience tells me that, without a doubt, how professionals in the criminal justice system respond to criminals is often a direct function of these professionals' beliefs about the extent to which the offenders sitting before them are (or are not) responsible, in the free-will sense of the term, for their misconduct. Police, judges, probation officers, and parole board members often react relatively leniently or punitively, depending on their belief about the offenders' ability to exercise self-control. At one extreme are offenders with severe psychiatric symptoms whose behavior is almost entirely or completely determined and far beyond their control. At the other extreme are offenders who seem to be cool, calculating, exploitative, and deliberate, embodying the most essential features of free will.

An alternative to extreme views of either free will or determinism that contains elements of both schools of thought has become known in philosophical circles as the mixed view, or soft determinism. This view perhaps has the most currency and relevance in work with heinous offenders. This perspective essentially entails three assumptions. The first is that the thesis of determinism is generally true and that, accordingly, human and criminal behaviors—both voluntary and involuntary—are preceded and caused by preexisting conditions, such that no other behavior is likely (for example, the direct effect of severe child abuse on a child's subsequent development and tendency toward domestic violence, the effect on a fetus of exposure to drugs in utero and subsequent drug addiction, the influence of profound poverty on an individual's subsequent ability to be self-supporting and crime free, and the influence on an individual's subsequent use of alcohol abuse of being raised in a household where the adults are chronic substance abusers). The second assumption is that genuinely voluntary behavior is nonetheless possible to the extent that it is not coerced, and the third assumption is that, in the absence of coercion, behavior results from the decisions, choices, and preferences of individuals (Taylor 1991). That is, the free-will and determinism positions can be complementary, as suggested by such noteworthy philosophers as Thomas Hobbes, David Hume, and John Stuart Mill (Ginet 1962).

Clearly, the degree to which we view heinous crime as a product of voluntary, willful effort or as determined, coerced behavior has profound implications for whether we respond to it retributively and punitively. Aristotle argued centuries ago that an individual is responsible only for those actions that are voluntary (Feinberg 1970); an action can fail to be voluntary in two principal ways: as the result of compulsion ("I fired the gun because my partner pushed my arm," "My brother pointed a gun at me and told me to start the fire or he'd shoot me," "My heroin addiction was so out of control that I *had* to find a way to get money fast") or ignorance ("I had no idea I could become addicted to cocaine," "I thought she was eighteen years old—I never would have had sex with her if I had known she was thirteen"). Retribution as a response to heinous crime becomes more problematic to the extent that we acknowledge factors in offenders' lives that caused them to behave as they did and limited their ability to control their behavior and act voluntarily. Brettschneider (2001) states the problem clearly:

> Retributivists also face a challenge from those who argue that one's particular circumstances in life often contribute to criminal acts. Without making the broader claims that determinists raise, these critics point out that it is often those who commit crimes who have been most abused by a given society, including abuse as children. This is especially the case when it comes to those who have committed capital crimes. Furthermore, those who commit the most serious crimes often grew up in poverty and/or live in poverty at the time their crime is committed.
>
> It could be argued that abuse or poverty is responsible for these crimes. On this view, to hold the criminal responsible is to blame the victim. Perhaps society at large, rather than the individual who committed the crime, should be found responsible for criminal acts. . . . The retributivist, however, need not abandon the claim of responsibility to respond to this challenge. First, the retributivist can respond that the fact that some are not responsible for crimes does not imply that all are not. In fact, the retributivist argument only addresses one's responsibility in particular circumstances and leaves room for the claim that those who have not been abused by family or society are responsible for their crimes. The philosopher John Rawls, for example, has argued that one's responsibility in regard to the law increases proportionally to the degree that one is treated well in life. In his words, the top tier of society holds certain "obligations" not required of those who have not benefited as greatly from society.
>
> In a practical sense, this view is incorporated into the legal decisions of judges who see poverty and abuse as mitigating circumstances in criminal cases. In other words, poverty or abuse could be seen to lessen the degree of

responsibility for a crime. In extreme cases of abuse, perhaps no punishment is deserved. Consider, for instance, an extreme case in which an individual is seldom fed and is kept in a cage for his entire lifetime. Perhaps if such a person were to commit a crime, he could be judged not responsible and thus not be punished. Most people fall on a continuum between this extreme and no abuse, but there is no reason to think that their degree of responsibility cannot be judged accordingly. In incorporating these practices, the retributivist could consistently claim that punishment should be less extreme for poor, abused criminals than for wealthy criminals who have not been abused. This claim is consistent with Nozick's formula that appropriate retributive punishment should be determined by multiplying responsibility by the degree of seriousness of the crime. (40–41)

Interestingly, some victims also grasp these conceptual nuances concerning circumstances that limit offenders' ability to control their behavior. In my experience a small, albeit significant, percentage of victims of heinous crimes are remarkably forgiving and charitable, tempering their pain and anguish with some understanding of the factors that appear to have led to offenders' misconduct:

Even though I'm horrified by what he did to me, I trust your judgment about whether he's ready for release. Frankly, I don't think this guy had a chance in life. In the courtroom I heard about how he was horribly abused as a child and lived in more than a dozen foster homes and group homes. He even lived on the streets for awhile. No wonder he developed a drug problem and robbed me. If you think he got good [substance abuse] treatment here, I wouldn't oppose his release.

Victim of armed robbery

I know it's hard for you to believe this, but when he's not drinking Johnny is really a good man. I know. I've lived with him for twelve years. It's true that he never should have stabbed me with the kitchen knife. That was horrible. But I know that's not the real Johnny. He's an alcoholic who needs help, just like his father. He was brought up thinking that what men do is drink and control women.

Victim of domestic violence

For years after the murder all I could think about was getting revenge. But, you know, during the past couple of years I've met with Darryl several times [as part of a formal prison-based mediation program]. I've gotten to know

Darryl as a person, and I've discovered how sorry he is about what happened when he shot my son. There's no excuse, of course, but I now understand how they were both involved with drugs. Without the drugs this never would have happened. I think he deserves a chance.

Mother of murder victim

Those of us who work with heinous offenders need to be particularly cognizant of the possibility that our resentment of offenders' behavior will shape our perception of their ability to control their behavior. The philosopher Harry Frankfurt puts it succinctly in his essay on coercion and moral responsibility: "We do on some occasions find it appropriate to make an adverse judgment concerning a person's submission to a threat, even though we recognize that he has genuinely been coerced and he is therefore not properly to be held morally responsible for his submission. This is because we think that the person, although he was in fact quite unable to control a desire, ought to have been able to control it" (1973:79).

Just Deserts

One other key ingredient for many people who favor retribution and punishment in response to heinous crime is the goal of just deserts (von Hirsch 1998). The principle of just deserts has ancient origins, dating at least as far as the Torah, the Koran, and the Code of Hammurabi. Perhaps the best-known characterization is *lex talionis*, or the law of talion (commonly known as the principle of "an eye for an eye"), a precept of ancient Hebrew scripture. Prominent references in the Torah include

When men strive together, and hurt a woman with child, so that there is a miscarriage, and yet no harm follows, the one who hurt her shall be fined, according as the woman's husband shall lay upon him; and he shall pay as the judges determine. If any harm follows, then you shall give life for life, eye for eye, tooth for tooth, hand for hand, foot for foot, burn for burn, wound for wound, stripe for stripe. (Exodus 21:22–25)

If a malicious witness rises against any man to accuse him of wrongdoing, then both parties to the dispute shall appear before the Lord, before the priests and the judges who are in office in those days; the judges shall inquire diligently, and if the witness is a false witness and has accused his brother falsely, then you shall do to him as he had meant to do to his brother; so you shall purge the evil from the midst of you. And the rest shall hear, and fear, and shall never again commit any such evil among you. Your eye shall not pity; it shall be life for life, eye for eye, tooth for tooth, hand for hand, foot for foot. (Deuteronomy 19:16–21)

He who kills a man shall be put to death. He who kills a beast shall make it good, life for life. When a man causes a disfigurement in his neighbor, as he has done it shall be done to him, fracture for fracture, eye for eye, tooth for tooth; as he has disfigured a man, he shall be disfigured. He who kills a beast shall make it good; and he who kills a man shall be put to death. (Leviticus 24:17–21)

Similarly, the Koran makes explicit references to principles of *lex talionis* in its formulation of Islamic law (Henberg 1990:117). Islamic law provides for exact retaliation (*qisas*) and payment of blood money (*diyah*) in response to wrongdoing: "And We prescribed to them in it that life is for life, and eye for eye, and nose for nose, and ear for ear, and tooth for tooth, and for wounds retaliation. But who so forgoes it, it shall be an expiation for him. And whosoever judges not by what Allah has revealed, those are the wrongdoers" (Koran 5:45).

The Code of Hammurabi (ca. 1728–1686 B.C.E.) also contains similar prescriptions (Henberg 1990). The code includes the first written evidence for penalizing offenses with an exact "talion": For personal injury the code prescribes taking an eye for an eye (no. 196), breaking a bone for a bone (no. 197), and extracting a tooth for a tooth (no. 199). Other sanctions are less exact and identical, for example, cutting out the tongue of an adoptive son who has denied his adoptive parents (no. 192), cutting off the breasts of a wet nurse who, without informing the parents, contracts for another child to replace a child who has died (no. 194), and cutting off the hand of a son who strikes his father (no. 195). Interestingly, as the following two cases illustrate, the Code of Hammurabi was quite elitist in that it legislated different consequences and penalties depending on the involvement of different classes of nobles, commoners, and slaves (Henberg 1990:63–64):

209: If a seignior struck a[nother] seignior's daughter and has caused her to have a miscarriage, he shall pay ten shekels of silver for her fetus.
210: If that woman has died, they shall put his daughter to death.
211: If by a blow he has caused a commoner's daughter to have a miscarriage, he shall pay five shekels of silver.
212: If that woman has died, he shall pay one-half mina of silver.

213: If he struck a seignior's female slave and has caused her to have a mis-carriage, he shall pay two shekels of silver.

214: If that female slave has died, he shall pay one-third mina of silver.

229: If a builder constructed a house for a seignior, but did not make his work strong, with the result that the house which he built collapsed and so has caused the death of the owner of the house, that builder shall be put to death.

230: If it has caused the death of a son of the owner of the house, they shall put the son of that builder to death.

231: If it has caused the death of a slave of the owner of the house, he shall give slave for slave to the owner of the house.

Also consider the spirit of *lex talionis* in this succinct excerpt (cited in Henberg 1990:85) from Aeschylus's *Agamemnon* (458 B.C.E.), where Clytemnestra's husband, Agamemnon, is fated to die for slaying his eldest daughter, Iphigenia:

The spoiler is robbed; he killed, he has paid.
The truth stands ever beside God's throne
Eternal: he who has wrought shall pay; that is law.

In the nineteenth century, Kant wrote his classic and oft-cited passage about the law of talion in *The Philosophy of Law*:

But what is the mode and measure of punishment which public justice takes as its principle and standard? It is just the principle of equality, by which the pointer of the scale of justice is made to incline no more to the one side than the other. It may be rendered by saying that the undeserved evil which any one commits on another, is to be regarded as perpetrated on himself. Hence it may be said: 'If you slander another, you slander yourself; if you steal from another, you steal from yourself; if you strike another, you strike yourself; if you kill another, you kill yourself.' This is the right of retaliation (*jus talionis*); and properly understood, it is the only principle which in regulating a public court, as distinguished from mere private judgment, can definitely assign both the quality and quantity of a just penalty. All other standards are wavering and uncertain; and on account of other considerations involved in them, they contain no principle conformable to the sentence of pure and strict justice. (1887, cited in Ezorsky 1972:104–5)

Many ancient and contemporary interpretations of retribution move beyond exact and identical penalties for like acts (eye for eye, tooth for tooth, and so on). Retributive responses to crime, the argument goes, should be guided by the concept of just deserts, where penalties are determined by assessments of how much suffering and misery an offender deserves based on the gravity and severity of his or her wrongdoing. That is, retribution and punishment ought to be proportional (Blomberg and Cohen 1995; von Hirsch 1998). As Ezorsky concludes with regard to determining appropriate punishment for an offender, "the misery he deserves depends on the moral wrong he has committed. Thus desert is a moral, not a legal notion. Suppose that torture of children were perfectly legal and shoplifting were illegal. It would be true, nevertheless, that those who torture children deserve to suffer more than shoplifters" (1972:xxii). Criminal offenses that are more serious warrant more severe punishment than offenses that are less serious. For Murphy, "all criminals have a fundamental right not to be punished in excess of their just deserts. A person is punished in excess of his just deserts if he is punished with greater severity than the blameworthy character of his conduct would justify" (1995:145).

An alternative view of the concept of just deserts was espoused by F. H. Bradley, the noted nineteenth-century British philosopher, who argued in *Ethical Studies* (1927) that criminals deserve to be punished because they have earned a right to be punished by being guilty:

> If there is any opinion to which the man of uncultivated morals is attached, it is the belief in the necessary connexion of punishment and guilt. Punishment is punishment, only where it is deserved. We pay the penalty because we owe it, and for no other reason; and if punishment is inflicted for any other reason whatever than because it is merited by wrong, it is a gross immorality, a crying injustice, an abominable crime, and not what it pretends to be. We may have regard for whatever considerations we please—our own convenience, the good of society, the benefit of the offender; we are fools, and worse, if we fail to do so. Having once the right to punish, we may modify the punishment according to the useful and the pleasant; but these are external to the matter, they can not give us a right to punish, and nothing can do that but criminal desert. (26)

Many criminal justice professionals and members of the public hold a commonsense view that punishments and penalties should take diverse mitigating factors into consideration. In the context of the free will–

determinism spectrum, some would distinguish between the remorseful indigent mother who robbed a convenience store solely to feed her starving children and the opportunistic, arrogant criminal who viewed armed robbery as a much more expedient way to obtain cash than earnest labor. Some would distinguish between the arsonist with mental retardation—who functioned at the cognitive level of a nine-year-old and generated excitement in his life by lighting fires—and the fully cognizant arsonist who torched an occupied dwelling to make quick cash from a man who wanted his estranged wife to die.

It is not unusual to hear victims of heinous crimes comment on the correlation between the gravity of the crime and the offender's punishment:

> My son is in the ground, sentenced to death by that bastard. My son can't be paroled. He should serve his entire sentence for what he did—no breaks. If you let him out now, after serving only a third of his sentence, what does that say to us?
>
> Father of murdered son

> He stole my daughter's childhood from her. She can't sleep at night, she's afraid to be alone, she's a mess. He did that to her—he's ruined my daughter's life; now his life should be ruined. He has no right to get out of prison so soon. Let him out when my daughter can sleep at night without nightmares—that might be never.
>
> Mother of child molestation victim

> I can't believe this guy is already up for parole. What kind of justice is that? I mean, he shot one of my clerks and held a gun to my head—I thought it was all over for me. I'm just lucky he panicked when he heard the police sirens. I want him to sit here [in prison] a lot longer—this is where he deserves to be for what he did.
>
> Victim of armed robbery

The philosopher H. J. McCloskey (1965) reflected on the appropriateness of correlating penalties with the gravity of the offense:

> The criminal is one who has made himself unequal in the relevant sense. Hence he merits unequal treatment. In this case, unequal treatment amounts to deliberate infliction of evils—suffering or death. . . . If the deserved punishment is inflicted, all we need to do to justify it is to point out

that the crime committed deserved and merited such punishment. Suppose that the just punishment for murder is imprisonment for 15 years. Suppose also that the judge knows that the murderer he is about to sentence will never be tempted to commit another murder, that he is deeply and genuinely remorseful, and that others will not be encouraged to commit murders if he is treated leniently. If the judge imposed a mild penalty we should probably applaud his humanity, but if he imposed the maximum penalty we should not be entitled to condemn him as unjust. (cited in Ezorsky 1972:131–32)

That is not to say that it is always easy to calculate proportionate penalties for diverse offenses. Clearly, we can agree that some offenses are particularly reprehensible—such as choking an infant to death when she would not stop crying, stealing elderly nursing home patients' pain medication, or raping a twelve-year-old babysitter—and warrant severe penalties. However, once we move past such black-and-white distinctions, inevitably we will encounter shades of gray where we may disagree about the relative seriousness of diverse offenses and the appropriateness of various punishments. Is an armed robbery of a bank teller in which no one was physically injured more or less serious than burning down an unoccupied home? Is marital rape more or less serious than holding the child of a corporate executive hostage for ransom? Is the stabbing death of a homeowner, committed during a robbery, more or less serious than molestation of a five-year-old child? As McCloskey (1965) concludes,

Most of us would agree that murder is a very serious crime and that shoplifting a cake of soap is a considerably lesser offence. We should perhaps differ about such questions as to whether kidnapping is more or less serious than blackmail, whether embezzlement should be treated as a lesser crime than housebreaking, whether stealing a car worth £2,000 is less serious than stealing £2,000 of jewelry. We do disagree, and most of us would have doubts about the right order of the gravity of crimes. (cited in Ezorsky 1972:134)

The eminent scholar H. L. A. Hart (1968) echoes these sentiments in *Punishment and Responsibility* when he concludes that

the suffering imposed by punishment should be in some sense equal to or proportionate to the wickedness of the crime. But in what sense? How [to] measure either wickedness or suffering in the absence of units of either? Even if we had more than the limited insight which is available to human judges into a criminal's motives, powers and temptations, there is no natural relationship to be discerned between wickedness and punishment of a certain degree or kind, so that we can say the latter naturally 'fits' the former. Those who see these difficulties and yet insist that punishment must somehow be related to wickedness or 'culpability' present their principle in a different form: what is required is not some ideally appropriate relationship between a single crime and its punishment, but that on a scale or tariff of punishments and offences, punishments for different crimes should be 'proportionate' to the relative wickedness or seriousness of the crime. For though we cannot say *how* wicked any given crime is, perhaps we can say that one is *more* wicked than another and we should express this ordinal relation in a corresponding scale of penalties. Trivial offences causing little harm must not be punished as severely as offences causing great harm; causing harm intentionally must be punished more severely than causing the same harm unintentionally. (161–62)

In the end we have to accept that reasonable people may disagree about the relative gravity and seriousness of diverse offenses and their correlation with specific punishments and penalties. As Bean concludes, "We can accept a rough scale of penalties but it can be nothing more than that" (1981:25).

Offenders too have views on the relative gravity of crimes and appropriate, just, and proportionate punishment. In my experience most offenders who commit heinous crimes understand the logical connection between the gravity of their offenses and the prison sentence that they received. Rarely do I hear a convicted murderer, rapist, child molester, or arsonist—that is, those who admit their guilt—argue that he or she should have received a much lighter sentence. They may quibble about a handful of years—say, whether they should have received a thirty-five- as opposed to a forty-year sentence—but rarely do they question the appropriateness of a hefty prison sentence (which is not to say that they would not prefer to be released earlier rather than later).

Occasionally, however, I encounter an aberration, an inmate who does not share views held by the general public, the court, or the parole board that his crime was heinous and warranted a very lengthy prison sentence. One compelling example appears in the psychiatrist Willard Gaylin's (1982) chilling account of the Richard Herrin case. Herrin killed his estranged girlfriend, Bonnie Garland, when both were students at Yale

University. According to media reports, Herrin entered Garland's bed-room and viciously cracked her head open, like a watermelon, with a hammer. By every account Herrin's assault was among the most brutal imaginable. Eventually, Herrin was found guilty of manslaughter based on a "heat of passion" defense. After serving three years of his sentence, Herrin shared these observations about his punishment in an interview with Gaylin:

HERRIN: I feel the sentence was excessive.

GAYLIN: Let's talk about that a little.

HERRIN: Well, I feel that way now and after the first years. The judge had gone overboard. . . . Considering all the factors that I feel the judge should have considered: prior history of arrest, my personality back-ground, my capacity for a productive life in society—you know, those kinds of things—I don't think he took those into consideration. He looked at the crime itself and responded to a lot of public pressure or maybe his own personal feelings, I don't know. I'm not going to accuse him of anything, but I was given the maximum sentence. This being my first arrest and considering the circumstances, I don't think I should have been given eight to twenty-five years.

GAYLIN: What do you think would have been a fair sentence?

HERRIN: Well, after a year or two in prison, I felt that was enough. . . .

GAYLIN: How would you answer the kind of person who says, for Bonnie, it's her whole life; for you it's eight years. What's eight years compared to the more years she might have had?

HERRIN: I can't deny that it's grossly unfair to Bonnie but there's nothing I can do about it. . . . She's gone—I can't bring her back. I would rather that she had survived as a complete person, but she didn't. I'm not, again . . . I'm not saying that I shouldn't have been punished, but the punish-ment I feel is excessive. I feel I have five more years to go, and I feel that's just too much. There's no . . . I don't see any purpose in it. It's sad what happened, but it's even sadder to waste another life. I feel I'm being wasted in here.

GAYLIN: But what about the people who say, Look, if you got two years, then someone who robs should get only two days. You know, the idea of commensurate punishment. If it is a very serious crime it has to be a very serious punishment. Are you saying two years of prison is a very serious punishment considering what you did?

HERRIN: For me, yes.

(Gaylin 1982, cited in Moore 1995:124–25)

THE CAPITAL PUNISHMENT DEBATE

Any serious discussion of heinous crime—particularly with respect to retribution and revenge—must incorporate honest acknowledgment of the death penalty debate. Clearly, the most retributive response to heinous crime is execution of the offender.

Volumes have been written both for and against capital punishment. As with other enduring, chronic, fundamental controversies—Is abortion ever moral? Does God exist? How did life begin?—the capital punishment debate will probably never be settled. It is best to accept that large numbers of thoughtful, reasonable, and principled people will disagree on the issue (along with many people whose views are not very thoughtful, reasonable, and principled).

The capital punishment debate is critical to our discussion of heinous crime. After all, heinous crimes are the harshest, most extreme crimes possible and the death penalty is the harshest, most extreme retributive penalty. Clearly, human beings have struggled with this issue for a long, long time. The Bible makes a number of well-known references to capital punishment, and proponents use these passages to advance their argument in favor of the death penalty (Baird and Rosenbaum 1995). Prominent examples include

> He that smiteth a man, so that he die, shall be surely put to death. And if a man lie not in wait, but God deliver him into his hand; then I will appoint thee a place whither he shall flee. But if a man come upon his neighbor to slay him with guile; thou shalt take him with guile; thou shalt take him from mine altar, that he may die. And he that smiteth his father, or his mother, shall be surely put to death. And he that stealeth a man, and selleth him, or if he be found in his hand, he shall surely be put to death. And he that curseth his father, or his mother, shall surely be put to death. . . .
>
> And if any mischief follow, then shalt give life for life, foot for foot, burning, for burning, wound for wound, stripe for stripe. . . .
>
> If an ox gore a man or woman . . . if the ox were wont to push with his horn in time past, and if it hath been testified to his owner, and he hath not kept him in, but that he hath killed a man or a woman; the ox shall be stoned, and his owner shall be put to death. (Exodus 21:12–17, 23–25, 28–29)

> Thou shalt not suffer a witch to live. Whosoever lieth with a beast shall surely be put to death. He that sacrificeth unto any god, save unto the Lord only, he shall be utterly destroyed. (Exodus 22:18–20)

Whosoever he be of the children of Israel, or of the strangers that sojourn in Israel, that giveth any of his seed unto Molech; he shall surely be put to death; the people of the land shall stone him with stones. . . .

And the man that commiteth adultery with another man's wife, even he that commiteth adultery with his neighbor's wife, the adulterer and adulteress shall surely be put to death. And the man that lieth with his father's wife had uncovered his father's nakedness; both of them shall surely be put to death; their blood shall be upon them. And if a man lie with his daughter-in-law, both of them shall surely be put to death; they have wrought confusion; their blood shall be upon them. If a man also lie with mankind, as he lieth with a woman, both of them have committed an abomination; they shall surely be put to death; their blood shall be upon them. And if a man take a wife and her mother, it is wickedness; they shall be burnt with fire, both he and they; that there be no wickedness among you. And if a man lie with a beast, he shall surely be put to death: and ye shall slay the beast. And if a woman approach unto any beast, and lie down thereto, thou shalt kill the woman, and the beast; their blood shall be upon them. . . .

A man also or a woman that hath a familiar spirit, or that is a wizard, shall surely be put to death: they shall stone them with stones: their blood shall be upon them. (Leviticus 20:2, 10–16, 27)

The Code of Hammurabi also mandates capital punishment for a wide range of offenses, including theft of temple property (no. 6), kidnapping (no. 14), abetting the escape of a slave (no. 15), robbery (no. 22), hiring a substitute for military service (no. 33), adultery (no. 129), harboring outlaws (no. 199), and mother–son incest (no. 157). Islamic law requires stoning by death as a penalty for adultery (Henberg 1990). Plato also supported the death penalty in the *Laws*: "But suppose the law-giver finds a man who's beyond cure—what legal penalty will he provide for this case? He will recognize that the best thing for all such people is to cease to live—best even for themselves. By passing on they will help others, too: first, they will constitute a warning against injustice, and secondly they will leave the state free of scoundrels" (cited in Henberg 1990:97).

In the United States capital punishment has been an accepted practice—with changing sentiments and tide—ever since the first European settlers arrived. The English penal code, which was in force in the British colonies, identified fourteen capital offenses, such as idolatry, witchcraft, blasphemy, rape, kidnapping, rebellion, murder, assault in sudden anger, certain forms of perjury, and buggery (sodomy), arson, treason, and grand larceny (Information Plus 1995). The first signs of a serious movement to abolish the death penalty appeared in the late eighteenth century, led principally by Dr. Benjamin Rush.

Public policy on capital punishment has fluctuated in the United States. Although a number of states outlawed capital punishment early in the twentieth century, by 1921 five states had reinstated capital punishment. Until the 1960s the death penalty was considered legal under the U.S. Constitution. However, in 1963 Supreme Court Justice Arthur Goldberg wrote a dissent in a rape case in which the defendant had been sentenced to death. His dissent in *Rudolph v. Alabama,* which was joined by Justices William J. Brennan and William O. Douglas, argued that capital punishment is inhumane and barbaric. It sent a strong signal to the American legal community that at least some Supreme Court justices were now willing to consider a challenge to the constitutionality of the death penalty.

Since the landmark 1972 case of *Furman v. Georgia* the Supreme Court has been refining what is and is not acceptable under the U.S. Constitution (Information Plus 1995). In its 5–4 decision in that case, the Court ruled that capital punishment as then administered was unconstitutional primarily because of its arbitrary and discriminatory use and application. Many states responded to *Furman* by revising their capital punishment statutes to remedy unconstitutional features. A number of court decisions since *Furman* have upheld the use of capital punishment so long as it meets constitutional standards (Paternoster 1991).

As one would expect, contemporary death penalty proponents typically cite the appropriateness of a retributive response to heinous crime. As David Gelernter—the Yale University professor who was severely injured by one of Theodore Kaczynski's bombs—asserts, "We execute murderers in order to make a communal proclamation: that murder is intolerable. A deliberate murderer embodies evil so terrible that it defiles the community" (1998:26). Offenders who commit heinous crimes, proponents argue, deserve the ultimate penalty and the public has a right to impose the ultimate penalty as a reflection of its collective rage and vengeance. As Brettschneider (2001) notes in his reflections on executing convicted murderers, death penalty supporters

> focus on the cruel acts of the criminals being executed, hoping to horrify the public into support for the penalty. This horror is at the root of what is perhaps the most commonly invoked argument for the death penalty: the need for revenge. Although the victim cannot feel the satisfaction of re-

venge, proponents of the family can experience it vicariously. Many supporters of the death penalty often cite the need to protect family members or children as part of their defense for the punishment. It is not a great leap to claim that imagining oneself or one's own loved ones in the position of the victim would lead to an even greater emotional need for vengeance and for a feeling of vindication during the execution of a murderer. (17)

Death penalty opponents typically advance several key arguments (Bidinotto 1998; Costanzo 1998; Johnson 1998; Permanent Deacons 1998; van den Haag 1995):

- Mercy is ethically superior to revenge or vengeance.
- Execution is inhumane.
- Capital punishment undermines the sacredness of life.
- The death penalty does not alleviate the fear of violent crime.
- The death penalty does not protect society more effectively than other alternatives, such as life imprisonment without parole.
- The death penalty does not restore the social order breached by offenders.
- All human life—even that of a killer—has "intrinsic value," so that it is immoral to kill another individual under any circumstances.
- Society's response to a crime should not necessarily be proportionate to the harm caused by the criminal (an eye for an eye, a life for a life).
- The death penalty does not effectively deter serious crime.
- The death penalty is not imposed with fairness and discriminates against the poor and ethnic and racial minorities.
- The death penalty is not imposed in such a way as to prevent the execution of innocent death-row inmates.

Most arguments against the death penalty are philosophical and theological. These are the enduring, gut-wrenching, passionate, and ultimately unresolved debates about the relative inhumanity and immorality of capital punishment. These issues do not lend themselves to any sort of reasonable empirical test.

In contrast, we can explore empirically the arguments of critics that focus on the deterrent value of capital punishment, discriminatory application of the death penalty, and the potential execution of innocent people who have been sentenced to death—and the available data are troubling indeed.

Let us look first at what we have learned about the likelihood that capital punishment—or, more precisely, the threat of capital punishment—

deters crime. That is, what evidence is there that the states that impose the death sentence deter their citizens from the commission of heinous crimes significantly more than states where judges do not have the option to sentence criminals to death? Scholars have conducted diverse studies of this question. Most studies include state-by-state comparisons of homicide rates in death penalty and nondeath penalty states that are considered similar with respect to other key attributes, such as region, unemployment rates, per capita income, and ethnic and racial composition.

Thorsten Sellin (1959) conducted the most significant early studies of the deterrent value of the death penalty. He examined homicide rates from groups of matched death penalty and nondeath penalty states. His results were compelling in that they demonstrated the inconsistent correlation between the death penalty and homicide rates. Ohio, a death penalty state, had the highest homicide rate; Michigan, a nondeath penalty state, and Indiana, a death penalty state, had identical homicide rates. In a second comparison Iowa, a state with the death penalty, had the lowest homicide rate, but it was nearly the same as the rate for Wisconsin, a nondeath penalty state. In another comparison North Dakota, a nondeath penalty state, had a lower homicide rate than South Dakota and Nebraska, both death penalty states. Finally, Maine, a nondeath penalty state, had a slightly higher homicide rate than two death penalty states in New England, New Hampshire and Vermont, but the homicide rate in Rhode Island, a nondeath penalty state, was considerably lower than Connecticut's, which was a death penalty state.

Since Sellin's classic study, various other scholars have examined homicide rates in death penalty and nondeath penalty states, using diverse methodological approaches to control for various extraneous differences between these states. For example, Peterson and Bailey (1988) examined annual homicide rates in death penalty and nondeath penalty states, along with national homicide data, between 1973 and 1984 and found no evidence that the death penalty deters crime. For each year in the twelve-year period examined in the study, the average annual homicide rate in the death penalty states was higher than the rate in the nondeath penalty states and for the nation as a whole (Paternoster 1991).

In a prominent study, Ehrlich (1975) used sophisticated statistical analysis techniques to assess the deterrent value of the death penalty on homicide rates between 1933 and 1969. Specifically, Ehrlich examined the relationship between the risk of execution (the ratio of the number of executions to convictions for murder) and the homicide rate. Ehrlich concluded that capital punishment had a significant deterrent effect; he maintained that a 1 percent increase in the risk of execution could produce a 6 percent decrease in the national homicide rate.

However, serious doubts about Ehrlich's methodology and conclusions began to appear shortly after publication of his research. The criticisms and controversy led the National Academy of Sciences to commission research specifically to examine Ehrlich's data (Paternoster 1991). This extensive reexamination of Ehrlich's data was led by Lawrence Klein, a Nobel Prize–winning economist, and concluded that "we see too many plausible explanations for his [Ehrlich's] finding a deterrent effect other than the theory that capital punishment deters murder" (Klein, Forst, and Filatov 1978:358).

Numerous other studies have also failed to produce compelling evidence that the death penalty deters crime, leading Paternoster, who conducted a comprehensive review, to conclude "that the earlier conclusion of Sellin remains intact; capital punishment does not seem to have a general deterrent effect on the level of general homicide" (1991:227).

In addition to evidence suggesting that the death penalty does not have a deterrent effect, we have mounting evidence that the death penalty has been applied inconsistently, arbitrarily, and discriminatorily (Bailey and Peterson 1999; Zimring and Hawkins 1986). One can cite many studies on the subject; here is a cross-section of findings (for a comprehensive overview of pertinent research, see Paternoster 1991):

- Bowers and Pierce (1980) assessed the probability of a defendant's receiving a death sentence in Florida, Georgia, Texas, and Ohio. For all homicides the authors found that black offenders who murdered white victims in Florida were thirty-seven times more likely to receive a death sentence than blacks who killed other blacks; in Georgia black offenders who murdered white victims were thirty-three times more likely, in Texas eighty-seven times more likely, and in Ohio fifteen times more likely to be sentenced to death than blacks who killed blacks.
- Arkin (1980) followed 350 homicide cases presented to the grand jury for indictment in Dade County, Florida (Miami). Arkin found that killers of whites were more than twice as likely to be sentenced to death than were killers of blacks (although the rates were relatively similar when the analysis was limited to first-degree murder cases).
- Radelet (1981) examined homicide cases in twenty Florida counties and found that killers of whites were significantly more likely to be sentenced to death than were killers of blacks (again, the differences

were not significant when the analysis was limited to first-degree murder cases).

- Bowers (1983) found that in a sample of Florida homicide defendants indicted on first-degree murder charges, black killers of whites and white killers of whites were significantly more likely to be sentenced to death than were black killers of blacks.
- Gross and Mauro (1984, 1989) examined the influence of race on the imposition of the death penalty in eight states. The authors found that for all homicides both the race of the victim and the combination of the victim's and offender's race had an effect on the likelihood that a defendant would be sentenced to death. In Georgia killers of whites were nearly ten times more likely to be sentenced to death than were killers of blacks, in Florida they were almost eight times more likely, and in Illinois six times more likely. Black offenders were significantly more likely to be sentenced to death if they killed a white rather than a black.
- Baldus, Woodworth, and Pulaski (1983, 1985, 1990) examined 594 murder defendants in Georgia and found modest evidence that a death sentence was four times more likely to be imposed on a defendant who killed a white than on someone who killed a black person.

After conducting a comprehensive review of literature on the subject of discrimination related to the death penalty, Paternoster (1991) concludes that

> when deciding which capital defendants should die and whose life should be spared, juries may be more inclined to sentence to death black than white offenders, particularly those black offenders who cross racial boundaries and slay a white person. Given the history of racial animus in the United States, both in society generally and in the criminal justice system, as well as the emotionally volatile nature of both capital crimes and capital punishment, it is reasonable to believe that the administration of the death penalty has in the past and may continue to be tainted with racial discrimination. (116)

Further, a review of twenty-eight studies by the General Accounting Office found that "in 82 percent of the studies, race of victim [white] was found to influence the likelihood of being charged with capital murder or receiving the death penalty. . . . This finding was remarkably consistent across data sets, states, data collection methods, and analytical techniques" (General Accounting Office 1990:6, cited in Hood 1998).

In addition, there is growing evidence of wrongful convictions that lead to the death penalty—in other words, the United States has a small but significant percentage of individuals who were sentenced to death but are innocent. In their compelling volume *In Spite of Innocence: Erroneous Convictions in Capital Cases*, Radelet, Bedeau, and Putnam (1992) document twenty-three cases of individuals who were executed for murders they did not commit. These authors also document nearly four hundred cases of people whose innocence was demonstrated so convincingly that the state ultimately admitted its errors. As Radelet, Bedeau, and Putnam (1995) conclude from their sobering analysis,

> It was fickle good fortune rather than anything having to do with the rational workings of the criminal justice system that played the crucial role in sparing these innocent defendants. Yet luck was not sufficient to spare them time in prison (often many years), the agony of uncertainty over whether they would ever be vindicated and released, and blighted hopes for a decent life all too frequently destroyed by the ordeal and stigma of a murder conviction. . . .
>
> How many other cases there may be in which good fortune, hard work, or unflagging courage was absent and the erroneous conviction was never corrected or even adequately identified (except by the prisoner and a few supporters), we cannot say. We are confident, as a result of [our] years of work . . . that there are hundreds (perhaps even thousands) of other cases in which innocent people have been convicted of homicide or sentenced to death without having been able to prove their innocence to the authorities. We also have reason to believe that there are other cases, not yet known to us, in which states have officially acknowledged, one way or another, that an innocent person was convicted of homicide. Even today, after eight years of continuous and well-publicized research into this subject, we learn of new cases at the rate of one each month. Some of these cases date back twenty or thirty years; others crop up as current news reported in the daily papers. (142, 143)

Currently, a number of national projects have documented significant numbers of wrongfully convicted inmates, including the prominent Innocence Project at the Benjamin N. Cardozo School of Law (along with various other Innocence Projects throughout the United States) and the Center on Wrongful Convictions and the Death Penalty at Northwestern University Schools of Law and Journalism. In one of the boldest moves nationally, in 2000 Illinois governor George Ryan imposed a moratorium on capital punishment in that state based on compelling evidence that sentences were being imposed unfairly. Before leaving office in 2003, the Republican commuted the death sentences of 167 Illinois inmates. Since 1977, when Illinois reimposed the death penalty, thirteen inmates have been freed from death row after their innocence was proved.

Capital punishment opponents often frame their arguments by using data that demonstrate that (1) capital punishment is not a significant crime deterrent; (2) preventing crime can be achieved by long-term imprisonment (i.e., killing a high-risk offender is not necessary to prevent that person from committing crimes in the future); (3) the death penalty has been applied unfairly, inconsistently, arbitrarily, and discriminatorily; and (4) some innocent people have been sentenced to death. I find these arguments compelling, impossible to ignore, and sufficient to reject the death penalty as a legitimate, justifiable option.

However, death penalty opponents must still grapple with the overarching moral question. That is, in principle we could establish a criminal justice system that imposes the death penalty fairly, consistently, and without arbitrariness or any hint of discrimination. In principle we could establish safeguards that prevent the execution of innocent people. Then what? If we subtract from the equation the basis for any and all objections related to unfair, inconsistent, arbitrary, and discriminatory administration of capital punishment, can we still mount reasonable objections to the death penalty?

It is at this point that, in my view, we must accept that thoughtful people are going to disagree. That is the reality. Some will favor capital punishment because it offers society the purest, most basic, and authentic way to express its rage and honor its legitimate retributive instincts in response to the worst heinous crimes. We can debate this issue forever and people will continue to disagree. I believe that the deliberate execution of people who commit heinous crimes is morally reprehensible. As I will explain more fully later in this chapter, I do not think retribution is inherently offensive or immoral; in fact, I believe that society has a legitimate right to express its outrage in response to many heinous crimes (although not all) and that principled forms of retribution have a place in the criminal justice system. However, I do not believe that our wish for retribution ought to be satisfied by capital punishment.

There is one other key point. Apart from my belief that capital punishment is hard to defend on moral grounds, I have often argued that execution provides some people who commit heinous crimes with an "easy way out." I have encountered some offenders who find the prospect of life-long imprisonment so odious—the daily grind of prison life, the ever-present tension and potential for conflict, the annoying politics of relationships among inmates and correctional staff, the occasional brutality, the monotony—that lethal injection, the electric chair, and the firing squad begin to look like appealing alternatives. For some—not all—people who commit heinous crimes, my retributive wish is for them to suffer in prison minute by minute, hour by hour, day by day, week by week, year by year, and decade by decade. I want them to get up in the morning dreading what awaits them—the endless repetition, frustrations, disappointments, the aches and pains of imprisonment. I want them to lie in their bunks at night replaying their poor choices, reflecting on the misery they have inflicted on others, and wrestling with their agony. Some people are so cruel and vicious that life imprisonment without the possibility of parole *is* retributive justice. Execution is the undeserved, easy alternative—the path of least resistance.

Moving beyond the capital punishment debate, what is the appropriateness of retribution as a response to various types of crimes and offenders? Not surprisingly, the answer is complex. In chapter 2, I outlined pertinent conceptual categories of crimes in my presentation of the typology of criminal circumstances: crimes of desperation; greed, exploitation, and opportunism; rage; revenge and retribution; frolic; addiction; and mental illness. Let's consider them in turn with respect to the appropriateness of retribution as a response.

CRIMES OF DESPERATION

I think it is a mistake to generalize about the appropriateness of retributive responses to heinous crimes of desperation. The reason is that heinous crimes of desperation vary enormously. Put simply, retributive responses are more appropriate in some instances than others, depending primarily on the nature of the offender's desperation, the offender's motive, and the offender's ability to control his or her behavior.

Consider, for example, the case of Alfred B. (case 2.1), a heroin addict who robbed a convenience store to obtain money to support his drug habit and shot and killed the clerk during a scuffle (an example of a crime of financial desperation). Alfred apparently did not walk into the convenience store intending to murder the clerk; he brandished a gun to intimidate the clerk and, regrettably, fired the gun when the clerk resisted: "I hope you can understand this. I'm a heroin addict. I'm not a murderer.

I mean, I know it's true that I murdered a man, and I feel horrible about that. I would never do something like that when my head is clear. But, man, when you're strung out on smack [heroin], it's like you have no control. You'll do anything to get what you need. I'm a junkie, pure and simple. I know I need help. But I'm not a cold-blooded murderer, you know what I'm saying? I was out of my mind when I went into that store." The outcome in this case was tragic, of course. Without question, Alfred deserves to be incarcerated for public safety purposes, and he ought to receive substance abuse treatment. But should retribution be the primary aim in a case where heinous behavior appears to be a direct result of an addiction? It is certainly understandable that victims would feel enraged toward Alfred and would yearn for retribution. That is a human, if not a humane, response to the commission of a heinous crime in which a loved one was killed. But it is important, I believe, to distinguish between a homicide committed by someone who is not under the influence of drugs and simply kills someone who stands in the way of money or valuables and a homicide committed by someone who acts out of a sense of desperation driven by a physical addiction. A wish for retribution is understandable in both instances; however, it seems far more justifiable in the first instance.

The concept of mitigation is fundamentally important here. To mitigate is "to lessen in force or intensity; make less severe," according to *Random House Webster's College Dictionary* (1991). In legal contexts mitigating circumstances are those "that do not exonerate a person from the act with which he is charged but which reduce the penalty connected to the offense, or the damages arising from the offense. . . . Mitigating circumstances may also influence the choice of sanction by the court so that a defendant pleading mitigating circumstances might receive a more lenient sentence" (Gifis 1991:305). Thus the concept of mitigation suggests that we do not necessarily need to choose whether to respond to heinous crimes retributively. Rather, it is appropriate for us to consider the possibility of mitigating circumstances and factor them into our determination of the most appropriate *degree* of retribution. Retribution is not a black-and-white affair; it comes in many shades of gray. The desperate circumstances that lead offenders to commit heinous crimes may, in selective instances, constitute legitimate mitigating circumstances that call for less intense, although some, retribution.

For example, it is useful to contrast Alfred B.'s case of financial desperation with that of Carlos L. (case 2.2), who owed money to a loan shark and concluded that he had no choice but to rob a bank. During the armed robbery Carlos shot and killed a bank customer. In this case the offender made a calculated decision—uninfluenced by addiction or substance abuse—to resolve his financial plight by robbing a bank. He entered the bank with a handgun, fully understanding the risk to everyone's personal safety. The gun went off inadvertently and killed the customer. In this case there is less mitigation because of Carlos's cool-headed attempt to rob a bank, with full awareness of the possibility that people could be harmed in the process. Although he did not intend to kill the bank customer—which provides at least some modest mitigation—more retribution is warranted than in Alfred's case because of the stronger element of intent to commit a serious crime.

These two cases contain at least some mitigating evidence because of the absence of explicit intent to harm (kill) the ultimate victims. Similarly, the case of Barry M. (case 2.9)—the community college student who ended up strangling a man who made sexual advances toward him—included evidence that the offender lost control in what appeared to be a desperate situation and killed a man he did not initially intend to kill. However, the case of Evan A. (case 2.5), the superior court judge who solicited and accepted a bribe from a lawyer related to an ongoing court case being tried before him, provides a useful contrast. Although the crime in this case—a bribe of money—is far less serious than the murder of two people, the offender's intent was clearer and more explicit. Evan knew *exactly* what he was doing and could foresee that accepting a bribe would constitute one of the most serious violations of public trust imaginable. In this case retribution is very appropriate because of the offender's explicit intent and complete control over his actions. That an officer of the court—a *judge*—accepted a bribe adds to the reprehensible nature of the offense. There is no room for mitigation; retributive punishment commensurate with the seriousness of the crime is appropriate, consistent with the concept of proportionate justice.

CRIMES OF GREED, EXPLOITATION, AND OPPORTUNISM

The case of Evan A. resembles circumstances sometimes found in heinous crimes of greed, exploitation, and opportunism. One subtle difference is that the latter include no evidence that the offenders' crimes arose out of a keen sense of desperation, financial or otherwise. Rather, crimes of greed, exploitation, and opportunism are committed by people who want more money, property, and other valuables merely to enrich themselves rather than to resolve a desperate financial predicament. Their self-centered lust for the high life is transparent. For example, in a case that received national attention, the Missouri pharmacist Robert Courtney confessed that during a nine-year period he diluted medications, including chemotherapy medications and drugs prescribed for infertility, nausea, and pain. Evidence showed that Courtney had assets of $18.7 million and had diluted at least ninety-eight thousand prescriptions for approximately forty-two hundred patients over nine years. At his sentencing in federal court Courtney—a man with very expensive tastes—simply said, "I don't know why I did this" (Draper 2003:83).

Cases involving greed, exploitation, and opportunism usually do not include evidence of mitigating circumstances. For example, Pat M. (case 2.12) was eager to make some quick cash and agreed to viciously assault the lover of a man's wife. The victim suffered very serious and permanent injuries. In this case there was no evidence of mitigating circumstances that would justify lessening the punishment (imprisonment) imposed for retributive reasons—the offender agreed to carry out the vicious assault merely for personal gain and profit. He was not driven by an addiction or desperate personal circumstances. He was greedy, pure and simple, and chose to exploit an opportunity to make money. The following exchange occurred when I interviewed Pat in prison:

QUESTION: Why did you decide to assault this man? What was in it for you?

PAT: What do you mean? Isn't it obvious? I was going to get big bucks.

QUESTION: Thinking back on it now, does it trouble you that you decided to do that?

PAT: Well, I'm not happy about being in here, if that's what you mean. This is real hard for me and my family.

QUESTION: What about the guy you assaulted? What about him?

PAT: Yeah, well, I know that wasn't the smartest thing for me to do. That wasn't a good idea. But did you ever hear about how the guy was foolin' around with some other guy's wife? He was sort of asking for it, you know? I mean, I shouldn't have assaulted him the way I did, but it's not like the guy was some angel.

The cases of Donnie A. (case 2.13) and Hank S. (case 2.21) also offer little room for mitigation. Donnie supervised a large-scale heroin and cocaine operation and was arrested during a sting operation. While awaiting trial, Donnie murdered a man he believed worked as a police informant and leaked information about Donnie's drug activities. Hank was the seminarian who seduced and raped a young man after inviting the victim to participate in a bogus photo shoot for a national men's magazine. In both cases the offender set his sights on a target, and evidence showed cool, calculated premeditation. The offenders took careful, deliberate steps to harm their victims for self-serving purposes. Retribution was entirely appropriate.

> I'm not thrilled about the fact that I killed him, but he's been around the block enough times to know how the game [drug dealing] is played. In this business there's nothing lower than a snitch. When he decided to sing [cooperate with the police], he sealed his fate.
>
> Donnie A., referring to his victim

> I'm not exactly proud of what I did [sexual contact with the victim]. But what you read in the police report isn't the way it really happened. Yes, I was interested in having a relationship with the guy. I'll admit that. And it's true that I lured him to the hotel. But once he got there he was a willing participant. I never pressured him or forced him into anything. You should take a look at some of the e-mail messages he sent me before we met. There's no way he didn't know what he was getting involved in. He changed his tune after it all happened.
>
> Hank S.

Offenders who show such little regard for their victims typically manifest symptoms of what mental health professionals dub "personality disorders," specifically, antisocial personality disorder. According to standard psychiatric criteria, a personality disorder is an enduring pattern of inner experience and behavior that creates significant problems for an individual's ability to function in familial, social, occupational, and other important life arenas (American Psychiatric Association 2000). Of the many personality disorders, antisocial personality disorder is the most prominent among offenders who commit heinous crimes of greed, exploitation, and opportunism.

The essential feature of antisocial personality disorder (formerly known as psychopathy or sociopathy) is a "pervasive pattern of disregard for, and violation of, the rights of others that begins in childhood or early adolescence and continues into adulthood" (American Psychiatric Association 2000:701–3). Deceit and manipulation are common elements. Individuals with antisocial personality disorder typically violate social norms and engage in unlawful behaviors that may or may not lead to arrest, such as destroying property, harassing others, stealing, or pursuing illegal occupations. These individuals often disregard the wishes, rights, or feelings of others. They are frequently deceitful and manipulative in order to enhance their personal profit or pleasure (for example, to obtain money, sex, or power in relationships). They may repeatedly lie, manipulate, and con others and use assumed names and identities. Individuals with this disorder usually have difficulty with impulse control and have a hard time planning for the future. They tend to make decisions on the spur of the moment, without much forethought and without considering the effect of their decisions on others.

Offenders with antisocial personality disorder show little remorse for the consequences of their actions. They may be indifferent to, or provide a superficial rationalization for, having hurt, mistreated, or stolen from someone (for example, "losers deserve to lose," "he had it coming anyway"). They may blame their victims for being foolish, helpless, or deserving their fate; minimize the harmful consequences of their actions; or manifest complete indifference. They generally show no interest in compensating people whom they have harmed or in making amends for their behavior (American Psychiatric Association 2000).

In contrast, the case of Angela U. (case 2.14) may be one that has some very modest room for mitigation. Angela had become involved as an accomplice in her husband's ambitious burglary and robbery ring. At her husband's request Angela agreed to drive a car during an armed robbery of a jewelry company employee who held a large bank deposit. Angela panicked during the robbery and drove her car into the employee when she realized that the worker had seen Angela's face and the car. Although Angela knew full well that her participation in the robbery was risky and could lead to serious harm, she did not intend, initially, to injure the bank employee by driving into her with the getaway vehicle. Angela's greed led her into a situation that quickly spun out of control and ended in a heinous crime. Angela's lack of intent was evident during my interview with her:

QUESTION: Can you tell me how this whole series of events unfolded? What happened?

ANGELA: It's hard to explain. Well, not really. I never should have let myself get talked into doing the robbery with Jose and all them. That was my own stupidity. I just never thought it would end this way. I didn't want that lady to get hurt, believe me. I just thought I'd drive the car, we'd get some money, that's it. But that's not what happened. When the whole thing came down I panicked. I knew that lady could identify me and the car, and I just drove into her. I feel so bad about it. Now she's in real bad shape; I lie awake at night thinking about what I did to her and her family. I just can't believe it.

Angela seemed to be sincerely remorseful. She understood that her judgment was bad and felt a sense of guilt and shame, unlike offenders with classic antisocial personality disorder. None of this was sufficient to subtract retribution from the equation, but Angela's insight, lack of premeditated intent, and remorse provided at least a modicum of mitigation that could be used to justify at least a very modest reduction of the amount of time she spent in prison.

CRIMES OF RAGE

Heinous crimes of rage usually arise from domestic situations, conflictual relationships with acquaintances and co-workers, and tension-filled encounters with strangers. Offenders typically lose control in the moment. Most of these offenses are crimes of passion. As with crimes of desperation—where offenders feel at their wit's end—crimes of rage sometimes contain some modest mitigating reason with respect to retribution. That is, the evidence suggests that the offender did not enter the conflict intending, in the premeditated sense of the term, to seriously harm the victim. Conflict arose, the dispute escalated, tempers flared, and people lost control. Unlike offenders who commit heinous crimes for purposes of greed, exploitation, and opportunism, some—not all—perpetrators of crimes of rage feel sincere remorse for their actions, which should have at least some mitigating effect on retributive responses.

For example, Yolanda F. (case 2.22), an adolescent, was romantically involved with an older man. During an intense argument with her grandmother about the teen's relationship with the man, Yolanda grabbed an iron frying pan and slammed it against her grandmother's head, killing her. After serving several years of her prison sentence, Yolanda understood the inappropriateness of her heinous behavior and seemed genuinely remorseful:

QUESTION: How do you feel now about what happened between you and your grandmother?

YOLANDA: It's a nightmare. I can't believe I did that to her. Granny was like my parent. Sure, we had our share of arguments but nothing big like

119

this. This was just one of those horrible moments you wish you could erase. I was just a kid—you know what I mean?—and I didn't want Granny telling me I couldn't hang out with my man. At the time I thought she was just bein' a strict old lady. *Now* I know she was just trying to do what was best for me, trying to keep me out of trouble. But at the time I thought she was just an old fool; I got real angry and lost control.

There's no way something like that would happen again. I've learned a lot in here about how to handle anger. I feel bad—real, real bad.

QUESTION: Well, everyone gets angry now and then. Suppose something like this were to happen again, over some other issue. How would you handle it?

YOLANDA: Of course everybody gets angry. That's part of life. But now I know that it's possible to lose control and hurt somebody bad. I also know there's another way to handle it. What I've learned in the program is that instead of just reacting and lashing out, you can walk away from the situation until you've had a chance to cool off. It don't make no sense to try to work it out when everybody's screamin' and yellin'. You've got to let things calm down first.

Sometimes, however, even sincere expressions of remorse are not enough to temper retribution. Sometimes the malice involved in the heinous crime extends so far beyond the pale that there is virtually no room for mitigation. Such was the case with Larry K. (case 2.23), who viciously assaulted his estranged wife with a machete, maiming her with life-long, debilitating injuries. Larry fully grasped the horror of his actions and deeply regretted his poor judgment. Years of incarceration had provided Larry with an opportunity to absorb and reflect on his brutality: "It's hard to describe what it's like to live with the knowledge that I could lose control like that. Never in my life have I gone after somebody like that. She was my wife, the mother of my children. It's scary to think a human being can lose it like that. It's almost like it was another person attacking her, not me. But I know it was me, and I have to live with that. Do I think it's safe for me to go back on the streets? I do. But I also understand why people would be afraid."

Some people who commit heinous crimes of rage do not offer even the slightest opportunity for mitigation of retribution. Not only were their crimes brutal, but they exacerbate their circumstances by failing to display any hint of remorse or insight, consistent with antisocial personality disorder. This is particularly common in cases of domestic violence, where the offender is controlling, arrogant, and self-righteous, as with Milton L.

(case 2.26). In this case the offender was furious that his partner had left him. In addition to harassing his partner, the offender viciously vandalized the property of his partner's close friend and neighbor, accusing her of aiding and abetting his partner.

> QUESTION: Can you tell me why you decided to destroy the victim's car window, flood her basement, carve threatening messages on the front door, and destroy furniture? What led up to that?
>
> MILTON: Nancy [the victim] still denies it, but I know she put Evelyn [Milton's estranged partner] up to it; I know Nancy talked Evelyn into leaving me and helped her do it. Evelyn never would have done this on her own.
>
> QUESTION: Let's assume for the moment that Nancy was involved, that she did talk with Evelyn about leaving you. Do you think what you did to Nancy and her property was justified? Does that make sense to you?
>
> MILTON: I know it don't make no sense to you, and I can see that it went too far. But that woman [Nancy] had no business poking her nose into our business. She was just asking for trouble. I never laid a hand on her; everything I did was to her property.

CRIMES OF REVENGE AND RETRIBUTION

As with crimes of greed, exploitation, and opportunism, offenders who commit crimes of revenge and retribution typically plot, calculate, and carefully orchestrate their heinous crimes. Their goal is to pay someone back, and scheming is often part of the plan. Rarely is there strong evidence of mitigating circumstances, given the offender's clear intent and malice. Remorse is rarely sufficient to mitigate a retributive response to the crime. For example, when Oliver Y. (case 2.34) pushed his pregnant partner off a ledge, he fully intended to kill her, and he succeeded. During the years following the murder, Oliver matured and gained considerable insight into his behavior. He understood how horrific his actions were and felt badly about them. However, early release from prison in this case would have undermined the legitimately retributive function of incarceration.

> At the time I thought my world had completely fallen apart. I understand now that there were other ways to handle a mess like the one I was in. I had just found out that she [Mary Lou, the victim] was pregnant with another

man's baby. There we were, talking about getting married, and she's fooling around with another guy. I was ripped. I remember thinking for days about what I could do to get back at her. I know I wasn't thinking real clearlike, but at the time it's all I could do. I remember feeling like I had no choice. I also remember how relieved I felt after I killed her. I was real scared too.

I'm really sorry the whole thing happened. I was just a dumb kid at the time. Really dumb. I know better now, but of course that doesn't make the situation any better. What's done is done.

With some heinous offenders who committed crimes of revenge, it is difficult to know whether they feel any remorse; in other cases the offender clearly shows no remorse. In the case of Ronald B. (case 2.39), for example, it was hard to know whether the offender grasped the heinous nature of his crime. Ronald shot and killed his acquaintance, Harris L., after learning from Ronald's close friend Lynne N. that Harris had been beating her. Ronald's simple, straightforward aim was to get back at Harris for mistreating his friend. Ronald seemed to have an intellectual understanding that what he did was horribly wrong, but his responses to my questions about his crime were superficial, vague, and inscrutable; I could not tell whether he felt remorse. Ronald seemed emotionally paralyzed and shut down (his blunted affect and unresponsiveness suggested that he was clinically depressed).

QUESTION: My impression from reading the police report and the transcript of the detective's interrogation of you is that you were so angry with Harris for beating up on Lynne that you felt like you had to get back at him. Do I have that right?

RONALD: Yeah.

QUESTION: Can you walk me through this? Can you give me some sense of what was running through your mind, what led you to take revenge in the way you did?

RONALD: I don't really remember. I try not to remember.

QUESTION: Were you drunk or under the influence of drugs at the time of the murder? Is that why you don't remember?

RONALD: No. I just don't remember. I've sort of blocked it out.

QUESTION: How do you feel about what you did to Harris? How do you feel about the murder?

RONALD: I feel bad. I know it was bad.

QUESTION: Is there anything else you would like to tell me about the murder or how you feel about it?

RONALD: No, not really.

In other cases the offender is not remorseful or refuses to let anyone know that he is remorseful. This may be a reflection of the offender's antisocial personality traits or bravado or both. Cases involving hate crimes often fall in this category, where offenders feel self-righteous indignation toward their victims and the ethnic, racial, or sexual group that they represent. Perpetrators of heinous hate crimes are often unrepentant and offer no mitigating circumstances in conjunction with their offenses; in such instances retributive punishment is justifiable.

CRIMES OF FROLIC

I find that offenders who commit heinous crimes of frolic often feel very remorseful about their conduct. With the passage of time and opportunity to mature, these offenders often grasp the nature of their remarkably poor judgment that led to serious harm and injury. These offenders are often young at the time of their crime. Their time in prison provides them with an opportunity to reflect on their poor choices and their consequences. Many of these offenders use the time to grow up. While incarceration for retributive purposes is warranted, these offenders often earn some degree of mitigation by virtue of their genuine remorse and earnest attempts to learn from their mistakes (as evidenced by their diligent participation in prison-based counseling and rehabilitation programs). Although this is not true of all offenders who commit heinous crimes of frolic, it is true of many. Such was the case with Eddie Z. (case 2.46) who, along his friends, fired BB pellets at a group of adolescents who were hiking through the woods, one of whom was blinded by the assault. Eddie had just turned eighteen when he committed the crime. He was sentenced to twenty-five years in prison and appeared before me after he had served a little more than eight years of his sentence. Eddie was twenty-six at the time of our interview:

QUESTION: What have you learned as a result of this experience? You've had a lot of time to think about this. After all, you were just a kid when you came in here more than eight years ago.

EDDIE: It's really embarrassing for me to think about what I was like back then. I can hardly believe that I could be so stupid and cruel. Anyone in his right mind would know that it's wrong to start shooting at people with one of those rifles. At the time I just wanted to fit in, be one of the guys, and all that. One of the things I've come to understand after talking every week with Lori [a prison social worker] is that I felt so alone at the time and would have done just about anything to be accepted by other kids my age. At the time my mother was struggling with a drug problem, and I barely even knew my father; I had only met him a couple of times. I wasn't doing well in school—I was a real lost soul. When I think about it now, it all makes sense; of course, at the time I didn't have a clue. Believe me, I've learned a whole lot about how to stay away from bad situations. There's no way I'd let myself get talked into that kind of thing again. Sometimes I cry myself to sleep thinking about what I did to that kid. I wish I could give him one of my eyes to make up for it, I really do.

Occasionally, I encounter offenders who commit heinous crimes of frolic who do not outgrow their pattern of criminal behavior. In these cases the frolic is more likely to occur in the context of predatory, gang-like behavior, as in the case of the young men who accosted a young couple, carjacked them and their vehicle, raped the woman, and shot both victims with a handgun (case 2.47). What is characteristic of this form of frolic is group pressure to conform in a way that is viciously assaultive, sinister, and sadistic. These perpetrators are less likely to understand that their behavior has tragic, regrettable consequences; for reasons that are not always clear, they are more likely to set out with the deliberate goal of inflicting pain and suffering on either targeted or randomly selected victims.

CRIMES OF ADDICTION

Offenders who commit heinous crimes that arise from their addiction pose a special challenge. On the one hand, offenders who commit armed robbery or vehicular homicide while under the influence of drugs or alcohol engage in reprehensible behavior that causes great harm. Certainly, it is reasonable to want to punish such offenders retributively for the injuries they have caused victims.

On the other hand, our society has come to accept that addictions are a type of disease, such that addicts do not have full control over their behavior.[3] That is, we tend to be willing to acknowledge the role of deterministic, positivistic, or causal factors that account for the offenders' conduct, as opposed to attributing their heinous crime entirely to their free will (consistent with the classical school of thought). More precisely, cases involving addicted offenders fall more appropriately under what is variously known as the neoclassical school of etiology or causation, the mixed view, or soft determinism (Matza 1964). In these cases we are inclined to believe that offenders should be held accountable because of their decisions to experiment, use, and abuse drugs or alcohol (consistent with the free-will, classical school of etiological thought) but also recognize that, once addicted, these offenders' ability to control their behavior is somewhat limited because of significant, often powerful, changes in brain chemistry, physiology, and functioning (determinism). If we believe that retribution should be imposed commensurate with an offender's ability to control her or his behavior, we should view offenders' addictions as a mitigating medical circumstance.

Typically, I adjust my retributive response based on offenders' willingness to acknowledge their addiction and their willingness to engage in sustained, meaningful treatment to address it. Offenders who are willing to enroll in drug and alcohol treatment programs—not to impress parole board members and judges but to help them to abstain from further use and prevent relapse—deserve less retribution. Offenders who are not willing to acknowledge compelling evidence of their addiction or take earnest steps to address it are more deserving of retribution.

For example, Colleen O. (case 2.53) was a cocaine addict who drove home from a party under the influence, broadsided an oncoming car, seriously injured the young mother who was driving the other car (she eventually died from the injuries), and killed the mother's twin infants, who were riding in the car. During my interview with her Colleen acknowledged her responsibility, expressed genuine remorse, and was determined to get help for her cocaine addiction.

QUESTION: Do you consider yourself a drug addict?

COLLEEN: You know, until this happened, I never used to. Like a lot of my friends, I thought I was just a recreational user—someone who can take it or leave it. I now realize that I was in denial, that I was much more dependent on cocaine than I let myself believe. Since I've been in the Insight Program [the prison's drug treatment program], I've begun to admit to myself something I've been unwilling to believe—that I have a serious drug problem.

When I get out of here I'm going to continue going to NA [Narcotics Anonymous] meetings. I have to. I've learned that people who let down their guard and stop going to meetings are heading for relapse. I don't want that. I have too much to lose. My three-year-old daughter is starting to understand that Mommy did something bad and is being punished. It kills me to see her come in here with my mother to visit me, and it's even worse when she leaves. I can't let this happen again—not to her or me.

Sometimes I think about somebody driving a car under the influence and killing my daughter. That's what I did. I just can't believe I did that to someone else. I just can't believe it.

Although many offenders with addictions pursue treatment and recovery ambitiously and earnestly—with mixed degrees of success—some offenders are unwilling to take any steps in that direction. These offenders do little to mitigate retribution in the form of continued incarceration. Tim M. (case 2.55) is a typical example. Tim was the police officer who became a pathological gambler and stole about $90,000 worth of diamonds at a crime scene to help cover his gambling losses. Tim was placed on probation after being convicted in criminal court but was then incarcerated when he violated the terms of his probation after resuming his gambling and being charged with fraudulent use of a credit card. Despite the precipitous loss of his law enforcement career, reputation, and freedom, Tim failed to acknowledge the seriousness of his addiction. He did not appreciate that, given his complicated personal history and addictive personality, any future gambling could trigger a relapse:

QUESTION: It must be painful to be in here [prison] after having served as a police officer. What have you learned about your gambling problem and the impact it has had on your life and other people?

TIM: The truth is, I just had a remarkably bad string of luck. I was doing well at the casinos for a long time. When I ran into a problem, I didn't handle it well; I admit that. But most of the time I had things under control. I know I can't be a cop again, but I'll get back on my feet.

QUESTION: Do you think you'll need to take any specific steps to ensure that you don't end up gambling again?

TIM: Nah. I'm smart enough to know how to avoid getting in over my head. I may fool around a little bit at the tables [casino tables], but I know when to stop.

CRIMES OF MENTAL ILLNESS

Retribution is least appropriate for offenders with major mental illness. Of all types of offenders, this is the group where determinism, the positivist perspective on etiology, is the most germane. Offenders' diminished capacity and the absence of *mens rea* (criminal intent) constitute legitimate mitigating factors.

Significant numbers of offenders who commit heinous crimes manifest evidence of major mental illness, including schizophrenia and other psychotic disorders; major mood disorders, such as bipolar disorder; dissociative disorders (particularly dissociative identity disorder); and paraphilias (sexual disorders such as pedophilia). Current estimates are that 20 percent of violent offenders display symptoms of mental illness. More generally, approximately 7 percent of federal prison inmates, and 16 percent of inmates in state prisons, in local jails, or on probation, manifest evidence of mental illness (Ditton 1999).

By definition, offenders who commit heinous crimes and who have a major mental illness are the least likely candidates for retribution. Offenders with psychotic and other severely disabling psychiatric disorders simply are not responsible for their conditions.[4] By now we have ample evidence of the biochemical determinants of many forms of major mental illness—factors that lie outside the control of the offenders who are plagued with such disorders (Farrington 1998; Guy et al. 1985; Powell, Holt, and Fondacaro 1997; Steadman et al. 1989; Teplin 1990). Thus retribution would hardly be appropriate in the case of Joy H. (case 2.60), who had been struggling with psychotic symptoms since she was twelve and was arrested for sexually abusing her baby boy. Similarly, retribution would be inappropriate in the case of Sam E. (case 2.59), whose paranoid schizophrenia caused him to hear voices directing him to sexually assault women at a nearby college. Both Joy and Sam required psychiatric treatment, not retributive punishment.

Matters are more complicated in cases involving crimes such as pedophilia. Here there is considerable debate about whether offenders are primarily "mad" or "bad." Those who embrace a more positivistic or deterministic view maintain that pedophilia is a psychiatric disturbance involving "recurrent, intense sexually arousing fantasies, sexual urges, or behaviors" over which offenders have little or no control (American Psychiatric Association 2000:566). According to this view, offenders who molest children require treatment, not retribution. Others, however, are less willing to view pedophilia primarily as a psychiatric disorder; some professionals argue that pedophiles should be held accountable and punished for their heinous sexual violation of children (Feierman 1990; Quinsey 1998; Schwartz and Cellini 1995, 1997, 1999).

My own position is in line with the mixed view, or soft determinism, such that we should view the typical pedophile as someone with a serious psychiatric disorder that requires in-depth treatment, *and* we must hold pedophiles accountable for their behavior. I do not think retribution alone is warranted in the typical case, primarily because pedophilia is an illness. At the same time I believe that pedophiles should face consequences—incarceration, for example—if they are continuing to engage in high-risk behaviors or are unwilling to participate, sincerely and earnestly, in treatment. Unlike offenders who suffer from florid psychotic symptoms and who, without neuroleptic medication, have no ability whatsoever to grasp the seriousness of their misconduct or to engage in meaningful treatment, many pedophiles do have the ability to grasp the seriousness of their compulsive behavior and are able to conceptualize about treatment options. Incarceration of pedophiles would not be for retributive purposes per se; rather, it would be for public safety reasons and to convey to offenders the message that the community will not tolerate high-risk behavior or a lackadaisical approach to supervision and treatment.

Retribution serves an important, albeit circumscribed, function in criminal justice. It should be used selectively and judiciously to express the community's intolerance and rejection of various forms of heinous crime. The community has a right to convey its disapproval and condemnation of behavior that is reprehensible and odious.

Having said this, it is important for the community to acknowledge that retribution should be imposed proportionately, keeping in mind the gravity of the offense and the extent to which the offender could reasonably be expected to exercise control over her or his behavior. Retribution is far more justifiable when offenders commit heinous crimes of greed, exploitation, opportunism, and revenge—where there is evidence of malice and deliberate intent to harm—than when offenders commit heinous crimes as a result of their severe addictions or mental illness. A civilized society should hold itself to a high standard when imposing retribution to avoid slipping into tyranny and the arbitrary, unrestrained exercise of authority.

4

IMPRISONMENT:
THE PUBLIC SAFETY IMPERATIVE

People who commit heinous crimes have to be in prison in order to protect the public—most for a significant period of time and some forever. Apart from whatever retributive reasons we may have to incarcerate heinous offenders, we need to ensure public safety. The optimal length of imprisonment is subject to debate, both in theory and practice, depending on one's interpretation of current knowledge about the deterrent and rehabilitative effects of incarceration, the trajectory of criminal careers, and risks associated with noninstitutional, community-based supervision.

For quite some time political jurisdictions in the United States—federal, state, and local—have been known for their extraordinarily high rates of incarceration. Compared with nearly all other industrialized nations, the United States incarcerates a stunning number of its citizens. Currently, more than two million prisoners are being held in federal, state, and local correctional facilities. The incarceration rate has increased dramatically. Since 1975 per capita prison populations have increased in every state, by an average of more than 300 percent (Spelman 2000). State and federal incarceration rates grew by more than 200 percent between 1980 and 1996. Much of the increase was attributable to drug-related convictions, which increased by a factor of ten during this period. Incarceration rates were fairly steady between the mid-1920s and the mid-1970s, after which they began to skyrocket; the incarceration rate by the end of the 1990s (445 inmates per 100,000 population) was more than four times the stable rate between the 1920s and the 1970s (Blumstein and Beck 1999).

In 1990 the incarceration rate was 292 inmates per 100,000 U.S. residents, and by 2002 the rate had increased to 474 inmates per 100,000, a jump of 62 percent. The number of incarcerated violent offenders increased from 173,300 in 1980 to 589,100 in 2000, or about 340 percent. Between 1990 and 2000 violent offenders accounted for 53 percent of the total growth in state prison populations in the United States (Bureau of Justice Statistics 2003). During the last twenty years of the twentieth century, the states doubled their prison capacity, then doubled it again, increasing their corrections-related costs by more than $20 billion per year (Spelman 2000).

Nearly half of all inmates in state prisons are serving sentences for violent offenses (the percentage of inmates in federal prisons serving sentences for violent offenses is much lower—closer to 15 percent). Almost 1 in 10 state prison inmates is serving a sentence for murder or criminal homicide,[1] nearly 1 in 11 state prison inmates is serving a sentence for rape or another type of sexual assault, and close to 1 in 7 state prison inmates is serving a sentence for robbery (Bureau of Justice Statistics 2003c).

It is impossible to ignore the racial and ethnic face of incarceration in the United States. Ethnic minorities and people of color are incarcerated at a significantly higher rate than whites. In 2001, for example, 3,535 per 100,000 black males were sentenced to prison time in the United States, compared with 1,177 Latinos per 100,000 Latinos and 462 white males per 100,000 white males. Approximately 12 percent of black males in their twenties and thirties were in prison or jail in 2002. Nearly 1 in 8 black males (12.9 percent) aged twenty-five to twenty-nine were in prison or jail, compared with about 1 in 24 Latinos (4.3 percent) and 1 in 63 whites (1.6 percent). Black females were two and a half times more likely to be incarcerated (349 per 100,000) than Latinas (137 per 100,000) and five times more likely than white females (68 per 100,000).

State and regional differences in incarceration rates are remarkable. A number of southern states have traditionally had very high rates of incarceration. In 2002, for example, Louisiana incarcerated 799 inmates (serving sentences of more than one year) per 100,000 residents, Mississippi incarcerated 728 inmates per 100,000 residents, and Alabama incarcerated 593 inmates per 100,000 residents. In contrast, Maine incarcerated 137 inmates per 100,000 residents; Minnesota, 139 inmates per 100,000 residents; North Dakota, 167 inmates per 100,000 residents; and Rhode Island, 184 inmates per 100,000 residents. (The combined average incarceration rate for state and federal prisons was 470 inmates per 100,000 residents.)

Gender is also a significant factor: men are incarcerated at a much higher rate than women. In 2002 the United States had 1,309 male inmates per 100,000 men and 113 female inmates per 100,000 women. However, the female prison population recently has grown much faster than the male prison population. In 2002 women accounted for 6.7 percent of prisoners, up from 3.9 percent in 1980. Incarceration rates between 1980 and 1996 rose faster for women (364 percent) and minorities (184 percent for African Americans and 235 percent for Hispanics) than for men (195 percent) and non-Hispanic whites (164 percent). The incarceration rate for females increased by about a factor of five, from 11 inmates per 100,000 adult females to 51 per 100,000; the rate for males nearly tripled, from 275 male inmates per 100,000 male adults to 810 male inmates per 100,000. Since 1995 the annual rate of growth in the number of female inmates has averaged 5.4 percent, while the annual rate of growth in the number of male inmates has averaged 3.6 percent.

Clearly, multiple factors account for the rapid growth in the U.S. prison population—a rate that quadrupled during the last quarter of the twentieth century after nearly fifty years of stability. Chief among them was the nation's "war on drugs," which quickly began to overload the prison system. During the last two decades of the twentieth century, incarceration for drug-related offenses increased nearly tenfold (Blumstein and Beck 1999).

In addition, changes in political climate were key: candidates for office in nearly every election cycle since the late 1970s have competed with one another to be the first to tout strict penalties for convicted offenders. As Caplow and Simon note, "It is widely accepted that political candidates for statewide office must establish themselves as favoring more severe punishments to stand a chance of election. Between elections, crime control has also become a more salient feature of governing, with legislative bodies at all levels devoting large portions of their time and budgets to crime control measures" (1999:70).

Also, over time many states abandoned indeterminate sentencing— where judges had wide-ranging discretion and sentenced offenders based on their prospects for rehabilitation—and implemented determinate or mandatory sentencing guidelines. Under indeterminate sentencing, judges were not bound by strict rules and could use their subjective judgment when setting terms of imprisonment. Sentences for comparable offenses varied widely, based on judges' often idiosyncratic assessment of each offender's likely response to rehabilitative options in prison. In principle parole boards would monitor each inmate's progress and approve release when inmates could be safely returned to the community (Reitz 1998).

However, in the 1970s criminal justice professionals, politicians, and other public officials started to abandon the rehabilitative ideal on which indeterminate sentencing was based. Particularly influential was the much publicized 1974 study conducted by Robert Martinson with the telling title, "What Works? Questions and Answers About Prison Reform" (also see Lipton, Martinson, and Wilks 1975). Martinson's conclusions, based on his systematic and comprehensive review of current knowledge about the effectiveness of prison-based treatment programs, were pessimistic. Many corrections officials seized on Martinson's dire forecast and began to lobby for stricter sentencing guidelines and mandatory minimum sentences that would be imposed irrespective of an offender's rehabilitation prospects. As Reitz (1998) notes,

> For a number of reasons, the time was probably ripe for the idea that "nothing works." Going into the 1970s, a number of societal currents had worn down patience with the rehabilitative experiment and were signaling widespread receptivity to alternative approaches. Reported crime rates, including homicide rates, had jumped sharply during the 1960s; these alarming changes had coincided with a decade of slightly diminishing incarceration rates. With only a bit of imagination, one could link one trend with the other (e.g., Wilson 1975). In the same period, controversial defense-oriented rulings by the Supreme Court under Earl Warren had produced sentiment in some quarters that the legal system was "coddling criminals," and spawned an enduring public reaction against "lenient judges." Support for the death penalty, which had sputtered at submajority levels in the 1960s, soared to supermajority status during the next decade. . . .
>
> The public, and public officials, are now less likely to view criminals as disadvantaged, ill-treated members of society who can be changed for the better. This has had an interactive effect on viewpoints about other extant sentencing policies. Once the softening tendency of rehabilitation theory is removed, the other mainstream goals of punishment can be pressed toward visions of increased severity. If it seems that criminals cannot be changed, and have only themselves to blame for their behavior, then the most pivotal compunctions against harsh dispositions have been swept aside. There is no compelling argument against incapacitating as many offenders as the system can accommodate, for as long as possible. (544, 545)

Abandonment of the rehabilitative ideal and the move toward determinate sentencing as an alternative led to longer prison sentences and fuller prisons that quickly became overcrowded. Determinate sentencing severely limits judges' discretion; instead of imposing sentences on a case-by-case basis, judges must adhere to strict sentencing guidelines and mandatory minimum sentences.

The shift toward determinate sentencing began in earnest in the mid-1970s. Several states—Arizona, California, Colorado, Illinois, Indiana, and North Carolina—passed statutes that limited judges' discretion and established strict sentencing guideposts (Reitz 1998). Many states obligated judges to follow sentencing "ranges" for each offense (for example, ten to fifteen years for kidnapping, ten to twenty years for felony assault, twenty years to life for first-degree murder). Each offense carried a "presumptive" range for typical cases (those that did not feature extraordinary circumstances), "aggravated" ranges for cases involving extreme cruelty or violence, and "mitigated" ranges for offenses involving mitigating circumstances (for example, psychiatric illness, desperate personal circumstances).

Determinate sentencing guidelines flourished in the late 1970s and early 1980s, largely as a result of the work of newly established state-based sentencing commissions. The earliest commissions were in Minnesota, Pennsylvania, Florida, and Washington. By the mid-1990s more than twenty states and the federal system had established sentencing commissions.

U.S. District Judge Marvin Frankel (1973) introduced the concept of a sentencing commission in an effort to enhance the consistency of prison sentences imposed by criminal court judges. Frankel was concerned about the prevalence of inconsistent, uneven, and haphazard sentencing patterns around the United States. Many sentencing commissions, although not all, began their work with the explicit aim of lengthening sentences for a variety of offenses (Reitz 1998). Sentencing commissions established firm penalties for specific offenses—for example, life in prison without the possibility of parole for offenders convicted of aggravated murder—and mandatory minimum sentences that established a floor below which an offender's sentence could not go (for example, manufacturing and delivering cocaine might have a minimum sentence of six years). Some states also enacted "habitual offender" statutes, which required judges to impose longer sentences on offenders with substantial criminal records (recidivists). In the 1990s a number of states and Congress adopted "three strikes and you're out" policies, under which offenders convicted of a third felony must be sentenced to life imprisonment without the possibility of parole.

Consistent with the move toward determinate sentencing, a significant number of states—ten by 1983—abolished their parole boards entirely, which of course added to the growth of prison populations because of the elimination of this early-release option (King 1998; Reitz 1998). In 1984 the Sentencing Reform Act required "truth in sentencing" for offenders in the federal system and created a sentencing commission whose guidelines took effect in 1987. Under these guidelines federal inmates are required to serve at least 85 percent of their sentences. In addition, the Comprehensive Crime Control Act of 1984 and the Anti-Drug Abuse Act of 1986 greatly enhanced the use of mandatory prison sentences for many drug offenses. Over time, humane custody and protection of the public supplanted rehabilitation as the principal goal of the corrections system (King 1998; Reitz 1998).

Prison overcrowding then led to a widespread push for prison construction and what became known as a "build and fill" approach to corrections (1998:603). The consequence in the United States was an incarceration rate that grew rapidly and for many years was nearly the highest among developed nations; the only nations where incarceration rates were even close—South Africa, Russia, and some former Soviet republics—are politically and socially very different from the United States. By the mid-1990s the United States had an incarceration rate 40 percent higher than that in South Africa, five and a half times that in England and Wales, ten times that in the Netherlands, and fourteen times that in Japan (1998).

Growth rates in prison populations have varied over time for different categories of crime and offenders' demographic traits. Without question, much of the growth has been the result of drug-related convictions. In 1980 state and federal prisons held an estimated 23,900 inmates on drug offenses, an incarceration rate of less than 15 inmates per 100,000 adults. By 1996 the drug incarceration rate had increased to 148 inmates per 100,000 adults, almost a tenfold jump in these sixteen years.

Two types of heinous crime also account for a significant portion of the increase in incarceration rates. Incarceration for aggravated assault increased from 14 inmates per 100,000 adults in 1980 to 50 per 100,000 in 1996; the rate for sexual assault increased from 13 inmates per 100,000 in 1980 to 52 per 100,000 in 1996, an increase of more than 300 percent for each offense. The incarceration rate for murder increased from 22 inmates per 100,000 adults in 1980 to 57 inmates per 100,000 adults in 1996, a growth of 164 percent. The rate for robbery increased 54 percent (Blumstein and Beck 1999).

According to Blumstein and Beck (1999), for offenses other than drugs, decisions to incarcerate (the likelihood of imprisonment following conviction) account for approximately 40 percent of the growth of incarceration in state prisons; approximately 60 percent of the growth results from longer times served. A significant portion of the amount of time served in prisons is the direct result of parole violations (nearly 35 percent in the mid-1990s). Thus the increase in incarceration is not entirely the result of an increase in actual crime. A significant portion of the increase is attributable to changes in sentencing patterns, decisions to release inmates, and incarceration of parole violators.

THE EFFECT OF IMPRISONMENT

The modern-day prison is the product of centuries of change in penal philosophy and practice. Prisons in the United States were first established in the early nineteenth century, but they were preceded by European penal sanctions and institutions. In the Middle Ages imprisonment was used primarily to segregate offenders from the general public rather than punish per se. By the late Middle Ages, prisons were used for more punitive purposes, with prisoners occasionally surviving on the now-infamous bread-and-water diet. Galley sentences were also imposed to spur development of the medieval fleets of southern European naval powers. Galleys rowed by oarsmen, all of whom were prisoners, continued until the eighteenth century.

In the German Empire the Constitutio Criminalis Carolina of 1532 laid out a range of penalties—sometimes known as blood sanctions—for serious crimes. The statute called for hanging murderers and burglars. A woman who killed her infant was to be buried alive and impaled, and a traitor was to be drawn and quartered. Other serious offenders were to be subjected to flogging; pillorying; amputation of ears, fingers, or tongue; death by burning or drowning; or being set out to die with their limbs smashed. Imprisonment as an alternative to such penalties began in the sixteenth and seventeenth centuries (Langbein 1998).

The institution of the workhouse, inaugurated in the second half of the sixteenth century, also laid the foundation for the development of the modern prison. Workhouses were used primarily for petty crimes, such as vagrancy and poverty. Inmates were required to perform various tasks—such as grinding malt or logs and making gloves, silk lace, and various textile products—in order to correct (rehabilitate) as well as punish (Langbein 1998). By the middle of the seventeenth century, serious offenders were sentenced to terms in workhouses.

In the United States penitentiaries began to appear in the 1820s in New York and Pennsylvania. Between 1819 and 1823 New York designed what became known as the Auburn, or congregate penitentiary, at the Auburn State Prison. Under the Auburn plan prisoners were to sleep alone in a cell at night and work together in workshops during the day. Inmates were forbidden to talk with each other or exchange glances while on the job, during meals, or in their cells (Rothman 1998). In Pennsylvania officials developed a different approach—known as the "separate system" because inmates were isolated from each other during their entire sentence—at prisons in Pittsburgh (1826) and Philadelphia (1829).

Over time various penal theories have influenced the goals of the corrections field in general and, in particular, the design and administration of prisons. Until the 1970s and the abandonment of the rehabilitative ideal (Martinson 1974), the corrections field was dominated by penal consequentialism (von Hirsch 1998), which was anti-retributivist in spirit and embraced the goals of rehabilitation and deterrence. Beginning in the nineteenth century, and for well more than a century, corrections professionals designed and administered corrections programs and prisons with a clear goal in mind: to release inmates who had gained new insights into their criminal conduct, learned new vocational and educational skills, and feared returning to the toxic penitentiary environment.

In response to the disillusionment that many corrections professionals experienced in the 1970s in relation to the rehabilitative ideal, the law-and-order perspective and bounded consequentialism predominated (von Hirsch 1998). The law-and-order perspective is what led to "get tough" sentencing guidelines, mandatory minimum sentences, and "three strikes and you're out" statutes. Prisons became places for custodial care that would protect the public and punish the offender.

Bounded consequentialism, in contrast, seemed to strike a balance between the law-and-order perspective and penal consequentialism. According to bounded consequentialism, strict sentencing guidelines and standards, and proportionate sentencing, are critically important in order to protect the public and avoid inconsistency and arbitrariness, yet rehabilitative programs to deter and prevent recidivism were an important part of the program.

What evidence is there that prisons do, in fact, prevent crime and reduce recidivism? The empirical record is complicated. We have some evidence that increasing prison capacity, in and of itself, reduces crime. Available studies tend to rely on three different types of data: a time-series data set of crime rates and prison populations for the entire United States; a cross-sectional data set of the fifty states for one year; and a panel data set that combines cross-sectional data for each state for multiple years (Spelman 2000). Some studies use actual arrest, conviction, and incarceration data to explore the effect of incarceration on crime rates, whereas other studies are based on simulations using a mathematical model (Avi-Itzhak and Shinnar 1973; Shinnar and Shinnar 1975). In short, the simulation model combines estimates of the typical offender's offense rate per year; probability of arrest, prosecution, and incarceration per crime committed; and average sentence served in jail or prison to estimate the likelihood that a typical offender will be incarcerated at any given time. When combined with data about the length of the typical criminal career, one can estimate the proportion of that career that the typical offender spends in jail or prison. This proportion is the estimated reduction in the crime rate that results from incarceration (Spelman 2000).

Based on his comprehensive review of available research, Spelman (2000) concludes that most studies show that doubling current U.S. prison capacity would reduce index crime rates by 20 to 40 percent (the index crimes, measured by the FBI, include murder, rape, robbery, aggravated assault, burglary, larceny, and automobile theft). Spelman further estimates that a 1 percent increase in prison population would reduce the index crime rate by 0.16 to 0.31 percent.

Other analyses have produced different conclusions, leading to an unclear picture of the actual effect of incarceration on crime rates. Zimring and Hawkins (1995) reviewed the relationship between index crime rates and imprisonment for the United States as a whole and for California in particular; they conclude that the effect of incarceration is negligible. Levitt (1996), however, asserts that each additional incarceration prevents about fifteen index crimes.

Perhaps the most comprehensive assessment appears in the National Academy of Sciences report, *Criminal Careers and "Career Criminals"* (Blumstein et al. 1986). Based on their analysis of arrest data, the authors estimate that nonincarcerated offenders commit eight to fourteen index crimes per year. Self-report data from prison inmates are wide-ranging and suggest that the average nonincarcerated criminal commits between five and seventy-five robberies per year and fourteen to fifty burglaries. Available evidence also suggests that a very small percentage of offenders commit a large percentage of serious crime. Analysis of a sample of California inmates found that the average offender committed 43.4 robberies per year when out of prison. However, about 50 percent of the inmates reported committing fewer than four robberies, and about 5 percent of the inmates reported committing 180 or more robberies per year (Blumstein et al. 1986). Tonry and Petersilia capture current sentiments about the causal relationship between incarceration rates and crime rates: "Presumably most people would conclude a priori that a quarter century's quintupling of the prison and jail population must have reduced crime rates. There has, however, been relatively little research in recent years on deterrence and incapacitation effects, and most authoritative reviews of both subjects conclude that, while such effects exist, they are probably modest" (1999:7–8).

While the empirical record on the causal connection between incarceration rates and crime rates is mixed and uncertain, we know more about the effect of imprisonment on the individual inmate and inmates' family members and significant relationships.

COPING WITH IMPRISONMENT

In the mid-twentieth century, a handful of scholars began to study the ways in which inmates respond to, and cope with, imprisonment (Clemmer 1940; Cohen and Taylor 1972; Jacobs 1977; Johnson and Toch 1982; Sykes 1958; Toch 1975, 1977, 1992; Ward and Schoen 1981). This research is particularly germane to heinous offenders, who typically serve lengthy prison sentences. Taken as a whole, this line of research provides ample documentation of the ways in which incarceration affects inmates' mental health, self-esteem, violent tendencies, sense of deprivation, safety, and physical health (Flanagan, Marquart, and Adams 1998; Kupers 1999; Zamble and Porporino 1988).

Among the most comprehensive, empirically based assessments of inmates' responses to incarceration was a study conducted by Toch, Adams, and Grant (1991), who gathered data on thousands of New York's state prison inmates. Toch, Adams, and Grant identified five major challenges faced by inmates: gratifying impulses, enhancing esteem, pursuing autonomy, seeking refuge, and maintaining sanity.

Gratifying Impulses

Many inmates have difficulty controlling their impulses. Impulse-control issues that led some individuals to commit crimes on the streets also often lead to troublesome and high-risk behaviors in prison, such as exploitation of others (for example, stealing another inmate's radio or food), predatory behavior toward inmates and prison staff (physical fights or sexual assaults), and hustling (becoming involved in prison-based scams designed to, for example, smuggle in contraband or manufacture alcoholic substances from ingredients stolen from the prison kitchen). Here are several typical examples, reported by prison staff to Toch, Adams, and Grant (1991), of inmates who have difficulty with impulse control:

I approached the inmate and told him that he had been keeplocked [locked in his cell for having a confrontation with another officer in the prison dining room] and I wanted him to come to reception with the officer and myself. The inmate refused to leave the kitchen and said, "fuck that. I'm not leaving and nobody better put their mother-fucking hands on me." He was very anxious and nervous, in a fighting position and constantly moving around. The inmate picked up a can opener (approximately 24 inches long) and stated, "don't nobody come near me. I will hit you." He continued moving and again stated, "The state considers this a deadly weapon and I am going to use it as a deadly weapon. If any of you try to take me out of here, I'm going to use this weapon on you, you, and you." (91)

He stopped at the line and demanded more food. I says, "you have to wait till almost everybody is served. If there is any left over you could possibly get more food." He started yelling and screaming in the line, "if we don't get more food, how would the cooks and officers like to be taken hostage over more food?" At that time I ordered him to go to the table. He stayed right there and kept yelling and screaming at us, "how would the officers and cooks like to be held hostage?" (100)

Since entering (program) the inmate appears to have continued his unsatisfactory custodial adjustment of the past. Specifically he has been the subject of eighteen misbehavior reports during his fourteen months tenure with this program. . . . The inmate seems to associate with only a few individuals at any given time. These relationships appear to be . . . limited to manipulation on the inmate's part to obtain commissary items and use of the other's personal belongings. . . . The subject tends to avoid demonstrating this type of behavior with more aggressive inmates, which leads us to the inference that he is an "opportunity predator" of sorts. (103–4)

Enhancing Esteem

Inmates often cope with incarceration by engaging in behaviors and activities designed to boost their sense of worth in the eyes of other inmates and correctional staff. Some inmates actively cultivate a "tough" reputation—for example, an inmate who will throw punches at a moment's notice—in order to become admired by other inmates. They may also achieve this by affiliating with a prison-based gang that intimidates others. Here are typical reports by prison staff to Toch, Adams, and Grant (1991) of several different inmates:

While an officer was releasing you from your cell for keeplock exercise you approached the officer with your right fist clenched and verbally indicated you wanted to fight the officer. At this time you attempted to strike the officer in the face with your fist. In response the officer deflected your blow and physically restrained you while forcing you into your cell. . . . Once in your cell you armed yourself with a pen and commenced to attack (another officer). In response he closed your cell door before you could make contact and stab him. (115)

You destroyed your bedside table, tore up your sheets, broke a total of nine windows, and destroyed your clothing. . . . You did attempt to inflict bodily harm on correctional personnel by trying to strike them with a sixteen inch iron pipe when they entered your cell, by throwing a steel table against the cell bars and by throwing a lightbulb at the lieutenant. You also attempted to assault said officers by swinging your fists and kicking with your feet, and also by trying to bite any personnel that you could. . . . You made threatening remarks toward correction personnel, the judge who sentenced you, and police personnel who had arrested you. You stated that after you had been released you would return with a gun and kill as many people as you could. (122)

We again find (the inmate) in the special housing unit [segregation for punitive or safety reasons] as a result of receiving a threatening letter which he himself instigated by allegedly spitting on other residents and writing obscenities to said residents. Intermittently and continually we have endeavored to plead our case with hopes of transferring this individual to a more suitable facility. . . . Currently we have the individual again in a structured environment where he can or will gain very little. Once again we are appealing for consideration for his transfer to a more suitable facility from which he can enjoy benefits of population. (124)

Pursuing Autonomy

Many inmates yearn for some semblance of autonomy in a setting that provides precious few opportunities for individual initiative. Some inmates attempt to enhance their autonomy by endearing themselves to prison officials in the hope of being granted special privileges (for example, premier housing or cell locations, unsupervised or minimally supervised work and recreation time).

Some inmates pursue autonomy more destructively by refusing to participate in prison activities, rebelling against prison officials, and defying authorities in an effort to escape their watchful eye and constant supervision (for example, by making sub rosa deals with prison staff and other inmates for choice job or cell assignments, clothing, medical care, and food). Typical reports by prison staff include these, which are reported by Toch, Adams, and Grant (1991):

He constantly sits in his own dream world waiting for time to pass. He shows no interest in anyone else, and by his disheveled appearance and lack of motivation has little interest in doing anything for himself. When confronted in a group he verbalizes his dream world of no problems when he is released. He is one of the more remarkable individuals (we have) encountered when it comes to blocking out the real world and the problems he will have to face. . . . He does as little as possible to pass the day. . . . In the community he is the local hermit. . . . [He] spends the majority of time by himself in his room. Psychologically he appears to be somewhat depressed, but other than that he is nothing more than an extremely unmotivated, unrealistic individual. He . . . is probably as naïve an individual as you can find. (134–35)

The mess hall officer came to me and told me he wanted the inmate locked up for passing out extra butter on the line and that he had told the officer to go fuck himself. I went to the inmate and asked him what he was doing giving out extra butter and talking to an officer that way. He said, "I told him to get out of my face." I told the inmate he was going to keeplock. He said that he wouldn't accept that, and walked out of the kitchen. I walked over to the inmate and asked him why he was making it harder on himself. He said he wouldn't accept keeplock, that he wanted to go to the box (the segregation unit), where the men were. He went with no problem. When we got over to the unit he refused to bend over and spread his cheeks. He said it was against his religion. (140)

At 7 AM an officer awakened you for a count, at which time you told him he didn't have to wake you up in a nasty manner. At 8 AM the officer returned to your cell and found you still in bed. He informed you that it was time to get ready for your job assignment which was as a porter. At 8:30 AM it was necessary to wake you up again. At 9 AM you reported to your work assignment and stated to the officer, "You don't have to wake me up at 7 AM for no count. You are harassing me." When the officer gave you two copies of his Notice of Report you threw them out the door through the crack, and told the officer to "Get the fuck away from my cell." After the officer ordered you keeplocked you started yelling in front of other inmates who were standing around listening, "Go fuck yourself, you bastard." The officer has cautioned you previously about reporting to work at 8 AM and not starting work until 9 AM. . . . At 12:35 PM when the officer went to feed you, you told him to stop pointing his finger at you and to stop looking at you like he wanted to hit you. You stated to him, "You want to do something about it, come on in my cell any time. I'll take you on, you punk." (144–45)

Seeking Refuge

Some inmates cope with incarceration by withdrawing from the mainstream prison population as much as possible. Often inmates seek refuge for their personal safety (for instance, if an inmate has not paid a debt, has a reputation as a snitch who has disclosed other inmates' misconduct to prison officials or testified in court against another inmate, or has slighted or insulted another inmate). Some inmates will ask to be placed in protective custody—a segregated portion of the prison that is cut off from the general population—when they have been threatened physically by other inmates or fear sexual assault because of their youth and physical appearance. Typical reports from prison staff include these, as reported to Toch, Adams, and Grant (1991):

> He states he is in fear of his life. He is unable or unwilling to name names. He states that on several occasions he has come back to his cell and found notes on his bed which were unsigned. These notes stated in various forms that if he were caught in the right place he would be, as he put it, "iced." The inmate also states that on one occasion when he was on his bed some unidentified inmate threw scalding water on him. (158)

> The inmate was admitted to protective custody after stating he was being harassed for homosexual favors. . . . The inmate's situation, as in the past, is complicated by his flirtations and overt activities which has always and will always cause him problems. As in the past he remains a management problem requiring a lot of attention and professional supervision. These needs will probably never change and he will require a significant amount of staff time with little or no return. The long term problem will really be how long this inmate can continue his lifestyle before severe psychiatric/psychological problems consume him. (159–60)

> He has tried to be "slick" by running to several inmates with some "bullshit" stirring things up and then playing dumb. He has also been involved

in selling and/or exchanging articles with other inmates. While involving himself in these activities he thinks he is pretty sharp. However, more times than not the weight eventually falls back on him. In fact, as a result of his "games" he found himself in a bad position, and since he could no longer handle the pressures that went along with the games he requested protective custody under the guise of being sexually harassed by another inmate in his dorm. (162)

Maintaining Sanity

Although most inmates seem to cope with imprisonment reasonably well in a psychological sense (Liebling 1999), a significant percentage of inmates struggle with major mental illness and psychiatric symptoms. Some of these inmates isolate themselves—for example, by spending all day in their cells—in order to avoid being harassed and threatened by others. On occasion, inmates with major psychiatric problems will seek protective custody in an effort to escape the toxic prison environment. Some inmates with major mental illness have a great deal of difficulty managing the stress of incarceration and become explosive in an effort to cope with the chronic pressure (Wiehn 1982). Typical reports from prison staff include these, as reported by Toch, Adams, and Grant (1991):

> So far so good. Now, however, the patient states what appear to be delusions of grandeur, specifically that he is Jesus Christ. . . . His purpose here on earth, he says, is to "forgive you for your sins. Everybody who prays is praying unto me." He points out the misty background to his Department of Correction photograph and states that this is proof of his identity. Later he says that every time he drinks alcohol "clouds become cloudy." On questioning he states that God does not speak to him directly but through the mouths of others. . . . On further questioning he states that God intends that he be released on these charges. . . . Despite repeated confrontations he seems to be persistent in his beliefs. (194)

It would appear that his almost complete inability to function intellectually makes him a poor candidate for survival in open prison population, and I can't off hand think of another program that would possibly be more appropriate for him to be in, so I guess we are left with no choice but to accept him into our program. Our goal will be to first of all help him be clean and neat and sanitary, to help him find his way around the prison, help him establish and follow programs, learn how to eat in the mess hall and eventually get him into some meaningful work . . . and hopefully be able to nurse him ever so gradually into population. (196)

He has been playing with feces but when observed said that everything was fine. A pint of ice cream that he had recently received was up-side-down next to the toilet bowl. When questioned about this he merely makes the statement that it had tipped over on him. . . . His cell is very disorderly, with everything strewn around, some feces mixed with ice cream on the floor. As soon as the cell is cleaned he messes it up again. . . . States that he wishes to serve out his full term and then sue the State of New York for half a million dollars for false imprisonment. Admits analyzing his feces to extract the paste in order to use this material to blot out images on some of his snapshots. When shown a photo of himself, states that the man was a marine and had died. (199)

Significant numbers of prison inmates suffer from major mental illness, such as schizophrenia, clinical depression, bipolar disorder, anxiety disorders, and mental retardation (Ditton 1999; Guy et al. 1985; Powell, Holt, and Fondacaro 1997; Steadman et al. 1989; Teplin 1990). According to recent estimates,

- 7 percent of federal prison inmates are considered mentally ill.
- 16 percent of inmates in state prisons, local jails, or on probation report a mental condition or have stayed overnight in a psychiatric hospital, unit, or treatment program.
- 22 percent of violent offenders manifest symptoms of mental illness.
- 29 percent of white female inmates in state prisons are mentally ill.
- 40 percent of white female inmates younger than twenty-five are mentally ill.
- 20 percent of black female inmates are mentally ill.
- 22 percent of Latina inmates are mentally ill. (Ditton 1999)

Inmates with psychiatric problems often have considerable difficulty staying out of trouble, complying with rules and regulations, and avoiding the threats of other inmates. They are often easy prey for prisons' predators. As Kupers (1999), a psychiatrist who has worked extensively in prison settings, notes,

Prison constitutes meanness training; the meaner a prisoner becomes, the greater the chance of survival. Mentally ill prisoners have difficulty coping with the prison code: Either they are intimidated by staff into snitching or they are manipulated by other prisoners into doing things that get them into deep trouble. They are disproportionately represented among the victims of rape, they are extra-sensitive to the everyday traumas of prison life, and they are massively overrepresented among the prisoners in punitive and administrative segregation or "lock-up" units. Meanwhile, with the overcrowding of prisons and the removal of rehabilitation programs, the meanness goes unabated and proliferates, more prisoners crack under the strain, and a larger proportion of the population are locked in solitary or segregation units of one kind or another. (xvii)

Here are representative examples of mentally ill inmates and illustrations of the difficulty they have functioning in prison (Kupers 1999):

John, a thirty-five-year-old African-American man, had been in prison for seven or eight years. He had a history of mental hospitalizations dating back to age twelve, had been diagnosed as having bipolar disorder with psychotic features, and was taking strong antipsychotic medications when I interviewed him in the Security Housing Unit of a state prison. He told me that he believed the guards were singling him out for persecution, so he "bombed" one of them with excrement. They performed a cell extraction (four or five guards spray a recalcitrant prisoner with mace or pepper spray in his cell and then rush him and subdue him) and placed him in the cell with a plexiglass (lexan) outer door, where I found him. He also told me he suffered from hallucinations, did not relate to the other guys because "they would yell and argue," and he was "very depressed and extremely paranoid." (9–10)

James is a forty-three-year-old African-American man serving time in a security housing unit of a state prison system who is unusual among prisoners in having a bachelors degree from a prestigious university. When I met him he was in the eighth year of a fifty-year sentence for murdering his father. He had no prior criminal record, and he swears the death was accidental. "I loved my father very much, it was just one of those freak accidents. We were arguing, my sister had told him I was ripping off some money he had been managing for the family—that was a lie, he wouldn't believe me— there was a gun he had for protection, I shot him."

James had been struggling to control his temper outbursts all of his life, and had done relatively well until his father's death. Once he entered prison he began getting into fights and arguing with the guards. He received many disciplinary write-ups, and eventually was sent to the Security Housing Unit. He says he wants to take an anger management course, but he has never been given the opportunity.

James was hesitant to answer my questions about suicide, but tears appeared when I raised the subject. He began the interview with a studied composure, but as we continued to talk his thoughts became more disorganized. He eventually admitted he heard voices, and believed someone was trying to use him to channel thoughts from another world. He reported a beating that had occurred a few months earlier while he was being transported in shackles—the officer who was accompanying him pulled upon the "leash" (a strap connected to the handcuffs, wrapped under the leg irons and held by a guard who walks behind the prisoner) throwing him face first into the concrete floor. Then two guards pounced on him and kicked and beat him. I asked why they would do that, and he admitted he doesn't really know, "But maybe it has something to do with the fact that I'm one of a very small number of prisoners—or guards for that matter—who have been through college, so maybe they feel like I'm trying to down them."

As the interview continued he let down his guard and shared with me some of the ideas that he usually keeps to himself: He has immense sexual powers on account of an undescended testicle that remains lodged in his abdomen, and that is the real reason most men feel immense envy in his presence and want to attack him. He only gets into fights to protect himself from their assaults. In fact, "I keep hearing voices telling me that this prisoner or that guard is about to jump me, so I have to make the first move." (29–30)

Earl is a thirty-three-year-old Caucasian man who has been in the Security Housing Unit of a state prison system for almost three years. He did very poorly in school (he believes he had a learning disability related to childhood fevers and seizures), and even with special education classes he was unable to complete junior high school. His psychiatric history dates to early childhood, as does a severe seizure disorder. His father, a Korean War veteran, was disabled, alcoholic, and abusive. His mother supported the family by working as a nursing assistant.

Earl grew up in a low-income neighborhood where "all the kids committed petty thefts, but they got away with it and I was always the one who got caught—I think I was just too disturbed to plan a getaway or to think up a good alibi." He has been diagnosed and is being treated for a "manic depressive disorder with psychotic features," but he also suffers from a severe anxiety disorder with panic attacks and intense phobia connected with being confined in a cell.

Earl dates the origin of his "cell phobia" to the time he first arrived in prison ten years earlier and was dragged into a cell and raped repeatedly by several other prisoners. Indeed, besides a history of severe mood swings and psychotic episodes, he exhibits many of the features of chronic posttraumatic stress disorder, including flashbacks, severe insomnia dating back to the rape, nightmares, an intense startle reaction, a greatly constricted life and, of course, the panic attacks. He was written up for his first disciplinary infraction in prison because he refused to follow a direct order by a correctional officer to reenter his cell. He explains that at the moment he refused the order he was more afraid of being confined in the cell than he was concerned about certain punishment for disobeying an order. But his punishment was more confinement in his cell.

Earl also mutilates himself by cutting. I ask him why he cuts and he describes very poignantly how, after he has been confined to a cell for awhile, his anxiety level rises to an unbearable degree and he feels compelled to cut himself. He thinks the cutting is the only way to alleviate the anxiety. Eventually he discovered that each time he cut himself, across the wrist or across the abdomen, he would be removed from his cell and sent to the infirmary for stitches.

"Once I get to the infirmary I calm down immediately, the panic disappears as soon as I get out of that cell." But since self-mutilation is a violation of prison rules, more time is added to his term in lock-up. When I point out that he is taken to the infirmary only for a short time for emergency treatment and then he is returned to his cell, Earl responds: "Still, it's worth it!" He believes the panic he feels in the cell leaves him no other option, and he feels that even the short period of relief is worth the pain and trauma. (36–37)

Within this population of mentally ill inmates are those who are suicidal. Although the frequency of suicide attempts in prison is difficult to measure precisely, Kupers (1999) estimates that the suicide rate in prison is twice as high as in the general population, accounting for more than half the inmates who die in custody. In the mid-1990s California state prisons saw 26.4 suicides per 100,000 inmates, and Texas state prisons saw 25 suicides per 100,000 inmates; these are the nation's two largest prison systems. The suicide rate in Georgia prisons was 10.8 per 100,000 and in Florida it was 9.9 per 100,000. Liebling (1999) examined various recent epidemiological studies of prison suicide and reports the following rates per 100,000 average daily prison population among various nations: United States, 140–200; Australia, 155; Scotland, 128; England and Wales, 116; Netherlands, 105; Canada, 94; New Zealand, 89; and Denmark, 19.

Various studies of inmates who attempt to commit suicide suggest that most completed suicides are male, a disproportionate number have been sentenced at the time of death (as opposed to awaiting sentencing), and a third have a history of inpatient psychiatric treatment. Further, inmates serving life sentences are overrepresented, most have previous criminal convictions, and 40 percent were seen by a doctor during the week preceding death. Most completed suicides are the result of hanging, many have injured themselves previously while incarcerated, many have serious drug and alcohol problems, and many prison suicides are completed by relatively young inmates (ages twenty to thirty-four).

Many inmates do not have a formal psychiatric diagnosis before the suicide attempt. Key contributory factors include the disruption of relationships with family members and acquaintances, lack of communication and support, bullying, threats from other inmates, fear, prison violence, uncertainty, isolation, boredom, enforced idleness, insomnia, and the prospect of a long sentence devoid of future hopes or plans. The principal motivation for prison suicide appears to be fear of other inmates, the consequences of one's crime, imprisonment, and the loss of a significant relationship. Research evidence suggests that shame, guilt, and psychiatric disorders are not key causes in most instances (Liebling 1999).

Some inmates attempt to commit suicide out of a sense of despair over their circumstances and bleak prospects—what some might call "rational" suicide. Other inmates attempt suicide in the midst of a psychotic episode, often in response to "command hallucinations," voices that instruct the inmate to kill himself or herself. Kupers (1999), a psychiatrist, describes a typical case:

> I found Mr. R. A., a Native-American prisoner in his late twenties, in an administrative segregation unit. He seemed agitated, and there was a strangeness to his wide-eyed stare, a kind of strangeness I have only seen in patients suffering from acute psychosis. I asked him why he was locked in Ad Seg, and he showed me his left wrist, where there was a thick scar from a self-imposed laceration. I asked what happened and he told me the voices told him to kill himself. Mr. R. A. had been in a protected, psychiatric unit for six months, receiving high-potency antipsychotic medications, when they transferred him to this prison. "They needed the bed in the psych hospital, and I was the most dispensable patient."
>
> There had been a delay in transferring the man's clinical chart, and he was unable to obtain his antipsychotic medications. Meanwhile, the other inmates made fun of him for "being a ding." He became progressively con-

fused over several weeks, and then he got into a fight with a prisoner who had insulted him. He believed the guards took the other prisoner's side, and he was thrown in "the hole." By this time he had remained off his medications for three weeks. Cut off from all social contact, the voices inside his head grew louder and began to tell him "what an asshole" he was. Then they told him to kill himself. He tried to do so by slashing his wrist with a piece of metal he broke off his bed. After the suicide attempt, Mr. R. A. was sent to the infirmary for two days and had the laceration sewn up. Then "a psychiatrist came and put me back on my meds." He was charged with a disciplinary infraction for attempting suicide, and returned to Administrative Segregation. (178–79)

Being placed in segregation—in "the hole"—is an occupational risk for any inmate, especially those convicted of heinous crimes who are management problems. Some inmates are placed in segregation only rarely, as a result of a sporadic fight or possession of contraband. Often they are placed in segregation for as long as thirty days. Other inmates are "frequent flyers" and may be placed in segregation for months at a time; these are the recalcitrant, out-of-control inmates who challenge prison rules and regulations, defy authority at every opportunity, and try to "get over" on prison officials. Abbott (1981), a career criminal, describes his own first encounter with "the hole":

My first acquaintance with punitive long-term solitary confinement had a more adverse and profound spiritual effect on me than anything else in my childhood.

I suffered from *claustrophobia* for years when I first went to prison. I never knew any form of suffering more horrible in my life.

The air in your cell vanishes. You are smothering. Your eyes bulge out; you clutch at your throat; you scream like a banshee. Your arms flail the air in your cell. You reel about the cell, falling.

Then you suffer cramps. The walls press you from all directions with an invisible force. You struggle to push it back. The oxygen makes you giddy with anxiety. You become hollow and empty. There is a vacuum in the pit of your stomach. You retch.

You are dying. Dying a hard death. One that lingers and toys with you.

The faces of guards, angry, are at the gate of your cell. The gate slides open. The guards attack you. On top of all that, the guards come into your cell and beat you to the floor.

Your mattress is thrown out. Your bedsheets are doubled. One end is run through a hole under the steel bunk that hangs from your cell wall. The other end is pulled through a hole at the opposite end of your bunk.

Your ankles are handcuffed and so are your hands. The sheet runs through them and you are left hanging from a spit by your feet and your hands. Your back is suspended several inches above the floor. You are smothering. You are being crushed to death.

They leave you like that all night. (25)

They finally put a name on what I have suffered in solitary: *sensory deprivation.* The first few times I served a couple of years like that, I saw only three or four drab colors. I felt only concrete and steel. When I was let out, I could not orient myself. The dull prison-blue shirts struck me, dazzled me with a beauty they never had. All colors dazzled me. A piece of wood fascinated me by its feel, its texture. The movements of things, the many prisoners walking about, and their multitude of voices—all going in different directions—bewildered me. I was slow and slack-jawed and confused—but beneath the surface I raged. (51)

Inmates who have been sentenced to death for heinous crimes face their own unique challenges. Johnson (1982) interviewed a group of inmates on Alabama's death row about how these inmates cope with the prospects of long-term imprisonment and capital punishment. Johnson found that a significant number of the death row inmates reported feeling harassed, isolated, in fear of guards, abandoned, and anxious about death. Here is a sampling of their comments:

We get 30 minutes a day to go outside. But that's in isolation, too. You walk around. You got a little place they set aside for us, but it's a cage. And you walk around like an animal does. And you know you're no different. You just go out there in another cage and you walk around. (135)

They have one day which is a store day. The one day actually is to those people on death row like Christmas and all they actually get is cigarettes and candy or cookies, and that's actually become to be a thing like Christmas. I've surveyed it from watching the guys and everybody gets excited and they are actually more happy on Tuesday when they get that little store package. But, you see this is actually what we have been reduced to as far as being men, trying to be a man, finally enjoying a little thing like a cookie. (136)

We're treated just like animals put in a cage. You know, like sometimes they come by with their sticks and they poke at you like you're an animal or something. That's the way they feel around here. And once you pick at an animal long enough, he starts fighting back. And we're not in a good place to fight back.

The people here make you feel isolated from the world. After a time, you don't want to trust nobody for nothing. Now you know that if a man gets to feeling like that, he just going to back off into a corner and he is going to protect that corner. That's the way I feel. Since I've been on death row, I feel like I have to protect myself because ain't nobody else going to help me. . . . I feel like I have lost faith in everybody. (137)

When you're on death row and you're laying down in your cell and you hear a door cracking you'll think of where it comes from. When you hear it crack. And when you hear the keys and everything, when something like this happens, the keys come through there: I'm up. I'm up, because you don't know when it's going to take place. The courts give you an execution date, that's true. But you don't know what's going to take place between then and when your execution date arrives. You don't know when you're going to be moved around to the silent cell over here. That's right down the hall, what they call a waiting cell. Up there, you don't know when you're going to be moved down there. And this keeps you jumpy, and it keeps you nervous, and it keeps you scared. (138)

THE PREDOMINANCE OF PRISON VIOLENCE

One of the most salient features of prison life is violence, both the fear of violence and the actual infliction of violence (Johnson 1987). Various attributes of prison settings make violence all but inevitable: overcrowding, close quarters, high concentrations of people with histories of impulse-control and anger-management problems, abusive relationships between staff and prisoners, involuntary residence, and the omnipresence of coercion and punishment.

Interpersonal violence in prison takes two primary forms: prisoners assaulting other prisoners and prisoners assaulting correctional staff (that is not to say that there is no staff abuse of prisoners). Prison violence occurs on a continuum, including such physical forms as shouting, threatening, pushing, shoving, slapping, scratching, punching, biting, elbowing, kneeing, kicking, knifing, and shooting (Bottoms 1999). Although victimization often takes these physical forms, it can also be sexual (sodomy, rape), psychological (setting inmates up by moving their cells to facilitate assaults, isolating inmates), economic (stealing from inmates, robbing inmates), or social (gang and ethnic conflict, assaults on "baby rapers" or child molesters) (Bowker 1982). Dale Simpson, the inmate serving a life sentence for triple murder (see chapter 1), wrote the following to me in a letter:

Crime in the institution is very widespread and covers many areas—from petty theft to rape and murder. I would say that about 75 percent of the inmate population has fears of being ripped off, assaulted in some way, or even killed.

Cell burglaries are by far the most feared crime. It would be safe to say this happens about 3 to 4 times a week. Stabbings, rapes, strong armed robberies happen less frequently and seem to occur in spurts. I can't tell you why. Stabbings can be totally unrelated to one another but seem to happen in groups. There may not be a stabbing for 4 or 5 weeks and then you will have 2 or 3 a week for a couple of weeks. Rapes occur at about 3 or 4 a year. Murders not that often.

Ninety-nine times out of a hundred no one will mess with you if they know you're going to stand up for yourself. I really hate playing the role of a killer in here. Unfortunately it's the only way I can survive. Unless I was to tell everyone how I really feel about murder they have no way of knowing how I feel. It's got to be enough to make others leery of you. Know what I mean? If I joke about it and act like it doesn't bother me, it makes others unsure. They think you're a little nuts or something. The better actor you are the better chance you have of not being messed with.

I believe that inmates put up shields around themselves—shields of fear, mystery, insanity, etc., and they try to radiate this out to others. What I mean is a person may act and talk mean to put doubt in others' minds about messing with him. He may be quiet, staying mostly to himself to make others wonder about him and therefore uncertain about whether he would be an easy victim or not. Some act crazy to keep others at a distance. There are a few who are themselves crazy. They don't need nor feel the need to hide their character from others.

If you show any weakness in here there is always someone who will prey on that weakness. I've seen it happen over and over and over. Let's say a group of us are sitting around watching the news on TV. Say there is a story about someone being hurt or killed in an accident or a hold-up. If a guy would say something like, "that's too bad" or "I feel sorry for him," someone would take that as a sign of weakness. Sympathy is a bad word in here. If you were in a group of friends you could get away with just some kidding. It's easy to share stories of crime, lousy things you've done in life, and so forth. But most of these are just that—stories. You will probably run into trouble if you relate feelings of sympathy and such to very many guys you don't know.

I have to play a role here that I do not like playing—a role I hope I do not come to believe myself. Each day is a danger. I am aware of it constantly. My life depends on that. I have to be very careful with who I let cross the boundary with me, from "killer" to me. I can count them on one hand, easy, and say with confidence that even they have at least a trace of doubt as to which is me.

It is difficult to produce precise estimates, given the large number of violent incidents that are never reported to prison authorities. Somewhat more reliable data are available on prison homicides, which authorities are much more likely to recognize as homicide. In the United States the rate of prison homicides increased sharply in the 1970s and then steadily declined, eventually falling below levels seen in the 1960s. Since the mid-1980s U.S. prisons have seen fewer than one hundred homicides per year (Bottoms 1999).

An all-too-frequent phenomenon in prison involves physical intimidation of younger and weaker inmates by older and larger inmates. Another common phenomenon is violent assault in order to settle a score. Physical threats, skillful manipulation, and exploitation are commonplace, as reflected in this graphically disturbing passage by Abbott (1981), a federal prisoner and murderer:

Sometimes a prisoner who happens to be physically big is encouraged to run the other prisoners' lives. That is the traditional dream of the typical warden. A hierarchy he can control. The big prisoners who believe this are usually fools who have been led (like sheep to the slaughter) to believe that because they can overpower with their hands the average man, everyone will obey them. What throws a wrench into all of this is the little skinny kid with a knife or some other weapon. The restraints, inner and outer, that govern ordinary men do not affect a prisoner bent on protecting himself.

To a prisoner it is an insult to grapple hand-to-hand with anyone. If someone ever strikes him with his hand (another prisoner), he has to kill him with a knife. If he doesn't, he will be fistfighting with him every day. He might be killed.

In prison we are all polite to each other: formal in our respect. We are serving years. If I have a verbal disagreement with someone, and I'm in the wrong, my apologies are given sincerely. But if I'm in the right and some asshole is wrong and he knows it, I have to see his face every day. If he

153

threatened to kill me, I have to see him day in, day out for years. This is what leads to killing him over a seemingly trivial matter. *All the violence in prison is geared for murder*, nothing else. You can't have someone with ill feelings for you walking around. He could drop a knife in you any day.

You learn to "smile" him into position. To *disarm* him with friendliness. So when you are raging inside at anyone, you learn to conceal it, to smile or feign cowardice.

You have to move into total activity from a totally inactive posture to sink a knife in as close to his heart as possible. It is this that also unsettles a man's mind in prison. A knife is an intimate weapon. Very personal. It unsettles the mind because you are not killing in physical self-defense. You're killing someone in order to live respectably in prison. Moral self-defense.

Let's say someone steals something from your cell. You catch him cold. Maybe he stole a carton of cigarettes. He gets loud with you. What you must do next is to become friendly with him. If he took your property, there is no telling what he may try to take next. It's possible that he would even try to fuck you if you let him steal from you. In prison society you are expected to put a knife in him. You might have to walk the yard with him for a week to take him off guard, to get him alone to kill him.

Here is how it is: You are both alone in his cell. You've slipped out a knife (eight- to ten-inch blade, double-edged). You're holding it beside your leg so he can't see it. The enemy is smiling and chattering away about something. You see his eyes: green-blue, liquid. He thinks you're his fool; he trusts you. You see the spot. It's a target between the second and third button on his shirt. As you calmly talk and smile, you move your left foot to the side to step across his right-side body length. A light pivot toward him with your right shoulder and the world turns upside down: you have sunk the knife to its hilt into the middle of his chest. Slowly he begins to struggle for his life. As he sinks, you have to kill him fast or get caught. He will say "Why?" or "No!" Nothing else. You can feel his life trembling through the knife in your hand. It almost overcomes you, the gentleness of the feeling at the center of a coarse act of murder. You've pumped the knife in several times without even being aware of it. You go to the floor with him to finish him. It is like cutting hot butter, no resistance at all. They always whisper one thing at the end: "Please." You get the odd impression that he is not imploring you not to harm him, but to do it right. If he says your name, it softens your resolve. You go into a mechanical stupor of sorts. Things register in slow motion because all of your senses are drawn to a new height. You leave him in the blood, staring with dead eyes. You strip in your cell and destroy your clothing, flushing it down the toilet. You throw the knife away. You jump under the showers. Your clarity returns. There is no doubt you did the only thing you could. Most of the regulars know you did it. No one questions, but whenever you see one, he may embrace you, pat your back, laugh. You just downed a rat everyone hates. In the big prisons, such murders are not even investigated at all. In _____, when I was there, between thirty and forty bodies were found stabbed to death. There was only one conviction, and even then, it was because the killer turned himself in and pleaded guilty to ten years. (75–77)

Many inmates—especially female inmates and younger male inmates—fear sexual harassment and assaults. A significant portion of prison violence arises from sex-related incidents, either in the form of violent sexual assaults or violent reactions by inmates who believe they are being sexually harassed and need to make preemptive strikes in self-defense (Lockwood 1982). The case involving a young inmate, Frank, who was convicted of murdering a man and who was being harassed in prison by an older inmate, is illustrative:

And so he comes in and sits down. And then he just keeps on staring at me. And I'm not going to run for nothing. And so I just sat there and kept on staring. And so he was sitting right over here and I was looking over there out the window and this guy was staring at me. And so all of a sudden he started laughing and licking his lips and I said, "What the hell does that mean?" I'm still not going to go anywhere. Because, if this dude is going to jump up, then I'm going to hurt him. So then, anyway, he started laughing and licking his lips and everything. And then I told him, I forgot what I told him, but it got him mad. And then he walked out of the room and he said, "I'll get you." And I said, "Get me now." And I stood up. And then I walked back into the room and I crouched into the boxing stance. And then he looked at me and then he walked back out of the room. . . .

So I went to the ward and I had the blade [to protect himself, Frank obtained a blade on the end of a comb from another inmate]. At night you leave your clothes in the dorm in the sitting room, and you lay there and go to sleep. And I laid there and went to sleep. But I had forgotten that I had laid the blade in my pants so that I couldn't reach it. So in the middle of the night he (Davis) gets up and goes to kiss me on the cheek. And I jumped up and I felt like I was going to puke. I started to choke and everything. And I hit him and he came back and hit me over the head. And just by the style of the way this guy hit me I know that this guy did box. And so I said, "Shit, if I don't do something to this dude, then he is going to fuck me up." So I just started getting mad and I hit him and hit him again. And then he hit me again and knocked me over the bed. I walked into the day room and he hit me and the officer saw the end of it. . . .

The next morning they put me in the room and it was like nothing ever happened. . . . And I had this blade in my pocket and I went over and talked to him and I said, "Listen, there is nothing going on between me and you. And there is never going to be, I don't care how big an army that you get. Nobody is going to make me a homosexual or I'm going to kill them." And then I took the blade out and he ducked and I went for his throat and I hit him on the arm. I cut him across there. I wanted to kill him. (Lockwood 1982:258–59)

Many male inmates engage in sexual activity yet do not consider themselves homosexual, although every prison has a small number of inmates who do consider themselves gay. Many inmates who have sexual contact with other inmates rationalize their conduct as a "normal" adaptation to abnormal circumstances. They maintain their heterosexual orientation while engaging in occasional sexual activity with other men. Abbott (1981) describes this common phenomenon as he observed it as an inmate:

The majority of prisoners I have known—something like ninety percent—express sexual interest in their own sex. I hesitate to call this "homosexual" because American society recognizes *only* the passive homosexual—the one who plays the female role—as being a "homosexual." So it is really the same outside as in prison, but open in prison.

So you can see already how this distorts a lot of meanings and can fuel a lot of violence, both physical and psychological. Because no prisoner really respects a homosexual, and yet—as I said—almost all have these desires themselves. It is the same as in the society of men outside prison.

Also, in all the penitentiaries I have been transferred to, in each one there were only at most half a dozen "known" homosexuals among prisoners.

Only once or twice in my life have I seen in any prison two men demonstrate sexual affection by kissing or otherwise touching each other. The open homosexual plays the role of a woman and is usually the wife of a prisoner respected on the yard. He gives her the security and protection he would a woman outside prison. But to be a punk is surpassed in contempt only by being a snitch. Prison regimes respect these relationships. In reality they encourage them. (80)

Abbott's observations are remarkably consistent with the sentiments expressed in a letter that Dale Simpson wrote to me about sexual activity and violence in a maximum-security prison:

I would say that at least 50 percent of the 19–20 year olds are "turned out." There are those who are able to take care of themselves. I would say (speaking of the 50 percent that aren't "turned out") 20 percent are man enough to stand up for themselves alone. Another 20 percent will fight if they have some help. The last 10 percent are those who have friends or relatives here to look out for them. Actually this 10 percent is close to being like the 20 percent who will fight with help.

There are convicts here who will help a youngster who is trying to stand on his own. If he won't fight for himself, no one will do it for him. Usually when someone helps another to stand up to those trying to make a "kid" out of him, there are no strings attached. There are times, of course, when the person helping the youngster has ideas of his own and wants to make a "kid" out of him. I would say that 9 times out of 10 when another inmate helps a youngster stand on his feet there is no other motive involved.

I have seen some of these young inmates who are "turned out" come to accept it and even like it. I would think that those who do not accept their lot will carry the hatred to the streets and will eventually return to prison by taking their hatred out on an innocent party.

Once a youngster starts having sex with someone they are stigmatized as weak, soft, queer, etc. Most convicts would not trust them with any sort of information that would get someone busted. If they are soft enough to let someone abuse their bodies then they would probably snitch under pressure.

To a large degree the administration ignores the problem of sex in prison. In some ways they even encourage it. They may let a guy they are trying to pacify go to the reception center and pick him out a "wife." I don't see how the administration could even think that it would help maintain control. More fights and stabbings occur over youngsters, money, and dope than all other things put together.

Female inmates are especially vulnerable to sexual harassment and, on occasion, rape. Although there are some instances of same-sex rape in women's prisons, most rapes are perpetrated by male staff. The organization Human Rights Watch investigated the sexual abuse of women in five state prisons in the mid-1990s and documented many occurrences of rape and sexual harassment by male staff (Kupers 1999). The following example is typical:

While incarcerated at Dwight Correctional Center in Illinois, Zelda was raped repeatedly by a correctional officer. The first time, he entered her cell at night, hit her in the face, handcuffed her to her bed, and raped her vaginally and anally. Then he took off the handcuffs and left her cell. She was taken to the emergency room of a local hospital where a physical exam revealed she had been raped. She was returned to her cell and raped twice more by the same guard. No real investigation ever occurred, and he was never punished. (Kupers 1999:144)

Some female inmates "agree" to have sex with male staff, although whether such sexual relationships are truly consensual is questionable in light of the women's vulnerability, the coercive setting, and dynamics between staff and inmates. As Kupers notes, "Women who go to prison are very likely to have been physically or sexually abused as children and to have been the victims of assault, domestic violence, or rape as adults. This makes the abuse they receive in prison seem 'all too familiar,' a reenactment of past traumas" (1999:145). According to a woman serving time in a California prison,

> They feel so isolated in prison, so guilty, they try in any way they can to feel loved—some just want to get daddy's approval—so they give in to guys hitting on them, bringing them flowers or little trinkets. They do it in an empty cell or a storage closet. Then, when they get pregnant, all hell breaks loose. The guard gets fired, the woman is thrown in the hole until she gives them permission to do an abortion, and then the whole thing gets hushed up and she's left to feel ashamed and afraid to tell anyone about it. Then she gets depressed but can't get to see a shrink because those guys don't really do anything but give out pills. (Kupers 1999:145)

Research evidence suggests several factors that are correlated with prison violence among inmates (Bottoms 1999). In general, perpetrators are most likely to be male inmates who are relatively young, convicted of violent crimes, have a history of psychiatric difficulties, and are serving a sentence in a maximum-security prison (as opposed to a lower-security institution). Poor prison management, overcrowding, and high turnover in the inmate population (transiency) have also been identified as contributing factors (Cooke 1998). Bowker (1982) suggests that most physical victimization results from several key features found in prisons: (1) inadequate supervision by staff members, (2) architectural designs that promote rather than inhibit victimization, (3) the easy availability of deadly weapons,

(4) the housing of violence-prone prisoners in proximity to relatively defenseless victims, (5) a generally high level of tension produced by the close quarters and multiple, crosscutting conflicts among both individual inmates and groups of prisoners, and (6) the pervasive need among inmates to seek revenge for real or imagined slights or past victimizations.

As one would expect, violence involving prison staff and inmates occurs for very different reasons and under different circumstances. Light (1991) examined data on prisoner-staff assaults in New York's state prisons and found that most were attributable to six dominant themes (in decreasing order of frequency): officer's command (assault on an officer following explicit command to inmate), protest (assault occurs because the inmate considers himself to be the victim of unjust or inconsistent treatment by a staff member), search (assault occurs during an officer's search of a prisoner's body or cell, excluding specific contraband searches), inmates' fighting (assault on an officer intervening in fight between inmates), movement (assault occurs during movement of inmates from one part of the prison to another), and contraband (assault on a staff member who suspects that an inmate possesses contraband items) (also see Bottoms 1999). Additional empirical evidence suggests that inmates are less likely to assault more experienced officers (with respect to years on the job) (Bottoms 1999).

THE IMPRISONMENT OF WOMEN

Women are incarcerated in much larger numbers than many people realize, and the female prison population has been increasing rapidly. Between 1990 and 2001 the female prison population more than doubled. Since 1995 the annual rate of growth in the number of female inmates has averaged 5.4 percent, compared with an average increase of 3.6 percent for male inmates (Harrison and Karberg 2003).

Incarcerated women who commit heinous crimes—a relatively small portion of the female inmate population—face a number of unique challenges beyond the risk of sexual victimization (Greenfield and Snell 1999). Although interpersonal violence and sexual aggression involving female inmates may be less common than among men in a purely statistical sense, they do exist and need to be addressed, particularly given the growing percentage of women in the prison system.

Women's corrections has always been a unique phenomenon, filled with stereotypes that for years have guided programming and prison administration (Fox 1982; Stanton 1980). In the nineteenth and early twentieth centuries, discussions of female inmates were replete with references to prisoners' "spoiled identities," sexual behaviors and orientation, morality, and "fallen women" (Bullough 1973; Lombroso and Ferrero 1895; Pollack 1950; Pomeroy 1975; Thomas 1923). For decades "rehabilitation" programs in women's prisons focused largely on sewing, typing, food service, hairstyling, and child care. In many jurisdictions women's prisons were given short shrift and were administrative afterthoughts, leading to severe overcrowding, inadequate medical care, abusive conditions, sexual exploitation of inmates by staff, and neglect (Fox 1982; Young 1932).

Construction of separate correctional facilities for women started in earnest around 1839, when New York State established the Mount Pleasant Female Prison on the hill behind Sing-Sing; the design resembled men's prisons with several tiers of cells (Rafter 1998). Early feminists subsequently lobbied for more enlightened facilities and programming for women in "reformatories" administered by women (Fox 1982). Among the earliest reformatories were several New York State prisons: the House of Refuge at Hudson opened in 1887, the Western House of Refuge at Albion in 1893, and the New York State Reformatory for Women at Bedford Hills in 1901. Some of the earlier institutional designs allowed for incarceration of women in supposedly "homelike" environments that were established in cottages and administered by parentlike staff. Over time the architectural design of women's prisons began to resemble traditional male prisons.

Currently, nearly two-thirds of women in prison are ethnic minorities and women of color. Recent surveys suggest that nearly two-thirds have young children; nearly 30 percent received welfare assistance just before the arrest that led to their incarceration; nearly three-fifths report having been physically or sexually abused; about half were using drugs, alcohol, or both at the time of their arrest; and about two-thirds have prior criminal convictions (Greenfeld and Snell 1999).

Interviews with female inmates demonstrate their unique experiences in prison. Some inmates claim that corrections staff patronize them because they are women, as reported by Fox (1982):

Some of these officers don't know how to talk to you as a woman. Sure, some women don't demand respect, but I do. Like the way some of them talk to you, like, "Do this, do that." All nasty like. Who in the hell do they think they are? They're no better than me. Just because they are a C.O. and

I have a number, they are no better than me. I'm no less a woman than they are. I get so aggravated, so angry. I just go right into anger, and they feed right into it. (213)

I give you respect because you're doing your job. But don't disrespect me, because I'm still a woman no matter what I'm in here for. Some officers say, "It's not my fault that you're in here." That really does it. I don't take that from anybody. I'm a woman, and I give you respect, but don't disrespect me just because I'm an inmate. Don't make it sound like I've got to do this or that because I'm just a "little girl." (213–14)

I find myself sometimes, if I'm writing a letter, I'll say, "the girls here. . . . " The officers make you feel as if you're definitely not equal. They look down to you, so you begin to look at yourself as a child. You're told when and what to do, when to go to bed, when to eat, when to shower, when to do everything. You begin to feel as though you're not a woman. And then people start acting like children. At those times, I have to realize that I'm doing this merely for a fact that I'm in here. At other times I can't deal with it, and I'm really messed up for the whole day. (214)

Most female inmates—nearly two-thirds—have young children, and most are single mothers (Greenfeld and Snell 1999; Kupers 1999); the mothers' separation from their children is particularly stressful. Although most children of female inmates are cared for by relatives or friends, some women need to place their children in foster care or have had their parental rights terminated by the courts (Fox 1982; Greenfeld and Snell 1999). As Kupers notes, "In many cases the gender differences that exist on the outside are exaggerated in prison. For instance, a large proportion of female felons are single mothers and serve as the primary parent in their households. When they go to prison, separation from their children becomes excruciatingly painful" (1999:114–15).

A significant number of women are pregnant when they enter prison and give birth while incarcerated. Although some states permit female inmates to care for their infants for up to one year following birth in order to enhance mother-child bonding, most new mothers place their infants with family, friends, in foster care, or make an adoption plan (Kupers 1999).

It's very hard. My daughter is two now, and it's hard. It's something that I hope won't affect her future. It's really hard, because I think of my daughter often, and sometimes I wish things could . . . I hope that things will turn out for the better, because I want her back, and I want to have a really good future together. It's been hard not being able to see her, but I've learned to accept it. (Fox 1982:215)

There are a lot of women who can't cope with the problem of being a mother in here. And a lot of women lose their children, and if you're in a group where there's a lot of emotion, you react to that emotion too. When a woman loses a child, like if she's doing a life sentence, the state takes over the child, we feel her reaction. We relate to that situation because we are mothers ourselves. (Fox 1982:215)

Even though I did well in prison, I would have these periods every six months or every nine months when I would hit this bottom. I would get so severely depressed about not seeing my son and my family, about just wanting to be free. After a while, you cannot take the confinement any more. You're so totally secluded from everything. I was fortunate. My family came to visit me three or four times a year. My older sister and her husband raised my son from the time he was two, and the blessing was that they always allowed me to be a part of his life. I had seen women in prison break up telephone receivers because they would tell them, no, you can't talk to your child, we don't want you in her life any more. (Kupers 1999:117–18)

Female inmates with major mental illness face added pressures and challenges. Some manifest symptoms of severe psychosis and clinical depression, as described in these reports by a prison psychiatrist:

Mary was hospitalized in a psychiatric unit with paranoid schizophrenia when she was twenty-three and again at twenty-four. When she returned home from the hospital after the second stay, she discovered that her husband had left with their two children. He eventually won custody. She fell into a deep depression, turned to illicit drugs, and stopped taking her prescribed psychiatric medications. Unable to pay rent, she became homeless. In the middle of the night, a police officer woke her and ordered her to move out of the park she had been sleeping in for over a week, and in the ensuing argument she struck him. Since she had two prior arrests for drug possession, the judge sentenced her to a prison term. I found her in a darkened cell in a women's prison in the middle of the day, and had to coax her to come to the bars to talk to me. She was quite disheveled and seemed frightened and distrustful. She told me she hears voices constantly but does not want to ask to see a psychiatrist because "all he'll do is lock me in a cell and make me take tranquilizers that make me numb and dumb." (Kupers 1999:10)

Sandra was sexually molested repeatedly by her grandfather from the time she was five until she was ten. She tried to tell her mother that she did not want to spend time alone with him, but her mother never listened. At ten Sandra began disobeying her mother, hitting boys at school, and getting in trouble with teachers. Her mother, an alcoholic who paid very little attention to her only child, gave her to a neighbor to raise. Sandra ran away several times, prompting the neighbor to send her to the adolescent ward of a locked psychiatric hospital. The psychiatrist decided Sandra was suffering from schizophrenia and prescribed antipsychotic medications, but he never uncovered the history of childhood sexual abuse.

Sandra remained in the hospital until she was eighteen. She left to live on her own. She stopped taking the medication and began to drink heavily. When she drank she became belligerent. Whenever a male stranger annoyed her while she was drinking, she would hit him. On two occasions she was taken to the county psychiatric hospital, admitted, and given injections of antipsychotic medications. Each time she left the hospital she immediately discontinued the medications and began drinking again. At nineteen she slugged the police officer who was called because she was acting too rowdy in a bar. She was arrested and sent to jail. After several more incidents of this kind, Sandra was convicted of assaulting a man in a bar and was given a term of three years in prison.

In prison, when she believed another prisoner was out to get her, she sought out that prisoner and attacked her. She was punished with a term in the administrative lock-up unit, where I met her. She appeared disheveled and admitted she heard voices commanding her to hit other prisoners. She told me she had never received any psychiatric treatment in prison, but she believed the guards were harassing her. She said they often walked by her cell whispering that another prisoner a few cells away was out to get her. She continued: "Telling me that makes my face get all red and I start screaming at the guard to stop getting me all agitated. Then they write me up another 115 [a disciplinary ticket] for disrespecting an officer and I have to do more time in this rotten hole!" (Kupers 1999:24–25)

Many female inmates suffer the ill effects of chronic physical or emotional abuse by their spouses or partners. One inmate serving a life sentence for killing her abusive husband reports that her treatment in prison, particularly with respect to the constant restrictions placed on her, are reminiscent of the abusive treatment she received from her husband:

> During my seventeen-year marriage, I developed a psychological profile similar to that of a prisoner of war. I went through many things which lowered my self-esteem including being told what to wear, when to wear it, and how to wear it. During my incarceration, I have accomplished many things, one of which is I feel a certain independence at being able to make decisions for myself, including what to put on every day. If my clothes are taken from me, I fear emotionally, mentally, and psychologically I will be going backward, again feeling like I did all those years ago in my abusive marriage. If this backward movement within myself takes place, I question whether I will again harm someone I may conceive as an abuser. (Kupers 1999:121–22)

COLLATERAL IMPACT

As a criminal justice professional and parole board member, I have spent a great deal of time with prison inmates. I have also met with inmates' family members, usually in the context of my meetings with domestic violence or sexual molestation victims just before the inmate's parole hearing. In most of these instances the family members who ask to appear at victims' hearings oppose the inmate's release, either out of anger or because they fear for their personal safety. Occasionally, family members will plead for the inmate's release, asserting that the inmate has been rehabilitated or has otherwise seen the errors of his ways.

I have to remind myself continually that inmates are not the only ones affected by their imprisonment. Many inmates have not harmed family members and have supportive relatives and "significant others" on the streets who count the days until the inmate returns home. Over the years I have read countless letters from wives, children, parents, cousins, clergy, employers, friends, and acquaintances who plead for the inmate's release and recount the ways, in painful detail, that the inmate's incarceration is wreaking havoc on family members and loved ones. The refrains are familiar, understandable, and predictable:

> I miss my Daddy so much. I cry at night because he isn't with me. I need him to play with me and to teach me things. Please let him come home. I know he'll be good.
>
> Inmate's child

I want to assure you that I will supervise John carefully. When he doesn't drink he is a wonderful member of the family. My husband and I will do everything possible to be sure that John goes to his meetings [Alcoholics Anonymous] and to his counselor. We really need him home with us, now that my husband and I are getting up there in years.

Inmate's mother

I have known Sarah since grade school when she babysat for our children. Deep down inside she is a wonderful person. I know she made a serious mistake [stabbing her boyfriend while under the influence of drugs] but that's not the *real* Sarah. Please know that Sarah would be coming home to loving family and friends.

Family friend of inmate

I beg of you to parole Marvin. He's learned his lesson this time, I'm sure. When I visit him I can see that he's a different person—more mature. He now knows that he can't be running the streets, that he needs to be home with me and our children. We're about to lose the house because we have no money. I don't know how I'm going to survive much longer. Please, please let him come home.

Inmate's common-law wife

Brenda was one of my most reliable employees. I was shocked when I found out she had a serious drug problem. It never caused a problem at work. I'd hire Brenda back in a minute to be a shift manager in my dry-cleaning business. I will also do what I can to help her with her recovery.

Inmate's former employer

Before his arrest Barry was an active member of my church. He would often go out of his way to help people in need. I know he has had his share of problems, but I assure you this is a man who really does know right from wrong. With the Lord's help, Barry will be a constructive member of society. I pledge my support.

Pastor in inmate's church

Incarcerating an offender is like throwing a large rock in a placid pond—it generates many ripples. With the exception of offenders who are virtually alone in the world—and there are such offenders—the more typical inmate's incarceration creates profound hardship on family members and others in the community (Tonry and Petersilia 1999). The effect of imprisoning offenders who commit heinous crimes tends to be the most profound because of their long sentences.

Although removal of the inmate may actually be salutary in some instances—for example, when the offender has abused, molested, or assaulted family members—more often the family mourns the loss of the inmate's emotional, physical, and economic presence (Fishman 1990). The consequences for inmates' children are particularly dire. Some children lose an important, meaningful parental figure in the household. The remaining parent, who is usually low income, often needs to work extra hours to make up for the lost income and thus is less available to her children (Bloom and Steinhart 1993; Browne 1989; Carlson and Cervera 1991; Ferraro et al. 1983; Hagan 1994; Sampson 1992). Children who are supervised less are then at greater risk of becoming involved in drug and alcohol use, sexual activity, and delinquency.

Children of incarcerated parents may also experience feelings of shame and rejection that impede their relationships with peers and school performance. It is not unusual for young children of incarcerated parents to begin manifesting behavior problems at home and in school (Barnhill 1996; Gabel and Johnston 1995; Hagan and Dinovitzer 1999; Sack 1977).

Despite stereotypes to the contrary, there is evidence that many incarcerated fathers want to be actively involved in their children's lives. Lanier (1993) found that nearly three-fourths of 188 fathers in a New York State maximum-security prison lived with their child before they were incarcerated, and almost exactly the same percentage reported that they spent a lot of time with their children before their incarceration. Other studies suggest lower, but still substantial, rates of male inmates' residency with children before incarceration and that these men made financial contributions to the children and their mothers (Gabel and Johnston 1995; Hagan and Dinovitzer 1999; Hairston 1989, 1991, 1998).

Somewhat more is known about the effects of incarcerating mothers. Because many incarcerated women are single parents, their children are typically raised by nonparents—grandparents, relatives, friends—during the mother's incarceration (Gabel and Johnston 1995; Hale 1988; King 1993; Raeder 1995). One study found that two-thirds of the caregivers to children of incarcerated mothers did not have the financial resources they needed to meet the children's needs (Bloom and Steinhart 1993). Baunach (1985) found that the loss of imprisoned mothers' daily contact with their children and the subsequent loss of parental skills, combined with feelings of inadequacy, have a profound effect on the mothers' ability to reconnect with their children meaningfully following their release from prison (also see Hagan and Dinovitzer 1999; Phillips and Bloom 1998; Wald 1995).

BALANCING PRISON AND INTERMEDIATE SANCTIONS

Offenders who commit heinous crimes typically require substantial periods of incarceration, whether for purposes of public safety, punishment, or rehabilitation. Nearly all—the relatively few exceptions are those sentenced to death or to life imprisonment without the possibility of parole—will return to the streets. One of the most difficult tasks that I have faced as a parole board member, and that I share with many colleagues who are in a position to decide when an inmate is to be released from prison, is determining at what point release is appropriate. It is tempting to assume that inmates who commit heinous crimes should be made to serve out their entire sentence, as a form of punishment and retribution.

The reality, however, is that we have a responsibility to enhance the likelihood that inmates who return to the community—including those who have committed the most heinous crimes imaginable—will not commit new crimes. Requiring inmates to complete their entire sentence in prison often is not in the public's best interest. This is not a form of leniency. Rather, I would argue that public safety is often, although not always, best served by a gradual release from prison with close monitoring and supervision in the community. Releasing inmates who have served very long sentences, sometimes decades long, directly to the streets—"cold turkey"—without any gradual transition is a likely set-up for failure.

The most responsible approach is to consider a wide range of intermediate sanctions (Carter and Ley 2001; Tonry 1998a) that can be implemented at some point during the inmate's sentence. An intermediate sanction falls somewhere on a continuum between unsupervised liberty on the streets and incarceration. For most offenders who have committed heinous crimes, such intermediate sanctions should be used only after the inmate has served at least a very significant fraction of his or her sentence, typically in the vicinity of two thirds.

Intermediate sanctions provide a wide range of alternatives to formal incarceration on a continuum from more to less supervision. In principle, inmates would be released with the sanction that is necessary to ensure public safety and enhance the likelihood that the offender can function effectively in the community, continue rehabilitation, maintain employment, and be held accountable. Alternative sanctions can be introduced when needed, either in the direction of more restriction (if an offender shows signs of needing closer supervision, for example, for violating curfew or missing appointments with a parole officer) or less restriction (when an offender demonstrates over time that she or he does not require the current level of supervision). This process of calibration and recalibration (Reamer 2003a) provides ongoing, continual opportunities to monitor the inmate's status and enhance or lessen supervision as needed. The complete menu of options, rank-ordered from most to least restrictive, includes

- Prison/jail: Incarceration in local or county jails, state or federal prisons (maximum, medium, minimum security, or work-release status)
- Residential programs: Residential treatment programs for specialized groups of offenders (for example, sex offenders, offenders who are drug or alcohol dependent, offenders with significant psychiatric disorders)
- Electronic monitoring: Requires offenders to wear a locked electronic transmitter that permits their parole and probation supervisors to monitor their whereabouts
- Curfew restrictions: Require offenders to report to their place of residence by a certain time and limit their travel
- Specialized caseloads: Supervision of offenders with common issues, needs, and profiles (for example, sex offenders, compulsive gamblers, offenders who are drug dependent or violent)
- Intensive supervision: Parole or probation supervision with more frequent contacts and restrictions (for example, travel and curfew restrictions)
- Probation: Minimal supervision with referral for appropriate social, mental health, educational and vocational services

The initial assignment of an intermediate sanction would be made by a parole board that has the authority to mandate the offender's supervision, residence, drug testing, and program participation. Ideally, the releasing authority would carefully review a wide range of factors that appear to be correlated with risk to the community. Various guides exist, such as the Level of Service Inventory—Revised (LSI-R) (Andrews and Bonta 1995, 1998; Simourd and Malcolm 1998). This instrument includes fifty-four items that measure ten components of offender risk, among them

- Criminal history: Nature and extent of the offender's criminal background (for example, number of previous offenses, types of offenses)
- Education and employment: Highest level of education, education history, employment history
- Financial resources: Sources of income and financial status and stressors
- Family and marital relationships: Current family constellation and connections, family history, marital status and history, key relationships and stressors
- Accommodations: Housing status and options
- Leisure and recreation: Lifestyle choices and patterns related to leisure and recreational time
- Companions: Nature and extent of social contacts, friends, acquaintances
- Alcohol and drug problems: History and current status of drug and alcohol dependence and abuse
- Emotional and personal: Psychiatric status and history, current emotional and personal issues (for example, depression, relationship conflict, impulse-control issues)
- Attitudes and orientation: Nature of offender's attitudes toward the law, orientation toward criminal thinking, and values

A second example of a standardized risk-management tool is the client management classification (CMC) system (Lerner, Arling, and Baird 1986). The CMC is divided into four sections (Harris 1994). An attitude section includes forty-five items concerning the offender's attitude toward the offense, his or her offense pattern, school adjustment, vocational and residential adjustment, family functioning, interpersonal relations, emotions, plans, and perceived problems. The second section focuses on the offender's history, emphasizing his or her legal involvement, medical history, academic achievement, family history, and marital status. The third section focuses on the offender's behavior, including his or her general demeanor, dress, affect, cooperation, and so on. The final section summarizes the criminal justice professional's impressions and provides an opportunity to rate the offender on seven key factors (for example, vocational and educational deficits, criminal value orientation).

If changes in an offender's circumstances suggest that a change in sanctions is necessary (either an increase or decrease in supervision or restrictions), criminal justice professionals can choose from a wide range of available institutional and community-based options (Carter and Ley 2001:62–63):

- Counseling or reprimand: This is the most common response to minor offenses and minor parole and probation violations. It involves confronting the offender with the apparent violation, listening to her or his side of the story, and delivering a stern admonition or warning. For example, if Melvin S. (case 2.6), the former physician who served a sentence for defrauding insurance companies, failed to report for a meeting with his parole counselor or skipped a restitution payment, a reprimand would be appropriate.
- Increased reporting requirements: For the parolee or probationer who commits minor violations, such as not keeping appointments or finding full-time employment, the supervising counselor can increase the frequency of his or her reporting requirements. For example, if Hank S. (case 2.21), the former seminarian who sexually assaulted a minor in a hotel room, was not participating consistently in his community-based sex offender treatment program, the parole counselor might increase his reporting requirements.
- Loss of travel or other privileges: Supervising counselors can withhold permission for the offender to leave the city, county, or state. They can also impose a curfew. For example, if the parole officer assigned to Marsha R.'s case (2.4) was concerned that she might cross state lines to gamble at nearby casinos—in light of Marsha's history of gambling problems and her embezzlement of funds from her former employer—the parole officer could impose a strict curfew and deny permission for Marsha to travel out of state.
- Increased drug or alcohol testing: This is the most common response for the offender who tests positive for drugs or alcohol. The supervising counselor can either increase the frequency of random drug tests or place the offender on a more frequent, fixed testing schedule. For example, if Alfred B. (case 2.1), who had a history of heroin addiction and robbed and shot a convenience store clerk, tested positive for marijuana use while on parole but otherwise complied with parole conditions, his parole officer could increase the frequency of random drug screens.
- Treatment and educational referrals: Supervisors should refer offenders to appropriate treatment and rehabilitation programs (usually alcohol, drug, and mental health programs) whenever the need arises. They should also refer offenders for educational and vocational education programs to enhance their knowledge and skills. For example, Angela U. (case 2.14), who was an accomplice in a robbery that critically injured the victim, had not graduated from high school and had

no marketable job skills. Her parole officer could help Angela enroll in a job-training program sponsored by a state agency.

- Restructuring payments: Offenders' payment plans (e.g., restitution, victim compensation, fines, probation fees, child support) may require adjustment when parolees lose a job, become disabled, or have their employment hours reduced. For example, if Theo N. (case 2.10) were laid off of his job and fell behind in his restitution payments to the jewelry salesmen he robbed, his parole counselor could help Theo negotiate a revised payment plan pending new employment.

- Extension of supervision: In some jurisdictions staff may petition the court to extend supervision of the offender who has not complied with all conditions. For example, assume that Larry K. (case 2.23) was eventually released from prison following his conviction for assaulting his common-law wife. For more than a year Larry complied fully with parole conditions. However, during one five-week period Larry missed two appointments with his parole officer and was pulled over by the police for driving his car on an expired license. Larry's parole officer could petition the local court for an extension of Larry's supervision.

- Community service: This is an appropriate sanction to use as punishment, to hold the offender accountable, or as a restorative justice option (see chapter 6). For example, it would be appropriate for Howard G. (case 2.56), the former lawyer who stole money from clients' escrow accounts to cover his gambling debts, to pay restitution to his former clients and to perform community service as a form of restorative justice (such as lecturing to law school students about legal ethics and problematic temptations of the trade).

- Electronic monitoring: This option is appropriate for offenders who require close supervision but not incarceration. This option is used for many offenders convicted of heinous crimes who are released from prison, usually after serving very lengthy sentences. Examples include the cases of Lyle K. (2.7), who was convicted of driving under the influence, death resulting; Paul C. (2.50), who served a sentence for rape; and Jason O. (2.64), who was convicted of child molestation.

- Drug and alcohol treatment: Supervisors should refer offenders with significant drug or alcohol problems to appropriate outpatient and residential programs. Examples include the cases of Dean E. (2.52), a heroin addict who shot the maitre d' of a restaurant during a botched robbery attempt; Colleen O. (2.53), a cocaine addict who drove her car under the influence and caused the deaths of several passengers in another car; and Antonia L. (2.54), the hospital nurse who became a drug addict and stole narcotic pain medication from several patients.

- Intensive probation and parole supervision: Some offenders do not require incarceration but do require very strict supervision. Intensive supervision entails frequent contacts, strict schedules, and close monitoring. This may be combined with other sanctions (for example, frequent drug testing, electronic monitoring). This would be appropriate for Tim M. (case 2.55), the former police officer who became a pathological gambler and stole valuable jewelry from a crime scene.

- Incarceration: Offenders who consistently violate probation or parole conditions, or commit new crimes while on parole or probation, may require incarceration for punitive and public safety purposes. Some jurisdictions have introduced daytime incarceration centers (offenders return home at the end of each day, a system that provides close supervision without the cost of twenty-four-hour institutional care). Reincarceration would be necessary for offenders who have considerable difficulty complying with parole conditions following their release from prison. Consider, for example, what would happen if Daniel S. (case 2.8), who murdered his wife, was paroled after serving twenty-five years and was rearrested for larceny; if Malcolm G. (case 2.11), the restaurant owner who served time for arranging an arson at his business, reestablished active contact with organized crime figures after his release from prison; and if Warren C. (case 2.25), the man who assaulted his landlady, was arrested for breaking into a liquor store after being released on parole.

Incarceration certainly is necessary for every offender who commits a heinous crime. Beyond imprisoning offenders for punitive and public safety purposes, it only makes sense to provide inmates with opportunities for genuine rehabilitation. I now turn to a review of what we know about the effectiveness of such efforts.

5

TREATMENT AND REHABILITATION

By definition, offenders who commit heinous crimes need help. Some offenders commit their crimes because of major psychiatric disorders. Others
have significant problems stemming from traumatic life experiences (rape,
molestation, child abuse and neglect), poor innate impulse control, anger
management, sexual deviance, and addictions.

It is one thing to assert that offenders who commit heinous crimes
need professional assistance to help them conquer, or at least manage,
their demons. It is quite another to assert that concerted professional efforts
to help offenders are effective. In some instances treatment and rehabilitation are feasible and successful. In others the results are mixed or discouraging. Some offenders are amenable to treatment and some are not.
Some offenders participate in treatment programs earnestly and enthusi-
astically, whereas others refuse to participate or do so halfheartedly only to
impress the parole board. Some interventions may themselves be ineffectual, even for offenders who want help and are receptive to treatment.

The principal challenge is to determine what distinguishes more and
less effective interventions, which offenders are most likely to respond well
to treatment and rehabilitation programs, and whether certain treatment
techniques and strategies are more effective than others for specific populations, such as inmates with sexual disorders, addictions, mental retardation,
and impulse-control problems.

AN OVERVIEW OF CORRECTIONAL TREATMENT

The concept of prisoner rehabilitation started in the late eighteenth and
early nineteenth centuries, when reformers believed that prisoners would

benefit from strict isolation, order, discipline, and moral education (Gaes 1998). During the Progressive Era in the early twentieth century, professions such as social work, psychiatry, and psychology introduced a medical-model approach to corrections, based on the widespread belief that treatments analogous to medical interventions could be brought to bear on problems of human misbehavior. This preoccupation with rehabilitation, in the form of diverse counseling, educational, and vocational programs, flourished until the early 1970s, when critics challenged the effectiveness of the so-called rehabilitative ideal (Lipton, Martinson, and Wilks 1975; Martinson 1974), claiming that most rehabilitation efforts failed to reach their stated goals.

More recently, a group of criminal justice scholars has challenged the "nothing works" doctrine (Andrews et al. 1990; Cullen and Gendreau 1989; Gaes 1998; Gaes et al. 1999; Gendreau and Ross 1987; Hodgins and Muller-Isberner 2000; Lipsey and Wilson 1993; Palmer 1975, 1992; Petersilia 2003), based on rigorous reanalysis of completed studies and the generation of new data on treatment effectiveness.

Most current thinking about the effectiveness of correctional treatment is based on what is known in the research trade as meta-analysis. Meta-analysis involves the comprehensive review and assessment of all empirical research on a given subject in an effort to get a sense of the big picture from comparing and contrasting diverse results.[1] The most comprehensive meta-analyses of correctional treatment have been conducted by Lipton, Martinson, and Wilks (1975), Lipsey (1995), and Lipsey and Wilson (1993), although several others have been useful as well (for a comprehensive review of meta-analyses in the corrections field, see Gaes et al. 1999).

Gaes et al. (1999) conducted a comprehensive review of the most prominent, valid, and reliable assessments of correctional treatment; they assert that interventions should be guided by a core set of principles (see evidence presented by Andrews and Bonta 1998; Antonowicz and Ross 1994; Gendreau and Ross 1987; Hodgins and Muller-Isberner 2000; Lipsey 1995; Loesel 1996; McGuire 1995; Palmer 1975, 1992):

Intervention efforts must be linked to the offenders' criminogenic needs. The term *criminogenic needs* refers to the unique attributes of each offender that enhance the likelihood that she or he will commit crimes. Prominent criminogenic attributes identified in the literature are criminal attitudes, criminal associates, impulsivity and weak self-control skills, weak socialization, below average verbal intelligence, a taste for risk, weak problem-solving skills, early onset of antisocial behavior, poor parental practices, and deficits in educational, vocational, and employment skills (Andrews and Bonta 1998). For example, Donnie A. (case 2.13), who was involved in organized crime and high-level drug dealing and then murdered a man he believed was a police informant, is a quintessential example of an offender with criminal attitudes and associates, impulsivity, and early onset of antisocial behavior. He did not lack educational or vocational skills, and he had reasonably impressive verbal intelligence. Intervention needed to focus on his specific needs and, especially, his criminal thinking and values.

Multimodal programs should be used to address all criminogenic attributes and needs of the offender. Most offenders who commit heinous crimes have multiple needs. To the extent possible, treatment should address all the deficits. Some deficits can be addressed simultaneously, but some may need to be addressed sequentially (for example, an offender's psychiatric symptoms may require stabilization before he can benefit from a drug abuse treatment program). For example, Edgar C. (case 2.63), the former state hospital psychologist who had major psychiatric problems (bipolar disorder) and made sexual advances toward a hospital patient, also had a problem with alcohol. Treatment needed to address both his psychiatric and substance abuse issues (so-called co-occurring disorders). Larry K. (case 2.23), who was estranged from his common-law wife and viciously attacked her with a machete, also had multiple needs that had to be addressed: impulse control and anger management issues, problems with interpersonal communication skills, and difficulty in work settings. Although Larry was unusually well educated (he had nearly completed college), he had a long-standing history of problems in relationships and with authority figures that created significant problems in his life.

Treatment providers should match inmate criminogenic learning styles with staff teaching styles. Programs should be designed for and delivered according to the specific needs and learning styles of eligible offenders. Offenders with severe learning disabilities are not likely to gain much from programs that depend heavily on didactic, concept-oriented presentations of material. Offenders with clinically diagnosed anxiety disorders may function better in one-on-one counseling than group counseling. For example, Jeffrey E. (case 2.71), who suffered from dissociative disorder and had molested several children, could not function in a typical sex offender treatment group; his psychiatric symptoms and interpersonal style were too disruptive, limiting his ability to gain from the group and interfering with the therapeutic experience of other group members. Services needed to be tailored to his unique needs. Theo L. (case 2.17), who joined an urban gang at a very young age and murdered a man at a strip club, was diagnosed with significant learning disabilities. He had difficulty processing information presented in a traditional didactic (lecture) fashion. Theo's teacher needed to use a variety of special education teaching techniques to help Theo work toward his general equivalence degree (GED).

Higher-risk inmates are more likely to benefit from treatment than are lower-risk inmates. The highest level of treatment intensity should be used for the highest-risk inmates. Although there are exceptions (for example, moderate drug abusers may benefit more from treatment than heavy drug abusers), in general more ambitious treatment should be reserved for offenders with the greatest needs.

That said, it is important to acknowledge that a small group of offenders who manifest monumental needs, or who may resist any and all offers of assistance, may not be amenable or responsive to treatment. For example, Frankie D. (case 2.24), who strangled his stepson in a fit of rage, acknowledged that he had lost control and made a mistake but denied that he had any deep-seated, chronic problems that warranted clinical attention. He claimed that overall he had his life under control. Even though Frankie was a high-risk offender, and had significant impulse-control and anger-management issues, he resisted help. Similarly, Tim M. (case 2.55), the former police officer who stole valuable evidence from a crime scene and used it to pay off his substantial gambling debts, considered himself "different" from other inmates and was not interested in participating in counseling or other rehabilitation programs.

In contrast, Antonia L. (case 2.54), the former nurse who stole pain medication from several patients to feed her own drug addiction, was deeply remorseful and eager for help. She was a high-risk offender, because of her long-standing drug dependence, and was motivated to participate in substance abuse treatment and collateral counseling.

Treatment providers should use programs that teach inmates skills that allow them to understand and resist antisocial behavior. Widely used social learning principles (such as positive, negative, and intermittent reinforcers, extinction) should be used to model and shape prosocial behavior. For example, Saravane S. (case 2.16), who joined a Laotian gang and participated in a vicious home invasion and robbery, was eager to make a new life for himself that did not involve crime, violence, or gang activity. He was an earnest student in several prison-sponsored educational, vocational, and group counseling programs that used various cognitive-behavioral principles to teach prosocial thinking and problem-solving skills, and challenge criminal thinking. Similarly, Karen R. (case 2.57), the office manager who became addicted to gambling and embezzled large sums of money, actively participated in an addictions group that used a wide range of cognitive-behavioral techniques to help participants cope with and manage their substance abuse and gambling addictions. She also attended weekly twelve-step meetings at the women's prison to strengthen her commitment to recovery.

Inmates should be treated in well-supported programs because continuity is important. Programs must have adequate funding, quality personnel, and staff commitment to enhance success. In some instances the availability of well-supported treatment programs in the community that are not available in the prison setting may be a factor in parole board decisions about release. Arranging for continuity between prison-based and community-based treatment is critical in order to reinforce and sustain gains made in the institutional setting.

Several states have developed ambitious community-based programs for offenders with major psychiatric needs or who have been found not guilty by reason of insanity (Heilbrun and Griffin 1998). For example, the Isaac Ray Center in Chicago has offered a three-phase intervention model that includes assessment, treatment, and follow-up services. At the time of the program's evaluation (Cavanaugh and Wasyliw 1985; Rogers and Cavanaugh 1981) all the inmates had committed crimes of violence, with 61 percent charged with murder or attempted murder. The vast majority of inmates (87 percent) had a primary diagnosis of schizophrenia or affective disorder.

The program's treatment approach included both pharmacological and psychosocial interventions. The principal goals were (1) a reduction of potential for future violent behavior, (2) remission of psychopathology, and (3) development of healthy and responsible personal relationships. Court orders mandated treatment and regular communication between program staff and court officials. Offenders were rehospitalized when necessary, if symptoms reemerged. Over a period of one to two years clinical services were gradually reduced.

Oregon has provided community-based services to mentally ill offenders under the supervision of the Psychiatric Security Review Board, which was created by the Oregon legislature to oversee offenders "not responsible due to mental illness" (Heilbrun and Griffin 1998:175). The board, whose members were appointed by the governor, included a psychiatrist and a psychologist with experience in the criminal justice system, a staff member from probation and parole, a lawyer experienced in criminal practice, and a member of the general public. The board had authority over inmates for as long as the maximum sentence that they could have received upon conviction in criminal court and had the authority to commit individuals to a maximum-security hospital, to grant a conditional release with appropriate terms (for example, outpatient treatment and supervision), or to release individuals unconditionally. The board received monthly reports on each offender and had the authority to revoke any release it had approved earlier. A treatment facility director, law enforcement officials, or any person responsible for the offenders' supervision could provide information to the board. Nearly half the clients evaluated had been acquitted of serious violent crimes because of their serious mental illness (Rogers and Bloom 1982, 1985).

A program in Portland, Oregon, that was under the board's jurisdiction provided services to offenders through a large community hospital day-treatment program. Clients received individual and group therapy, social skills and time-management training, and vocational education. They attended nine-week modules that began with basic skills training in meal preparation, nutrition, medication management, and familiarization with community resources. Clients then progressed to intermediate-level training in communication, assertiveness, sex education, stress management, coping strategies, and anger management (Heilbrun and Griffin 1998).

A Maryland program subjected offenders acquitted of criminal charges by reason of insanity to a five-year conditional release period. The program included a residential treatment program located on the grounds of a state hospital. Other innovative community-based treatment programs have been developed in Connecticut, Florida, California, New York, and Oklahoma (Heilbrun and Griffin 1998).

Several ambitious programs have been developed for mentally ill offenders on parole or probation. For example, outpatient treatment programs specifically for parolees and probationers have operated in Sweden, Great Britain, and Canada. Minnesota has sponsored residential programs for special needs individuals on parole or probation. One program was housed in a dormitory on the grounds of a state hospital within walking distance of schools, a college, vocational schools, and downtown Rochester, Minnesota. The program's board of directors included law enforcement and corrections officials, mental health professionals, educators, and members of the general public. A second Minnesota program was operated under the auspices of Lutheran Social Services and located in a large house in a residential neighborhood with nearby educational and vocational resources. The program, which required a minimum of five months' participation, included four or five nonmedical staff members, counselors, and trained volunteers. Offenders participated in individual and group therapy, took a money management course, and maintained family ties. Many offenders had been convicted of serious offenses, for example, manslaughter and sex-related crimes (Reid 1981).

Interventions should be comprehensive and of sufficient duration. Although there is no precise formula for determining how much treatment offenders should receive (for example, the length of treatment, the frequency of therapeutic meetings), corrections personnel should always attempt to monitor offenders' needs and gauge the frequency and magnitude of intervention accordingly. For example, Charles Z. (case 2.58), who suffered from schizophrenia and murdered and dismembered several young children, required ongoing, sustained psychiatric treatment while he was in prison. Psychiatric staff needed to prescribe and monitor Charles's use of neuroleptic (antipsychotic) medication. In addition, he required weekly meetings with a counselor to help him learn how to manage and cope with his mental illness. Lyle K. (case 2.7), the former town councilman who had alcoholism and killed a pedestrian while driving under the influence, required ongoing substance abuse counseling and treatment. Lyle's treatment needed to begin in a prison-based program and then continue for an extended period once he was released into the community.

The most comprehensive assessments of currently available empirical evidence on the effectiveness of correctional treatment (Gaes et al. 1999) suggest that

- Adult correctional treatment can be very effective in reducing recidivism.
- Cognitive-behavioral treatment, on average, is more effective than interventions based on principles of punishment, intensive community supervision, educational training, substance abuse treatment, or group counseling. Cognitive-behavioral treatment tends to be more effective in community-based settings than in institutional settings and with motivated, as opposed to resistant, offenders.[2]
- Intensive prison-based drug treatment can be very effective, especially when combined with follow-up community-based treatment.

- Education, vocational training, and prison labor programs have modest effects on reducing recidivism after release from prison and increase positive behavior in prison.
- Evidence on sex offender treatment interventions is less positive, perhaps because the target population is remarkably heterogeneous (rapists, child molesters, exhibitionists, and so on) and treatments need to be tailored to each offender's needs.

Studies that are particularly relevant to work with offenders who have committed heinous crimes focus on the effectiveness of programs, such as cognitive skills training, that are designed to challenge offenders' criminal thinking, and focus on the effectiveness of substance abuse treatment programs, sex offender treatment programs, education and vocational training programs, treatment of offenders with major mental illness, and treatment of offenders with mental retardation.

COGNITIVE SKILLS TRAINING

Cognitive-behavioral intervention programs now predominate in prison settings, in part because of the substantial body of research evidence on their effectiveness. Perhaps the most prominent program is the Cognitive Thinking Skills Program (CTSP) designed by Robert Ross and Elizabeth Fabiano (1985). Based on their systematic and comprehensive review of pertinent research, Ross and Fabiano designed an intervention approach that focuses on repeat offenders and their problems with impulsivity associated with poor verbal self-regulation, impairment in means-end reasoning, a concrete thinking style that impinges on the ability to appreciate the thoughts and feelings of others, conceptual rigidity that inclines people to a repetitive pattern of self-defeating behaviors, poor interpersonal problem-solving skills, egocentricity, poor critical reasoning, and a selfish perspective that tends to make people focus only on how their actions affect them instead of considering the effects of their actions on others (Gaes et al. 1999).

Ross and Fabiano identified core treatment components to address these deficits. They found that impulsivity can be reduced by teaching consequential thinking. Fatalistic thinking can be reduced by teaching offenders metacognitive skills that enhance their ability to evaluate the influence of their thinking on their actions. Antisocial behavior can be reduced by teaching offenders to replace these behaviors with prosocial ones (such as gainful employment, constructive recreational activities, educational pursuits). Rigid thinking can be minimized by teaching offenders creative thinking skills to provide them with prosocial alternatives when they encounter interpersonal conflict and problems. Illogical thinking can be modified by critical reasoning skills (applied logic). Egocentrism can be reduced by teaching offenders ways to empathize with others and by enhancing their values. Social adjustment can be improved by teaching offenders a variety of self-control techniques (Gaes et al. 1999; Ross and Fabiano 1985).

This particular model is delivered to groups of four to ten offenders two to four times per week in thirty-five blocks of two hours each. Although staff members make some didactic presentations, they rely heavily on role playing, videotaped feedback, modeling of constructive and appropriate behavior, group discussion, games, and practical homework designed to teach and reinforce skills.

Cognitive skills training can be especially useful for offenders such as Angela U. (case 2.14), who married a man who was heavily involved in a large burglary and robbery ring. Over time Angela became part of a criminal subculture. She had been sexually abused as a child and had limited educational and vocational skills. Angela had become quite dependent on her husband and his criminal associates. In prison Angela participated in a multimonth cognitive skills group designed to help women address their dependency issues, abuse histories, and cognitive distortions and to help them develop new prosocial ways of thinking. While serving her sentence Angela decided to divorce her husband and shed her criminal associates and lifestyle. After her release from prison she obtained permission from parole officials to move out of state (to a city where one of her sisters lived) so she could start a new life with a relatively clean slate and avoid some of the temptations associated with her former life and neighborhood.

Stan E. (case 2.20), the college student who sexually assaulted a woman following a party, also seemed to benefit from his participation in a group that addressed criminal thinking. Although Stan had a much higher level of education than nearly all other inmates and impressive academic skills, in the group he faced the fact that he too had become quite self-centered and exploitative. The challenge for him was to learn how to empathize with others and not manipulate others to meet his own needs. Stan easily understood the concepts intellectually, but it took some time for him to candidly acknowledge that his egocentrism and impulse-control issues were problematic.

TREATMENT OF DRUG AND ALCOHOL ABUSERS

Evidence of the relationship between substance abuse and crime is over-whelming (Reamer 2003a). Offenders who are under the influence and people who need money to pay for drugs commit significant numbers of serious crimes.

Research evidence suggests that therapeutic communities or intensive residential substance abuse treatment programs within prison should be the intervention of choice for drug-dependent offenders (Gaes et al. 1999; Wexler 1994). The typical therapeutic community in a prison partly isolates the offender from the rest of the inmate population, which, ideally, increases group pressure to take the program seriously and minimizes the likelihood of negative influences by inmates in the general prison population. Subsequent community-based treatment seems to significantly enhance the effects of prison-based drug and alcohol treatment (Gaes et al. 1999).

Most contemporary residential substance abuse treatment programs feature a key set of program components: knowledge of drug abuse, wellness, and fitness; cognitive-behavioral treatments; relapse prevention; simulations and role playing connected with difficult situations (for example, encounters with former friends who are drug abusers); techniques to increase motivation; small group sessions; and individual counseling. Most programs last six to twelve months, and staff members often include a mix of people who are in recovery or never were substance abusers. Research evidence (Annis 1998:181) suggests that tailoring treatment to offenders' individual needs through some kind of matching mechanism is critically important. That mechanism should consider such factors as

- Sociodemographics (e.g., age, sex, marital status, social stability, family history of alcoholism/drug abuse)
- Environmental resources (e.g., finances, social support)
- Neuropsychological status (e.g., type and degree of neuropsychological deficits)
- Personality (e.g., self-esteem, locus of control, psychiatric diagnosis and severity)
- Alcohol and drug consumption (e.g., years of excessive drinking/drug taking, quantity, frequency)
- Alcohol and drug dependence (e.g., degree of alcohol/drug dependence, symptomatology, presence of physical withdrawal)
- Treatment expectancies/outcome beliefs (e.g., self-efficacy, recognition that substance abuse is a disease)

- Situational antecedents (e.g., types of high-risk situations)
- Setting options (e.g., inpatient, outpatient, day treatment)
- Intensity/duration of treatment (the need for brief intervention versus longer-term therapy)
- Treatment method (e.g., psychopharmacological, relaxation therapy, cognitive-behavioral therapy)
- Therapist style (e.g., directive, nondirective, professional, peer)
- Treatment goal (e.g., abstinence, moderation)
- Treatment context (e.g., group, individual)

Dean E. (case 2.52), a heroin addict who, in the course of robbing a restaurant, accidentally shot and killed a man, required intensive ongoing residential substance abuse treatment. He applied for enrollment in the prison's residential drug treatment program, which was housed in a separate wing of a medium-security prison. Dean was earnest about his participation in the program and eventually became a peer leader. Similarly, Colleen O. (case 2.53), who was a cocaine addict and killed passengers of another vehicle when she drove her car under the influence, was desperate to participate in the substance abuse treatment program sponsored by the women's prison. She graduated from the program and was eventually released to a community-based residential drug treatment program operated by a private nonprofit organization.

In contrast, Howard G. (case 2.56), the former lawyer who became addicted to sports betting and stole money from his clients' escrow accounts, seemed to be in denial about the severity of his gambling problem. He was not eager to participate in the prison's addictions program or attend the prison's weekly twelve-step meetings ("I'm not really like all of those other guys with heroin and cocaine problems"). Howard claimed that he might "look into" a Gamblers Anonymous group once he returned to the community, but he demonstrated little interest in addressing his pathological gambling.

TREATMENT OF SEX OFFENDERS

Treatment of sex offenders is, without question, one of the most daunting challenges faced by corrections professionals. The sex offender population is remarkably diverse, and its clinical needs are wide ranging (Quinsey 1998). A typical sex offender treatment program might include participants as diverse as child molesters, rapists, exhibitionists, incest offenders,

offenders obsessed with pornography, and offenders who engage in compulsive sexual behavior with inanimate objects.

Current evidence suggests that different interventions may be more appropriate for different sex offender subtypes (Hagan, King, and Patros 1994; Marshall, Laws, and Barbaree 1990; Quinsey 1998), although most corrections programs do not have sufficient resources to offer this kind of specialized programming. When deciding whether to provide residential or outpatient treatment, or to use cognitive-behavioral, pharmacological, or psychotherapeutic approaches (such as individual or group therapy), treatment planning needs to consider a wide range of clinically relevant issues, such as offenders' sexual orientation; levels of denial, minimization, and rationalization; cognitive distortions; and impulse-control issues (Gaes et al. 1999). At present no conclusive evidence exists concerning uniformly effective interventions. As Gaes et al. (1999) conclude,

> While there is some research that suggests that there may be a modest positive effect of sex offender treatment in prison, we are wary of drawing sweeping conclusions. There is certainly no definitive approach to treatment. Across the many jurisdictions in Canada and the United States, sex offenders are required to complete a variety of different programs before being considered for release. Then, they may be required to participate in maintenance programs on their release to the community. As yet, the full effects of relative contributions of postprogram efforts (i.e., relapse prevention) to reducing recidivism among sex offenders remain largely untested. (410–11)

In principle treatment options include organic treatments, nonbehavioral psychotherapy, and cognitive-behavioral therapy (Barbaree and Marshall 1998). The goal of organic treatments is to reduce offenders' sexual urges. Common methods include inhibition of the gonadotropic function of the pituitary by administering medroxyprogesterone acetate (MPA) and inhibition by antiandrogens (cyproterone acetate, or CPA) of the androgenic action at the target organs. MPA increases the metabolism of testosterone in the liver and inhibits the pituitary release of luteinizing hormone, which stimulates the testes to produce testosterone. The goal is to reduce libido, sexual arousal, sexual behavior, fantasy, and overall deviant sexual behavior. CPA is a synthetic steroid, structurally similar to progesterone; it is used to block the receptors at the sites of androgen uptake and block the hypothalamic function that releases pituitary gonadotropins (Barbaree and Marshall 1998).

Nonbehavioral psychotherapy includes a broad range of approaches, such as group and individual counseling, self-help, and mutual aid groups. In contrast, cognitive-behavioral therapy for sex offenders is based on a social learning model that focuses on offenders' ability to process information, avoid cognitive distortions, make appropriate decisions, and engage in appropriate behavioral repertoires. One prominent program model (Barbaree and Marshall 1998) involves four stages of treatment:

1. Pretreatment: Developing motivation for behavior change (addresses issues of denial, minimization, victim blaming, victim empathy).
2. Treatment planning: Understanding precursors to offending and the behavior chain leading to sex offenses.
3. Treatment: Achieving behavior change (reducing deviant sexual arousal and fantasy; reducing cognitive distortions; addressing issues of offenders' own victimization; enhancing healthy sexuality; increasing social competence and anger control; decreasing criminal thinking, lifestyle, and behavior; substance abuse and psychiatric treatment, as needed).
4. Posttreatment: Preventing the recurrence of sexual offending (developing a relapse prevention plan involving internal self-management and external supervision and arranging for follow-up services and counseling).

It is critical that sex offender treatment programs be coordinated closely with corrections staff. The goals of corrections and sex offender treatment can be mutually reinforcing. The treatment staff cannot ignore relevant security concerns and criminal justice mandates, and corrections officials cannot afford to ignore sex offenders' treatment needs. Moreover, the authority that corrections officials can exercise may be necessary in order to motivate sex offenders to participate in treatment, particularly because most sex offenders deny their crimes and any need for treatment. As Barbaree and Marshall (1998) assert,

> We endorse the simultaneous application of corrections and treatment models and these two activities should have mutually facilitative effects. If the objectives for the cognitive components of therapy are met in treatment, namely that the man comes to accept responsibility for his criminal behavior, then the man's rehabilitation will be recognized within the framework of the criminal justice system. Similarly, a forceful and clear response by the criminal justice system, including initiating charges, aggressive prosecution,

and the consistent and fair sentencing of offenders will enhance the effectiveness of treatment. . . . The interface between the correctional/judicial system and treatment provides important sources of motivation for the offender in treatment. (310, 311)

Some offenders are much more likely than others to be responsive to sex offender treatment. For example, Stan E. (case 2.20), the college student who sexually assaulted another student following a party, and Ted E. (case 2.36), who became sexually involved with his girlfriend's fifteen-year-old daughter, were eager and regular participants in the prison's sex offender treatment program. They were serious about exploring the problems that led to their criminal conduct.

In contrast, Hank S. (case 2.21), the former seminarian who lured a young man to a hotel room and sexually assaulted him, did not seem fully committed to treatment. The director of the sex offender treatment program reported that Hank's involvement was inconsistent and halfhearted. Hank seemed to be having difficulty admitting to himself and others that he was a sex offender. This denial got in the way of his successful participation in the program. Also, Leon K. (case 2.47), who participated in the kidnapping and gang rape of a young woman, was not interested in addressing the issues that led to the sexual assault. Leon simply preferred to serve his sentence ("do my time") without actively participating in any rehabilitation programs. Requiring him to participate was not likely to be productive.

EDUCATION AND LABOR PROGRAMS

Education, work, and vocational training programs are the most traditional prison-based offerings. Many offenders have not completed their high school education, have weak work-related skills, and have had difficulty maintaining employment (this may be due to undiagnosed or untreated learning disabilities, attentional disorders, or inadequate school programs). Corrections professionals believe that enhancing offenders' educational skills (reading and writing skills) will increase their chances of gaining employment once released from prison. Enhanced education may also facilitate offenders' maturation, conscientiousness, and commitment and provide them with an opportunity in the prison to interact on a regular basis with civilian, nonauthoritarian, and supportive professionals (Ryan 1998). Many offenders need competent assessments of learning disabilities that may have impeded their educational progress.

Prison-based vocational and work programs can also produce benefits. Research evidence suggests that inmates who participate in these programs tend to be better behaved while in prison, are less likely to commit new crimes following release, and have more positive work-related experiences once they get out of prison (Gaes et al. 1999). Some prison programs are designed to teach offenders new, marketable skills (for example, automobile mechanics, heating and air-conditioning skills, hair cutting), and some programs aim only to provide inmates with meaningful work opportunities (for example, work in the prison laundry, clothing factory, furniture repair factory). As Gaes et al. (1999) conclude after their thorough review of prison-based educational and work programs,

> Public investment in prison work and education programs may be a wise and, considering the total cost of recidivism, a cost-effective investment. When considered as a body of developing scientific work on the impact of prison programs, education and work programs appear able to contribute significantly to increasing offenders' prospects for success. Moreover, the research to date provides correctional authorities with a set of empirically derived guidelines for the design and delivery of such interventions. From a public policy perspective, a retreat from public commitment to investment in prison labor and effective education programs in prison would be misguided. (407)

Yolanda F. (case 2.22), for example, the young woman who got into a fierce argument with her grandmother and viciously assaulted her with a frying pan, had dropped out of high school and had no significant work history and virtually no marketable skills. Yolanda agreed to participate in the GED and job-training programs offered at the women's prison. She recognized that without a high school diploma and vocational skills her options on the streets would be severely limited.

Similarly, Darryl P. (case 2.37), the seventeen-year-old who had become involved in a gang and participated in the murder of another young gang member, recognized that his chances of surviving in the community would be greatly enhanced by obtaining rudimentary educational and vocational skills. Darryl understood that it would be many years before he would return to the community and that it would behoove him to spend his time behind bars productively. He had entered prison at a very young age and was at a severe disadvantage. Unlike many young inmates, Darryl quickly understood that it would be to his advantage to build a long track record of involvement in prison-sponsored educational and vocational programs.

TREATMENT OF OFFENDERS WITH MAJOR MENTAL ILLNESS

As I noted earlier, a significant percentage of offenders who commit heinous crimes suffer from major mental illness or brain damage. While some offenders are found not guilty by reason of insanity and hospitalized in psychiatric facilities, many offenders are found guilty and sentenced to prison. Still other offenders are not mentally ill when they begin their sentence but decompensate during their sentence (Bloom and Wilson 2000; Nedopil 2000).

Based on his extensive experience as a prison-based psychiatrist, Kupers (1999) sets forth what he considers to be the essential elements of mental health services for offenders.

Comprehensive Levels of Care

Mental health care needs to be offered on a continuum, including inpatient psychiatric units for offenders manifesting severe symptoms, outpatient clinics, emergency services, day treatment programs, case management, halfway houses, supported living in the community (private housing supplemented with social work and case management support), and vocational training programs. Simply medicating offenders, especially incarcerated offenders, will not suffice.

Several organizations have promulgated minimum standards for correctional mental health care: the National Commission on Correctional Health Care, the American Psychiatric Association, and the American Public Health Association. Commonly recommended components include

- Crisis intervention, with infirmary beds for short-term treatment (usually less than ten days)
- Acute care
- Chronic care or a special needs unit (a housing unit within the correctional setting for inmates with chronic mental illness who do not require inpatient treatment but do require a therapeutic milieu because of their inability to function adequately within the general population)
- Outpatient treatment facilities
- Consultation services (consulting with the prison's management team and/or providing training of correctional officers and program staff)
- Discharge/transfer planning, including services for inmates in need of further treatment at the time of transfer to another institution or when discharged to the community (Metzner et al. 1998:237)

The National Commission on Correctional Health Care (1995, 1997) stresses the importance of having a designated health authority on site that is responsible for the delivery of mental health services in prisons. This authority may be a health administrator or a government agency (such as a health department, community mental health center, or a nonprofit health care corporation). A task force of the American Psychiatric Association (1989) recognized the need to balance security and treatment concerns. Its report recommends that the director of mental health services or a designee have direct access to the warden or chief administrator to enhance coordination, quarterly discussion of mental health services by program staff and corrections officials, and at least monthly mental health staff meetings to review administrative and procedural issues (Metzner et al. 1998).

Kupers (1999) recommends "direct admitting privileges" for psychiatrists who work in prisons. That is, when a psychiatrist discovers an acutely psychotic or suicidal inmate whom the psychiatrist believes should be admitted to a psychiatric unit or hospital, the psychiatrist can write an order and have the inmate admitted.

Inmates who manifest serious psychiatric symptoms should be referred to some kind of protected or supported correctional setting where their symptoms can be monitored and treated with appropriate psychotropic medication (for example, neuroleptics for psychotic symptoms, antidepressants, mood stabilizers), case management, and counseling (Maier and Fulton 1998). Based on their review of a range of prison-based psychiatric units around the United States, Dvoskin and Patterson (1998) recommend that a twenty-four-bed ward in a maximum-security psychiatric facility be staffed as follows:

- 1 treatment team leader
- 1 psychiatrist
- 1 clinical psychologist with a Ph.D.
- 1 master's-level social worker (two in a predischarge unit)
- 5 registered nurses (such that one R.N. is always on duty)
- 2 clinical nurses (for patient education as well as primary therapy duties)
- 20 treatment/security assistants (four on duty at all times)
- 2.5 treatment/security supervisors
- 4 activities therapists (occupational, recreational, rehabilitative, and the like, with four on duty for four ten-hour shifts so that therapists are available to inmates seven days per week)
- 1 teacher

Suicide Prevention

Mental health professionals know a great deal about how to prevent suicide. Many inmates who are contemplating suicide display cues that correctional staff can be taught to recognize. Solitary confinement is not an appropriate response to a suicide attempt; constant surveillance is, with appropriate crisis intervention, medication, and therapeutic support.

For example, Donald S. (case 2.41), who had been fired from his job in a computer software company and later murdered the company president, had become quite despondent in prison. He was having great difficulty coping with his long incarceration and his bleak prospects for parole. Donald began to contemplate suicide. One evening a correctional officer, who had sensed Donald's despondence, walked by Donald's cell and noticed that he was tying his bedsheets together. The officer thought that Donald might be planning to hang himself. The officer interviewed Donald, who admitted feeling depressed but said he was not really planning to kill himself. Nonetheless, the officer quickly transferred Donald for psychiatric observation. The prison psychiatrist prescribed a new antidepressant medication and monitored Donald for suicide risk. During the next several weeks Donald's depression lifted, he returned to the prison's general population, and he reenrolled in several rehabilitation and education programs.

Group Therapy and Special Problems

Group therapy—designed to educate offenders about mental illness, medication regimes, and therapeutic options—is essential for offenders suffering from major mental illness. Many offenders with major mental illness also struggle with substance abuse and dependence; groups designed specifically for offenders with dual diagnoses (also known as co-occurring disorders) can be particularly helpful. Such groups can also assist mentally ill offenders with their impulse-control, anger-management, and interpersonal skills.

For example, Jason O. (case 2.64), the former county child welfare department supervisor who became sexually involved with a minor, was diagnosed with clinical depression and cocaine addiction. Group treatment designed to address Jason's co-occurring disorders was essential. Group treatment was also critical for Edgar C. (case 2.63), the former psychologist who was diagnosed with major mental illness (bipolar disorder) and had become sexually involved with one of his patients.

Groups should also be provided to offenders who are victims of violence. Many female offenders, for example, are victims of sexual molestation and domestic violence. Competently run groups can help such offenders explore and grasp the connections between their victimization and their criminal activity (for instance, the way in which a victim of sexual violence may turn to drugs or alcohol to numb her pain). For example, Marion T. (case 2.72), who had stabbed a neighbor with a screwdriver, had been sexually assaulted for years by her stepfather. The prison psychiatrist believed that the history of sexual assaults probably contributed to Marion's dissociative disorder. Over time Marion responded well to psychotropic medication. Marion's subsequent participation in group treatment was an essential component of her rehabilitation.

Psychiatric Rehabilitation Programs

Many well-run mental health programs focus on rehabilitation more than treatment. Rather than provide long-term therapy, many programs have shifted their focus to day treatment, halfway houses, supported independent living, vocational training, and case management. In these programs the emphasis is on the offenders' practical, immediate, and near-term needs—daily living skills, medication compliance, and avoidance of illicit drugs or alcohol—rather than psychopathology per se.

In prisons it can be very helpful to set aside specific tiers or cellblocks as intermediate psychiatric care facilities for inmates who do not require full-fledged psychiatric hospitalization but are not ready to live in the general population. Such housing arrangements can also prevent victimization of offenders with serious mental illness, who are often targeted by predatory inmates.

Mental Health Programs for Psychiatrically Disturbed and Disruptive Inmates

Some inmates who pose severe management problems—inmates who are defiant and extremely difficult to control—have major mental illness. They are more mad than bad. Often these inmates are placed in segregation or some kind of disciplinary cell as a result of their violent behavior. Unfortunately, the forced isolation often exacerbates the inmate's psychiatric symptoms. Ideally, correctional facilities would set aside secure housing designed to both contain the inmates' behavior and provide constructive mental health treatment (psychotropic medication, crisis intervention, case management, counseling). This is a very specialized, high-need subgroup of inmates.

For example, Sam E. (case 2.59), who suffered from paranoid schizophrenia and sexually assaulted several college students who lived near his apartment, began manifesting psychotic symptoms in prison. He claimed that voices from the radio in his cell were controlling his thinking, and he went on a hunger strike when he became convinced that the prison cooks were poisoning his food because they believed that he was a government spy. Sam also became quite verbally abusive to staff and other inmates. Prison staff transferred Sam to a psychiatric unit attached to the prison hospital to conduct a full assessment and stabilize him on neuroleptic medication.

Joy H. (case 2.60), the young woman with a history of psychotic symptoms who was convicted of sexually assaulting her infant son, decompensated during her prison stay. In the midst of a psychotic episode Joy stabbed another inmate with a shiv (homemade prison knife). Joy was transferred to the state's forensic unit, where she was found to be incompetent to stand trial on the new charge against her (attempted murder). Joy's psychotic symptoms were treated in an effort to help her reach a level of competency that would enable her to participate in her criminal trial. Joy was eventually stabilized, went to trial on the new charge, and was found not guilty by reason of insanity. She was eventually returned to the women's prison, with close supervision and a strict medication regime, to complete her original sentence.

Peer Review and Quality Assurance

One way to enhance the likelihood that a prison will make an earnest effort to address inmates' mental health needs is to invite outside peer and quality assurance reviews by colleagues in the various relevant professions (such as psychology, social work, nursing, and psychiatry) or accreditation organizations.

Continuity of Care

Most mentally ill inmates who commit heinous offenses will be released to the community someday. To facilitate smooth, uninterrupted delivery of mental health services prison staff and parole boards must work closely with community-based resources (such as community mental health centers). Disrupted psychiatric care can be disastrous, particularly for high-risk offenders who are living on the streets for the first time in years, if not decades.

For example, the former priest who sexually assaulted a young man (case 2.65) was eventually released to the community. He was referred directly to a local community mental health center for follow-up services. Similarly, Brenda G. (case 2.69), who stabbed another resident of a group home for people with mental retardation, was released with the stipulation that she receive intensive case management from a community mental health center that had a close working relationship with the private agency that planned to supervise Brenda's care in a secure residential facility for people with mental retardation who manifest violent tendencies.

Confidentiality and Access to Care

The typical inmate is reluctant to acknowledge that he or she has a psychiatric or mental health problem. Many inmates fear that word will spread throughout the prison and that they will be harassed and permanently stigmatized. Private, accessible space in which inmates can confer with mental health professionals is essential if inmates are to feel comfortable broaching and addressing their mental health issues. Protecting inmates' confidentiality is uniquely challenging, given staff members' obligation to disclose information that involves a threat to prison security. Written policies and protocols regarding protection of confidential mental health information within the prison can help ensure ethical practice (Reamer 2003b).

Separation of Mental Health and Disciplinary Issues

Ideally, mental health and security staff in prisons can respect and accommodate each other's respective duties. Mental health professionals must recognize the pressing, compelling security requirements in every correctional facility. At the same time, staff responsible for security—both correctional officers and administrators—must be willing to make reasonable concessions and accommodations in order to ensure that inmates' mental health needs are met.

Too often disciplinary infractions that are the direct result of inmates' psychiatric problems are met with punishment without any recognition of the ways in which the inmate's mental health issues contribute to the problematic behavior. For example, Ira D. (case 2.68), who was diagnosed with moderate mental retardation and sodomized a resident in the group home where he lived, often had difficulty following prison rules and instructions issued by correctional officers. In his case, issuing one disciplinary infraction after another was shortsighted and ineffectual. Staff needed to recognize Ira's cognitive limitations and make special accommodations, to the extent possible. Ideally, staff members' threshold of tolerance for Ira's violation of prison rules and regulations should be higher than for inmates who do not have difficulty grasping these guidelines.

Cross-training, Including Cultural Sensitivities

Administrators should take steps to ensure that staff members who are responsible for security receive training related to mental illness, signs to look for, and constructive responses. Likewise, mental health professionals working in correctional settings need training to appreciate the ongoing security risks and requirements that are inherent in prison management. To minimize discrimination and enhance respect, all staff should be acquainted with the range of cultural and ethnic traditions and beliefs found in typical prisons.

Several prison systems have designed and implemented impressive programs whose aim is to enhance inmates' mental health and address mental illness (Kupers 1999; Metzner et al. 1998). For example, California's state prison system for women offers a residential program in the community where low-risk pregnant felons with special needs can be housed until they give birth and have an opportunity to bond with their infant (realistically, this may not be an option for a woman who has been convicted of a heinous crime, but this is an impressive example of a corrections department that has sought to accommodate inmates' special needs).

The state of Washington's Department of Corrections has set up a collaborative program with the University of Washington to intervene when a mentally ill inmate has become a management problem. A team of four staff members from other institutions, who have no ongoing relationship with the inmate, travels to the prison to assess the situation, recommend a management plan, and offer advice about placement in a mental health treatment setting or a punitive detention unit. Using staff from outside the institution enhances objectivity and avoids having staffers who have built up deep-seated frustration or resentment toward the inmate decide on the inmate's mental health treatment.

A number of states have established community-based forensic treatment programs for offenders who are incompetent to stand trial or who have been declared not guilty by reason of insanity, a mentally disordered sex offender, or mentally ill (Heilbrun and Griffin 1998).

TREATMENT OF OFFENDERS WITH MENTAL RETARDATION

Current estimates are that 4 to 9 percent of the correctional population meets the standard clinical criteria for mental retardation (Metzner et al. 1998; Santamour 1989). Approximately 88 percent of this group is considered mildly impaired, with most of the remaining 12 percent being moderately impaired.

Only a small minority of people with mental retardation actually engage in criminal behavior (Crocker and Hodgins 1997). A disproportionate percentage of offenders with mental retardation are people of color and ethnic minorities; most come from low-income families with high rates of unemployment. Evidence suggests that this group of offenders is high risk for recidivism, with an estimated 60 percent national recidivism rate (Gardner, Graeber, and Machkovitz 1998).

Several studies indicate that the majority of offenses committed by people with mental retardation involve crimes against people rather than property; a significant number involve sex offenses. Offenders with mental retardation tend to recidivate more quickly and frequently than offenders without mental retardation (Santamour 1989).

Current conventional wisdom is that individuals with mental retardation sometimes become involved in criminal activity because their cognitive disabilities make them impressionable and likely to seek peer approval, be impulsive, and be influenced by others who are inclined toward criminal activity. People with mental retardation—especially those in the mild and moderate groups—are also more likely than the general population to reside in higher-crime areas (a reflection of the correlation between mental retardation and income).

Research studies (Gardner, Graeber, and Machkovitz 1998:337; Talbot 2003) suggest that when compared with offenders who do not have mental retardation, offenders with mental retardation

- Are more likely to be arrested following illegal acts
- May be at a disadvantage in police interrogations because of their impaired understanding of their legal rights; they may be more susceptible to acquiescence, suggestibility, compliance, and confabulation. As a result these offenders are less likely to understand the implications of their Miranda rights, will often confess quickly and be unduly influenced by friendly suggestions and intimidations, and often plead guilty more readily
- Request pretrial psychological examinations and presentencing testing less frequently

- Are more often convicted of the arresting offense than a reduced charge
- Use plea bargaining less frequently
- Seek appeals of conviction less frequently and make fewer requests for postconviction relief
- Are more likely to be sentenced to prison, with probation or other noninstitutional programs used less frequently
- Have more difficulty in prison adjusting to the routine, which limits parole opportunities and lengthens prison stays (these offenders are frequently the target of sexual harassment, scapegoating, and practical jokes)
- Are less likely in prison to participate in rehabilitation programs, as these are not designed to accommodate the learning, motivational, and experiential attributes and styles of people with mental retardation
- Make parole less frequently and thus serve longer prison sentences

Several community-based and prison-based programs have been designed to meet the unique needs of offenders with mental retardation (Gardner, Graeber, and Machkovitz 1998). For example, the Florida Department of Health and Rehabilitative Services designed the Mentally Retarded Defendant Program to evaluate and treat individuals considered to be incompetent to proceed to trial because of their mental retardation. One goal of the program was to strengthen the individual's knowledge of court procedures, to the extent possible, in order to enhance the defendant's ability to participate in his or her own defense. Program participants also received training in daily living skills, behavior management, communication skills, functional academics, life management, leisure/social skills, and the dynamics of criminal behavior (causes and consequences). Individuals considered by staff to be unlikely to achieve a level of competence required for participation in criminal court proceedings could be referred for residential placement (a secure unit, if necessary); in a number of these cases the criminal charges were dropped because of evidence of impairment.

A program in Lancaster County, Pennsylvania, sponsored by the county Office of Special Offenders Services, was designed specifically to enhance the likelihood that offenders with mental retardation would succeed on parole or probation. The program was a joint venture of the mental health, mental retardation, and criminal justice agencies. The program was staffed by case management specialists and probation officers and was based on the assumption that the offender is accountable for her or his behavior. Participants were expected to adhere to probation and parole rules, behave well at home and work, and maintain appropriate relationships in the community. Typical plans included strict daily routines and services designed to help participants exercise good judgment in their choice of friends and activities, manage money, and obtain and maintain employment.

The Center for Intensive Treatment was implemented in a secure setting by the New York Office of Mental Retardation and Developmental Disabilities. This state program was designed specifically for individuals with mental retardation whose assaultive, aggressive, or criminal behaviors require strict supervision. The program facilities included four houses with individual bedrooms and a day-program center, all surrounded by a fence. Services included functional educational/academic skills training; vocational training through a mentoring program with maintenance staff; physical education/recreation programs; and treatment programs focused on each individual's unique offense and clinical issues (for example, sexual misconduct, anger management, substance abuse, domestic and other violence).

South Carolina and Texas officials also have designed prominent prison-based programs. The Habilitation Unit at the Stevenson Correctional Institution in Columbia, South Carolina, was designed for offenders with mental retardation who were recommended by a multidisciplinary review team. Key goals included increasing socialization skills, work-related skills, and interpersonal skills; clarifying values; and resolving emotional conflict.

The Program for Offenders with Mental Retardation, designed by the Texas Department of Corrections, was the result of a class-action lawsuit. After staff members identified inmates for the program, treatment teams developed individualized habilitation plans to provide academic, vocational, and social skills training.

LEGAL AND ETHICAL CONSIDERATIONS

Efforts to meet the needs of offenders with major mental illness and mental retardation inevitably raise complex legal and ethical issues. Several issues are prominent: equal protection, use of least restrictive alternatives, involuntary commitment and retention, offenders' right to treatment and the right to refuse treatment, use of aversive and experimental therapies, disclosure of confidential information, and release and discharge (Hafemeister 1998).

Equal Protection

Major court decisions have found that offenders with mental illness, regardless of their criminal conduct, are entitled to the same substantive and procedural rights as other offenders in similar circumstances. For example, in 1966 the U.S. Supreme Court, in *Baxstrom v. Herold,* ruled that a prison inmate, upon the completion of his or her sentence, could not be directly placed in a psychiatric facility without being afforded the same procedural protections as any other individual being civilly committed (Hafemeister 1998). In 1972, in *Jackson v. Indiana,* the Supreme Court rejected the indefinite commitment to a psychiatric facility of an individual found incompetent to stand trial on criminal charges, ruling that various courts had found that prison inmates, people who pleaded insanity and were acquitted, and sex offenders all are entitled to the same protections against indefinite psychiatric commitment as civil patients.

Least Restrictive Alternative

Since the civil rights era of the 1950s and 1960s in the United States, mental health and legal experts have agreed that treatment options should be guided by the principle of the least restrictive alternative, given the likelihood that mental health treatment will curtail the mentally ill offender's freedom and liberty. For example, when feasible, placement in a psychiatric unit that permits various privileges is preferable to placement in punitive segregation; all things being equal, placement in a community-based facility is preferable to placement in a secure psychiatric facility.

Involuntary Commitment and Retention

Various courts have upheld statutes requiring immediate hospitalization of individuals who have been found not guilty by reason of insanity (*Jones v. United States* [1983]; *Glatz v. Kort* [1986]; *In re Martin B.* [1987]; *People v. Catron* [1988]). Most laws require a hearing within a reasonable period to review the need for psychiatric hospitalization.

Courts have recognized the community's right to public safety as an overriding concern that justifies the temporary confinement of certain high-risk individuals. Courts have also permitted indeterminate hospitalization when necessary (Hafemeister 1998); the U.S. Supreme Court has authorized indefinite hospitalization of individuals found not guilty by reason of insanity (*Jones v. United States* [1983]).

Particularly controversial are statutes that permit commitment of repeat sex offenders to a secure psychiatric facility for an indeterminate period if they have been found to have a "psychopathic personality." Hafemeister (1998) points out that the Minnesota Supreme Court, ruling in *In re Blodgett* (Minn. 1994), noted that

> Minnesota, like other states, has long wrestled with how to deal with the legitimate public concern over the danger posed by predatory sex offenders. The court found a compelling government interest in the protection of the public from persons who have an uncontrollable impulse to sexually assault and concluded that this statute fell within one of the permissible categories when the State may constitutionally deprive an individual of liberty, namely, when a person is mentally ill and dangerous. The court noted that even though "psychopathic personality" is not currently classified as a mental illness, it does identify a "volitional dysfunction which grossly impairs judgment and behavior," can be systematically assessed, and is not a mere social maladjustment. The court rejected the defendant's argument that treatment for the psychopathic personality never works, but also asserted that even if successful treatment is problematic, as it often is, the State's interest in the safety of others is no less legitimate and compelling, and all that is required is that treatment and periodic review be provided. (53–54)

In a major ruling with sweeping implications (*Kansas v. Hendricks* [1997]), the U.S. Supreme Court upheld a Kansas statute permitting the commitment for an indefinite period of individuals likely to engage in "predatory acts of sexual violence," even *after* the individual has completed his or her sentence for a related crime (Hafemeister 1998). The preamble to the Kansas statute states:

> [A] small but extremely dangerous group of sexually violent predators exist who do not have a mental disease or defect that renders them appropriate for involuntary treatment pursuant to the [general involuntary civil commitment statute]. . . . In contrast to persons appropriate for civil commitment under the [general involuntary civil commitment statute], sexually violent predators generally have anti social personality features which are unamenable to existing mental illness treatment modalities and those features render them likely to engage in sexually violent behavior. The legislature further finds that sexually violent predators' likelihood of engaging in repeat acts of predatory sexual violence is high. The existing involuntary commitment procedure . . . is inadequate to address the risk these sexually violent predators

pose to society. The legislature further finds that the prognosis for rehabilitating sexually violent predators in a prison setting is poor, the treatment needs of this population are very long term and the treatment modalities for this population are very different than the traditional treatment modalities for people appropriate for commitment under the [general involuntary civil commitment statute]. (Kan. Stat. Ann. §59–29a01 [1994]).

Right to Treatment and Right to Refuse Treatment

The most prominent court case involving the right to treatment for involuntarily hospitalized individuals is the U.S. Supreme Court's ruling in *Youngberg v. Romeo* (1982). In addition, one federal court issued several rulings stating a right to "reasonably suitable and adequate" treatment for people involuntarily committed after being found not guilty by reason of insanity or after being determined to be a sexual psychopath (Hafemeister 1998). The court ruled that because commitment could last indefinitely, confinement could be justified only if therapeutic treatment was provided as well.

Several more recent rulings have been unwilling to recognize such a broad right to treatment for mentally ill offenders who have *not* been convicted of a crime and who are placed in a relatively nonsecure mental health facility (see, for example, *Thompson v. County of Mediana, Ohio* [6th Cir. 1994]; *Knight v. Mills* [1st Cir. 1987]; *Partridge v. Two Unknown Police Officers of Houston* [5th Cir. 1986]; *Florida DHRS v. Schreiber* [Fla. Dist. Ct. App. 1990]; *In re G. S.* [Ill. App. Ct. 1990]; *Commonwealth v. Davis* [Mass. 1990]; *Bahrenfus v. Bachik* [Or. Ct. App. 1991]; for a ruling that the Constitution does not require that all patients in state-run psychiatric facilities receive the same rights or care, see also *Doe v. Gaughan* [1st Cir. 1986]). The courts have generally respected the judgment of professional staff regarding individuals' treatment needs, concluding that the potential dangerousness of offenders with mental illness requires a treatment modality that recognizes the recurring need to protect public safety (Hafemeister 1998).

Several important court decisions have also cited the obligation of prison officials and mental health staff to identify and monitor inmates with mental illness. Various rulings refer to the need for proper intake and assessment procedures when inmates manifest signs of mental illness, referral procedures, proper communication between mental health staff and staff responsible for security, written rules and procedures regarding the management of inmates with a mental illness, limiting the use of "lockdown" as an alternative to mental health care, separating mentally ill inmates from the general prison population, and providing proper programming (see, for example, *Coleman v. Wilson* [E.D. Cal. 1995]; *Casey v. Lewis* [D. Ariz. 1993]; *Hoptowit v. Ray* [9th Cir. 1982]; *Lovell v. Brennan* [1st Cir. 1984]).

Courts generally have been reluctant to recognize a broad right of offenders with mental illness to refuse treatment. According to Hafemeister (1998), the courts have concluded that

> the State's interests in overriding a treatment refusal can outweigh the offender's interests. However, the federal courts have not ruled that this is solely a question of federal law and the states are free to expand the offender's right to refuse treatment. Indeed, a number of state courts have independently recognized this right, given greater weight to the offender's interests, and added requirements with which treatment providers in these states must comply.
>
> Generally, the question is not whether offenders with mental disorders can voice an objection and have it heard. This has been widely accepted; even the federal courts do not give treatment providers carte blanche to override an offender's objection. Instead, the issues are who can override an objection, when, and how. It should be noted, however, that enhanced procedural protections associated with a right to refuse treatment tend to extend only to psychotropic drugs, ECT [electroconvulsive therapy], and psychosurgery. These same safeguards have not generally been required for other forms of treatment because they are not considered as intrusive, onerous, or nonreversible. (63)

Nonetheless, important rulings have held that although inmates have a protected constitutional interest in avoiding forced administration of psychotropic drugs, this interest must be balanced against the state's interests in prison safety and security (Hafemeister 1998). In *Washington v. Harper* (1990) the U.S. Supreme Court noted the need to consider the effect of any ruling on prison resources and the need to ensure the safety of prison staff, other inmates, and the inmate. The Court recognized the danger to others from a behavioral outburst and that "prison authorities are best equipped to make difficult decisions regarding prison administration" (Hafemeister 1998:66).

Use of Aversive and Experimental Therapies

The courts have criticized, with good reason, treatments that make use of aversive therapies. In one major case (*Mackey v. Procunier* [1973]) the U.S.

Court of Appeals for the Ninth Circuit considered a complaint filed by an inmate who was sent to a medical facility to receive "shock treatment." The inmate alleged that while at the treatment facility, and without his consent, the staff administered a "breath-stopping and paralyzing fright drug" (succinylcholine). The court ruled that if the inmate could prove his claim, it would "raise serious constitutional questions respecting cruel and unusual punishment or impermissible tinkering with the mental processes" (Hafemeister 1998:69).

In a similar case the Eighth Circuit ruled that without prior informed consent administering a drug (apomorphine) to induce vomiting as part of an aversive therapy program for inmates in a secure medical facility constituted cruel and unusual punishment (*Knecht v. Gillman* [1973]). An important conceptual issue in this case was the court's determination that use of the drug for punishment purposes was impermissible, as opposed to using it for treatment purposes (see also *Souder v. McGuire* [M.D. Pa. 1976]; *Price v. Sheppard,* 239 N.W.2d 1136 [8th Cir. 1973]; *Canterino v. Wilson* [W.D. Ky. 1982]; *Green v. Baron,* 879 F.2d 305 [8th Cir. 1989]).

Courts have also weighed in on programs' use of experimental interventions that are not widely used and accepted among mental health professionals. In a 1973 Michigan case (*Kaimowitz v. Dep't. of Mental Health,* cited in Hafemeister 1998:112), an individual committed under a criminal sexual psychopath statute challenged proposed experimental psychosurgery. The court expressed concern that the treatment was irreversible and often led to the blunting of emotions, memory, affect, and creativity and ruled that the individual had a First Amendment right to be free from interference with his mental processes (Hafemeister 1998). The extent to which a treatment is intrusive (the probable effects on the individual's body, the risk of adverse side-effects, the potential for irreversible effects, and so on) has also been considered by a number of courts (see, for example, *Price v. Sheppard* [Minn. 1976]).

All institutions and programs that receive federal funding are now required to comply with federal guidelines governing research and experimentation with patients and human subjects. Research proposals and protocols must be reviewed and approved by an institutional review board. Some states also require this form of review.

Disclosure of Confidential Information

Thorny confidentiality issues can arise in work with mentally ill offenders. One issue concerns the disclosure of confidential details to prison or other corrections officials (parole or probation, for example) because of security and safety concerns. A second issue pertains to staff members' disclosures during formal judicial and administrative hearings and proceedings.

In general, mental health professionals are obligated to respect clients' right to privacy and confidentiality. However, widely accepted standards in professions such as social work, psychology, and psychiatry permit exceptional disclosures, without clients' consent, in order to protect the client or a third party from a serious threat, to comply with a federal or state law (for example, a mandatory reporting law related to child abuse and neglect), and in response to a court order. These exceptions are well established and are reflected in prominent codes of ethics (Reamer 1998a) and have been accepted by various courts of law (see, for example, *Linch v. Thomas-Davis Med. Centers* [Ariz. Ct. App. 1996]; *Commonwealth v. Wiseman* [Mass. 1969]; *MacDonald v. Clinger* [N.Y. App. Div. 1982]; *Mississippi State Board of Psychological Examiners v. Hosford* [Miss. 1987]). Courts have also respected the need for administrative bodies (such as a parole board) to have access to confidential information (see, for example, *Powell v. Coughlin* [2d Cir. 1991]; *Oakland Prosecutor v. Dep't. of Corrections* [Mich. Ct. App. 1997]).

Release and Discharge

Mental health professionals and correctional staff often make decisions to transfer inmates from one secure facility to another, from more secure to less secure facilities, to different units within a facility, to award or revoke privileges and passes, grant conditional releases, and release outright (Hafemeister 1998). Challenging legal and ethical issues arise when mentally ill offenders do not consent to such transfers and release decisions.

Courts have ruled that offenders are entitled to due process protections, for example, timely notice of, and an opportunity for, a hearing and access to legal counsel (see, for example, *Vitek v. Jones* [1980]; *Sandin v. Conner* [1995]). Courts have also recognized that communities have a right to be protected when an offender is being transferred to a less secure setting that may pose greater public safety risks (see, for example, *Molesky v. Walter* [E.D. Wash. 1996]; *Ohio v. Johnson* [Ohio 1987]; *McSwain v. Stricklin* [Ala. Civ. App. 1989]; *Idaho v. Hargis* [Idaho Ct. App. 1995]; *People v. Villaneuva* [N.Y. Sup. Ct. 1988]; *Ohio v. Lanzy* [Ohio 1991]; *Ohio v. Green* [Ohio Ct. App. 1996]).

In general, courts have ruled that transfers among programs within a facility for treatment purposes (as opposed to punishment) do not require judicial review (see, for example, *Sandin v. Conner* [1995]; *Meriwether v. Faulkner* [7th Cir. 1987]; *United States v. Perez* [7th Cir. 1994]; *Mary & Crystal v. Ramsden* [7th Cir. 1980]; *Casey v. Lewis* [D. Ariz. 1993]; *Anderson v. County of Kern* [9th Cir. 1995]; *Wolff v. McDonnell* [1974]; *Kulow v. Nix* [8th Cir. 1994]; *Powell v. Coughlin* [2d Cir. 1991]).

Courts have also expressed a strong wish to monitor conditional and outright releases of potentially dangerous offenders, primarily because of the possible threat to public safety (for a comprehensive overview of more than one hundred court cases in which these issues have been litigated, see Hafemeister 1998). Courts have also upheld the legitimacy of policies that require community notification and registration (with police) to ensure that victims and the community are informed when certain high-risk offenders—particularly sex offenders—are released from prison or move into a new community (see, for example, *Arizona v. Noble* [Ariz. 1992]; *People v. Adams* [Ill. 1991]; *New Hampshire v. Costello,* 643 A.2d 531 [N.H. 1994]; *Louisiana v. Sorrell* [La. Ct. App. 1995]; *Washington v. Ward* [Wash. 1994]; *Jones v. Murray* [4th Cir. 1992]; *Doe v. Gainer* [Ill. 1994]; *People v. Calahan* [Ill. App. Ct. 1995]; *Washington v. Olivas* [Wash. 1993]; *Doe v. Poritz* [N.J. 1995]).

OFFENDER REENTRY INTO THE COMMUNITY

Nearly every offender—even those who commit heinous crimes—will be released from prison some day. That day may be years or decades down the road, but for most offenders the day will come.

Whether our individual instincts are more liberal or conservative with regard to incarceration, it behooves us to plan for inmates' eventual release to the community and to take practical steps to enhance each offender's adjustment and minimize the likelihood of recidivism. Any reluctance that we might have to concede that offenders who commit heinous crimes will once again live among us is naive.

Even the most conservative observers should resist the temptation to require every offender to serve her or his entire sentence. While that wish may satisfy our often understandable retributive instincts, this would be remarkably shortsighted public policy. It is one thing for offenders serving relatively short prison terms to walk out the front gate only after completing their entire sentence. The adjustment is likely to be difficult but, for many, manageable, if they are fortunate enough to have constructively supportive family and friends, a job, and appropriate social, health, mental health, and other relevant services. However, to think that an inmate can make an easy, smooth adjustment upon walking out of the prison after incarceration for decades—without the benefit of parole supervision and a gradual transition—is the height of delusion.

That is, one can support the concept of parole from any point on the liberal-conservative continuum; whatever the ideological rationale, it only makes sense to release most inmates who have served lengthy sentences—most of whom will leave prison still struggling with some combination of issues related to substance abuse, mental illness, illiteracy, and chronic health problems—to some form of parole supervision to ensure their access to services they need and to monitor their whereabouts and conduct. Our principal challenge is to design a parole system that strikes a reasonable balance between the delivery of supportive services that minimize the likelihood of recidivism and the maintenance of public safety.

Currently, only about 20 percent of inmates serve their entire sentence or "max out" their time. Eighty percent of the prison population is released at some point to parole supervision. Most released prisoners are rearrested and returned to prison. Currently available data show that 30 percent are rearrested in the first six months after release, 44 percent within the first year, and more than two-thirds (67.5 percent) are rearrested within three years of release. A nontrivial percentage of these offenders commits heinous crimes (Langan and Levin 2002; Petersilia 2003).

Here are the cold hard facts about the attributes of inmates who leave prison (Beck 2000; Bushway and Reuter 2002; Maruschak and Beck 2001; Petersilia 2003; Rubinstein 2001):

- 19 percent are completely illiterate, and 40 percent are functionally illiterate.
- About 50 percent do not have a high school diploma.
- 10 percent of state prison inmates (5 percent of federal inmates) have significant mental impairment.
- 12 percent of state prison inmates (11 percent of federal inmates) have significant physical impairment.
- 21 percent of state and federal inmates report having some condition that limits their ability to work.
- A significant portion of the seventeen thousand prisoners held in super-max (the most secure, restrictive units available) units are released directly from this long-term isolation to the streets.
- 31 percent of state prisoners (27 percent of federal prisoners) report that they were unemployed in the month before their arrest.

- 5 percent of state prisoners (3 percent of federal prisoners) report having never held a job.
- Only 17 percent of state prisoners and 30 percent of federal prisoners are married.
- 74 percent of reentering state prisoners report drug or alcohol use; 25 percent report that they are alcohol dependent.
- 2 to 3 percent of prisoners are HIV-positive or have AIDS.

Clearly, many offenders have the deck stacked against them when they leave prison. Release under supervision, accompanied by an earnest attempt to provide needed social and health care services, is essential.

Parole as we know it today got its start in the early nineteenth century. Its origins typically are traced to Captain Alexander Maconochie, who was in charge of the English penal colony at Norfolk Island, off the coast of Australia. As the administrator of the Irish prison system in 1854, Sir Walter Crofton built on Maconochie's system. By the mid-1860s many of its features were beginning to appear in the United States, largely as a result of the efforts of Zebulon Brockway, a Michigan penologist (Petersilia 2003).

For decades parole flourished in the United States. Over time, however, as many politicians climbed over each other to be the first to proclaim new "get tough" policies on crime, many states abolished their parole boards or limited their parole board's authority (for example, by limiting the types of offenders and offenses that would be eligible for parole).

Based on her astute and comprehensive review of current parole practices in the United States and research evidence concerning the correlates of recidivism, Petersilia (2003:171) argues that prisoner reintegration practices need to be reformed in four major areas:

1. Alter the in-prison experience. Provide more education, work, and rehabilitation opportunities. Change the prison environment to promote life skills rather than violence and domination.
2. Change prison release and revocation practices. Institute a system of discretionary parole release that incorporates parole release guidelines. These parole guidelines should be based primarily on recidivism prediction.
3. Revise postprison services and supervision. Incorporate better parole supervision classification systems, and target those with high-need and high-risk profiles for services and surveillance.
4. Foster collaboration with the community and enhance mechanisms of informal social control. Develop partnerships with service

providers, ex-convicts, law enforcement, family members, victim advocates, and neighborhoods to support and facilitate the offender's community reentry and reintegration.

Petersilia (2003) proposes a series of sensible recommendations designed to achieve these four goals. Although her guidelines do not focus explicitly on offenders who commit heinous crimes, they are applicable to heinous offenders who have not been sentenced to life in prison without the possibility of parole and who will be released from prison someday.

1. *Prison administrators should embrace the mission of prisoner reintegration.* Some prison administrators are concerned almost exclusively with confinement and security. To facilitate prisoner reentry, reintegration—based on individualized plans designed to enhance inmates' chances of success— must be a *genuine* priority.

2. *Rehabilitate reentry programs: implement treatment, work, and education tracks in the prison.* As I discussed earlier, we have substantial empirical evidence that some rehabilitation programs are effective when they are tailored to inmates' individual needs. Not all treatment programs work all the time, and not all inmates are motivated to participate in them. However, many inmates are eager for help and respond well to high-quality, skillfully delivered treatment and services (see chapter 4).

3. *Encourage inmate responsibility through "parallel universe" concepts.* The former director of the Missouri Department of Corrections, Dora Schriro, was eager to help inmates cultivate solid decision-making skills and a sense of personal responsibility. She developed a creative strategy called the Parallel Universe, based on the belief that life inside a prison should resemble life outside prison as much as possible and that a key goal must be to assist inmates to acquire values, habits, and skills that will help them function well in the community. This approach has four major components:

- Every offender is engaged during work and nonwork hours in productive activities that parallel those of free society. In work hours offenders go to school and work and, when appropriate, to treatment for sex offenses, mental health problems, and substance abuse issues. In nonwork hours inmates participate in community service, reparative activities (see chapter 6), and recreation.
- Every offender must adopt relapse prevention strategies and abstain from unauthorized activities, including drug and alcohol consumption and sexual misconduct.

- Most offenders can earn opportunities to make choices and are held accountable for them.
- Offenders are recognized for good conduct and can improve their status by obeying the rules and regulations.

4. *Prisoners should participate in comprehensive prerelease planning.* Nearly every criminal justice professional agrees in principle that it makes complete sense for every inmate to be actively involved in prerelease planning, setting near- and long-term goals, identifying and reviewing options that can help the inmate move toward those goals, and pursuing those options. Sadly, current data suggest that only 12 percent of all state prisoners released to the streets participate in *any* type of prerelease program; some of the 12 percent participate in prerelease planning that can be described, at best, as thin and anemic. This is unconscionable and a recipe for disaster. Is it any great surprise that so many inmates released from prison are rearrested within three years?

5. *Reinstitute risk-based discretionary parole release.* States that have abolished discretionary parole should reinstate it. Without discretionary parole the typical inmate has little or no incentive to pursue and participate in rehabilitation programs while in prison, because participation would not affect the inmate's release date. Although a small group of inmates actively pursues rehabilitation programs because these inmates are wise enough to understand the potential benefits—apart from the likely influence on a parole board decision—most inmates are not so motivated and would benefit from the incentives provided by a discretionary parole system.[3]

6. *Encourage victims to submit statements requesting notification of inmates' release and special parole conditions.* We must always keep victims in mind. One way to ensure their involvement—for those who wish to be involved (not all do)—is to invite victims to address the parole board before the inmate's hearing. I know from many years of personal experience as a parole board member that meetings with victims can have an absolutely profound effect on parole board members' decisions. In-person, passionate, anguished, sincere, and heartfelt testimony by victims is usually very moving.

7. *Support greater monitoring of high-risk, violent parolees.* Put simply, many parolees—especially those who have committed heinous crimes—require strict, constant monitoring. Innovations such as electronic monitoring and global positioning satellites greatly enhance our ability to provide this essential supervision.[4]

8. *Provide treatment and work training to motivated parolees after prison.* Given what we know about the skill deficits, mental health problems, and physical health issues that many parolees face, it is remarkably shortsighted to not provide access to high-quality, sustained social and health care services.

9. *Parole offices should incorporate neighborhood parole supervision.* Years ago Tip O'Neill, the former Speaker of the House of Representatives, became famous for the phrase "All politics is local." One might say the same thing about parole. In recent years a model known as "neighborhood parole" (Smith and Dickey 1998) has gained currency. Under this approach parole officers become more visible in the offender's home community; they are accessible to community members and develop constructive relationships with family, neighbors, and employers.

10. *Establish and test reentry courts and community partnerships.* Reentry partnership, a concept being promoted by the U.S. Department of Justice, is among the latest innovations in the corrections field. The underlying assumption is that each component of the criminal justice system—police, courts, and institutional and community corrections—plays a role in trying to effect immediate change in an offender. In addition, these components must engage family, community service providers, religious organizations, and other sources of formal and informal support in order to reintegrate offenders over the long term. The process includes institutional and community-based steps related to risk and needs assessment, treatment, transition planning, transition reassessment, case management, and monitoring.

Earnest partnerships between the police and corrections can facilitate this reentry, where police become more actively involved as members of the parole supervision team and function as more than arresting agents. Many police have an active interest in providing supportive advice and referrals to parolees who need community-based assistance.

Finally, reentry courts, modeled after other specialized courts such as drug courts and gun courts, are designed to focus explicitly on parole-related decisions (Travis 2000). When the time arrives for an inmate to reenter the community, the court and the offender draw up a contract that sets forth the conditions that the offender must follow. The judge then has the authority to impose or change conditions, depending on the offender's individual needs, behavior, and challenges.[5] The core goal of reentry courts is to "coordinate services and establish a seamless system of offender accountability and support" (Petersilia 2003:204).

The deliberate combination of these various elements would help to produce what David Wexler refers to as a system of therapeutic jurisprudence, which is the

> study of the role of the law as a therapeutic agent. It focuses on the law's impact on the psychological well-being or emotional life of persons affected by the law. Therapeutic jurisprudence is a perspective that regards the law as a social force that produces behavior and consequences. Sometimes these consequences fall within the realm of what we call therapeutic; other times anti-therapeutic consequences are produced. Therapeutic jurisprudence wants us to be aware of this and wants us to see whether the law can be applied in a more therapeutic way. (n.d.:1, cited in Petersilia 2003:206)

11. *Implement and test goal-oriented parole terms.* Parole terms and conditions should be set according to offenders' unique needs, the risks that the offenders pose, their compliance with parole conditions, and their behavior. Parole boards and officials should have the option to reward parolees who do well, that is, "goal parole." Under this model offenders would have the opportunity to reduce the amount of time that they spend on parole by remaining arrest-free, participating in community service, completing treatment programs, and sustaining employment.

12. *Establish procedures for ex-prisoners to regain full citizenship.* Incentives should be available to enable motivated offenders to put their criminal histories behind them. Some offenders will work hard to regain full citizenship, that is, to have their records expunged or to receive a pardon for exemplary conduct. This option would not be available to all inmates, nor should it be. Some offenders' records should not be expunged. However, some offenders admit their mistakes, work hard to address their "issues," and live honorable, constructive lives. Their sustained, genuine efforts should be duly recognized.

6

RESTORATIVE, REPARATIVE, AND COMMUNITY JUSTICE

One of the most compelling developments in criminal justice in recent years is the restorative justice movement. Restorative justice is a victim-centered response to crime that provides opportunities for the victim, the offender, their families, and representatives of the community at large to address the harm caused by the crime. The number of formal restorative justice programs has increased dramatically, especially since the early 1980s (Umbreit 2000). Although some forms of restorative justice are not appropriate or feasible in cases involving heinous crime, several are.

Restorative justice is based on a belief that an important goal of the criminal justice system should be to restore victims who have been harmed or injured by offenders. More specifically, restorative justice stresses the importance of

- Providing opportunities for more active involvement in the process of offering support and assistance to crime victims
- Holding offenders directly accountable to the people and communities they have violated
- Restoring the emotional and material losses of victims, to the degree possible
- Providing a range of opportunities for dialogue and problem solving to interested crime victims, offenders, families, and other support persons
- Offering offenders opportunities for competency development and reintegration into productive community life
- Strengthening public safety through community building (Umbreit 2000:1)

Victims can be defined broadly to include individual victims (as in cases of heinous offenses such as murder, aggravated assault, robbery, arson, rape, and child molestation), organizational victims (as in cases of fraud, destruction of corporate property, or embezzlement of funds), and the broader community (as in cases of destruction of public property or theft of public funds).

The concept of restorative justice has ancient roots and a number of contemporary applications that have intriguing relevance to heinous crime. The term *restorative justice* was probably used for the first time by Albert Eglash in 1977 (Kurki 2000). Restorative justice programs now operate in nearly every state in the United States and throughout Europe, Australia, New Zealand, Canada, and South Africa.

Restorative justice is one expression of the broader phenomenon of community justice. The goal of community justice is to empower communities and enhance citizens' participation in the administration of justice. It is based on the premise that

> crime is a social problem that corrodes the quality of life in communities, and it redefines the role and operations of criminal justice agencies. Rather than focus solely on punishment, deterrence, or rehabilitation of individual offenders, agencies should broaden their mission to include preventing crime and solving neighborhood conflicts. Operations should be moved to local communities, and citizen involvement should be encouraged. (Kurki 2000:236)

Original notions of restorative justice have their roots in Jewish, Buddhist, Taoist, Greek, Arab, Roman, and Hindu civilizations, among others (Braithwaite 1998; Van Ness 1986). According to Braithwaite, "Taken seriously, restorative justice involves a very different way of thinking about traditional notions such as deterrence, rehabilitation, incapacitation, and crime prevention. It also means transformed foundations of criminal jurisprudence and of our notions of freedom, democracy, and community" (1998:323).

Contemporary restorative justice programs have evolved from an exclusive focus on victim-offender mediation to a much more comprehensive approach that views crime as a "rupture in relationships and attempts to restore victims and communities, mend relationships, and build communities" (Kurki 2000:239). The first North American victim-offender mediation program, in Kitchener, Ontario, was established by Mennonite Central Committee workers in 1974. Many of the movement's earliest proponents were members of faith communities who designed and implemented programs in the 1970s and early 1980s (Van Ness and Heetderks Strong 1997; Wright 1990; Zehr 1990). Broader community involvement in restorative justice initiatives started primarily in the 1990s (Kurki 2000; Pranis 1997). These developments were an outgrowth of a peacemaking process that has been part of North American aboriginal, First Nation, and Native American (especially Navajo) traditions for centuries, traditions that emphasize the importance of confessing one's wrongs, apologizing, forgiving, and reconciling (Sullivan and Tifft 2001).

The majority of the earlier restorative justice programs in the United States and Canada aimed to divert juvenile offenders involved in minor, nonviolent, and nonsexual crimes. In New Zealand restorative justice programs are used for all juvenile offenses, with the exception of homicide. In Germany about 70 percent of both adult and juvenile cases of victim-offender mediation studied in a recent survey involved violent crimes, and in Austria 73 percent of adult and 43 percent of juvenile cases involved violent crimes (Kurki 2000).

Most restorative justice programs are based on five principal assumptions (Bazemore and Walgrave 1999; Braithwaite 1998, 2002; Consedine 1995; Kurki 2000; Pranis 1997; Sullivan and Tifft 2001; Umbreit 1994; Van Ness and Nolan 1998; Wright 1990; Zehr 1990):

1. Crime consists of more than violation of the criminal law and defiance of the authority of government.
2. Crime involves disruption in a three-dimensional relationship involving the victim, the offender, and the community.
3. Crime harms the victim and the community, and the primary goal should be to restore the victim and the community, repair harms, and rebuild relationships among the victim, the offender, and the community.
4. The victim, the community, and the offender should all participate in determining what happens, and government should surrender its monopoly over responses to crime.
5. The disposition should be based primarily on the victim's and the community's needs and not solely on the offender's needs or culpability, the danger the offender presents, or the offender's criminal history.

Restorative justice programs can take various forms, the most common of which include victim-offender mediation, conferencing, circles (a long-standing Native American and First Nation practice in which community members meet with the offender to discuss the crime and offer opportunity for reparations, restitution, and community service). Contemporary examples of restorative justice programs include crime repair crews, victim intervention programs, family group conferencing, victim-offender mediation and dialogue, peacemaking circles, victim panels that address offenders, sentencing circles, community reparative boards that offenders appear before, offender competency development programs, victim empathy classes for offenders, victim-directed and citizen-involved community service by the offender, community-based support groups for crime victims, and community-based support groups for offenders (Umbreit 2000). Restorative justice efforts can have diverse goals (Abel and Marsh 1984; Braithwaite 1998, 1999, 2002; Galaway and Hudson 1978; Kurki 2000; Reamer 2003a; Umbreit 1994), including the restoration of property, injury, sense of security, dignity, sense of empowerment, harmony, social support, and proportionality, consistency, and equality.

Property. Offenders who broke into a home can return stolen jewelry or, if it has already been sold, pay restitution for the loss. Offenders who embezzled money can be expected to repay the amount. For example, Marsha R. (case 2.4), who was imprisoned after embezzling a large sum from her employer, could work out a long-term payment plan in an effort to make her victim whole. Marsha R. may have difficulty paying off the entire amount, given her likely wages for some time after her release from prison, but she could make a sustained effort to pay back as much as possible. Similarly, Saravane S. (case 2.16), who, along with other gang members, robbed and terrorized a family, could be expected to repay the family as much as possible to compensate them for the loss of their cash and jewels. Although the monetary compensation would not heal the emotional wounds caused by the horrific terror inflicted by the gang members when they tied the family members up at gunpoint, restitution would provide the offender with an opportunity to partially pay back the victims and express his remorse.

Injury. Offenders who injured someone in a physical assault can pay the victim's medical expenses or compensate for lost wages. Offenders can also express their sincere remorse—either in person, by telephone, or in writing—for the pain that they have caused. Offenders who have somehow harmed the community but whose actions did not harm individuals can compensate by performing some form of community service (such as volunteering to work with disabled people, painting a neighborhood health clinic, or removing litter from a public park). For example, Larry K.

(case 2.23), who assaulted his estranged wife with a machete while she was sleeping, could be expected to cover her uninsured medical expenses and the income she lost when she had to quit her job as an office manager because of her injuries. Similarly, Merrill S. (case 2.31), who killed one teenager and injured two others during a "road rage" conflict, could be expected to make restitution payments in an effort to cover at least a portion of the victims' medical expenses, funeral expenses, and lost wages.

Sense of security. Offenders who become acquainted with their victims may provide reassurance that they did not target these individuals specifically and that the victims need not fear retaliation. For example, the unruly customer who viciously assaulted Anthony Y. (case 2.32), after he tried to calm the customer down in a department store, could reassure Anthony that he did not set out to harm him and that Anthony should not live in fear of a retaliative assault. Antonia L. (case 2.54) could reassure the elderly patients whose pain medication she stole that she did not set out to harm them individually and that they should not fear retaliation of any sort.

Dignity. Offenders who engage in sincere attempts to restore their victims can enhance their own sense of dignity and reduce their sense of shame. Restorative justice efforts may be an important step in the offender's rehabilitation. For example, Karen R. (case 2.57) was deeply remorseful about the large sum of money that she embezzled from her employer. Agreeing to a restitution plan provided Karen with a meaningful opportunity to regain some dignity. Similarly, Edgar C. (case 2.63), the former psychologist who suffered from his own mental illness and sexually abused a client, could be eager to express his feelings of remorse toward his victim, now that he has been stabilized on medication and understands the ramifications of his behavior.

Sense of empowerment. Offenders, victims, and members of the community may enhance their sense of empowerment. For victims and community members restorative justice provides an opportunity to confront crime and criminals and to assert their rights and indignation. For offenders who are eager to change their conduct, taking responsibility for their misdeeds can provide a strong sense of empowerment.

Harmony. Restorative justice seeks to create the feeling that justice has been done. Consistent with ancient traditions, restorative justice can help people make amends for their wrongdoing. An increased sense of justice among citizens has the useful by-product of increased harmony. This is especially true when restorative justice programs take the form of reconciliation meetings between victims and offenders.

Social support. Here too both victims and offenders may find healing. Through restorative justice efforts victims may gain a sense that the broader community in general, and the criminal justice system in particular, is behind them, in their corner, and supportive. Similarly, offenders may gain a sense that those responsible for administering justice have more than punishment and retribution in mind, that they are genuinely concerned about the offender's well-being and future.

Proportionality, consistency, and equality. Restorative justice interventions can enhance proportionality, consistency, and equality in the administration of justice. Careful review of each case's circumstances by a diverse group of interested parties can lead to a greater sense of fairness.

Restorative justice programs have been implemented for a wide range of populations that have made mistakes and committed crimes: corporate executives, juvenile delinquents, former business partners, and so on. How appropriate this model is for perpetrators and victims of heinous crime is a matter of debate. Clearly, in some circumstances victim-offender mediation, or any form of contact between these parties, would be out of the question and insensitive. The surviving family members of a child strangled to death by a man diagnosed with schizophrenia, or the victim of a vicious rape by a stranger, are not likely to want to meet and talk with the offender, at least not for a very long time. The encounter is too likely to be traumatic and painful, and the victims' sense of rage may be so intense and overwhelming that face-to-face contact with the perpetrator would be unwise for everyone concerned. Yet, there are remarkable examples of encounters between victims and offenders who have committed stunningly heinous crimes, for example, the efforts sponsored by members of Murder Victims' Families for Reconciliation (Sullivan and Tifft 2001; Umbreit et al. 2002, 2003; also see Gobodo-Madikizela 2003).

With these cautions in mind, restorative justice has its place in the range of potential responses to some heinous crimes. Restorative justice is but one expression of the true democratic process, actively engaging citizens in the administration of justice. That is, justice is not rendered only from on high—in the form of judicial sanctions and oversight—but within the commonweal itself. The challenge is identifying feasible, appropriate, and meaningful applications that serve a constructive purpose. For heinous crimes the most likely restorative justice possibilities are victim-offender mediation, family group conferencing, circles, restitution, and community service.

VICTIM-OFFENDER MEDIATION

Canada and the United States pioneered the use of victim-offender mediation in the 1970s (Umbreit 2001). Typically, the victim and offender meet with a facilitator to address their conflict and to explore meaningful ways to resolve the conflict and for the offender to compensate victims for their injuries.

Victim-offender mediation programs typically involve several stages. The process usually starts when judges, probation or parole staffers, prosecutors, or victim assistance staffers refer offenders to the victim-offender mediation program. Before scheduling the mediation session, the mediator meets with the victim and offender separately, listens to each individual's story, explains the program, and encourages participation. These meetings provide the mediator with an opportunity to establish rapport and trust with both victims and offenders.

Once the mediator has answered questions, the victim and offender have expressed their initial feelings, and both have agreed to participate in mediation, the facilitator schedules a face-to-face meeting. The session begins with the mediator's explaining his or her role, establishing communication ground rules, and outlining the meeting's agenda. The agenda includes talking about what happened when the crime was committed; the victim's and offender's reactions; losses, harm, and injuries that resulted from the crime; and various restitution options. The session concludes with discussion of the possibility of developing a mutually agreeable restitution plan that might involve money, work for the victim performed by the offender, work for the victim's charity of choice, and so on. If all goes well, the parties—victim, offender, and mediator—sign a written restitution agreement (Umbreit 1994). What follows is a description of the process involved in a typical victim-offender mediation session (Umbreit 1994:119–22). The case involves a young man, Brian, who shot an adolescent, Sarah, with a pellet from his rifle. He was accompanied by his mother, and Sarah was accompanied by her mother and stepfather. The mediator, John, invited Sarah to begin:

> SARAH: I was in my own yard working in the garden. I was bent over weeding when I felt a sharp sting in my right leg. Some blood was oozing from my leg. (She seems to lose concentration and is close to tears.)
> JOHN: What did you do then?
> SARAH: I turned around and saw him and his friend running toward his

house. He had a gun in his hand. I thought, "My God, he shot me!" And I started screaming.

JOHN: What happened then?

SARAH'S MOTHER: I heard the screams and dashed out of the house to see what was wrong. A little blood was coming from her wound, but she was screaming almost beyond control. I got her into the house where we washed the wound. I found a tiny hard lump and found the pellet but could not get it out.

SARAH'S STEPFATHER: I called the police and we took her to the trauma center at the hospital. Medical staff calmed her down and very simply removed the pellet. We then went home with a still very frightened girl on our hands. It was a helluva thing to happen; we had just moved in the weekend before.

JOHN (addressing the offender): Brian, why don't you tell us what happened that morning?

BRIAN (he does not look up): Well, me and my friend were in the backyard shooting around. I didn't really aim at her. I didn't really think the gun could shoot that far.

SARAH: You didn't really want to hurt me?

BRIAN: No, I didn't think we could hit you even if I tried.

SARAH: Didn't you hear me yell?

BRIAN: Yeah.

SARAH: Well, then, why did you run away?

BRIAN: We were scared. Real scared. Thought maybe we had really hurt you.

Silence ensues. Victim and offender seem to feel that they have little to add.

SARAH'S STEPFATHER: You could have put out an eye; you could have blinded her.

BRIAN: I know. I know. That's why we were so scared. I'm sorry it happened. It was stupid.

Both mothers are visibly moved by Brian's comments.

JOHN: I am sure that your apology is appreciated, Brian, but how might you begin to repay Sarah and her family for the pain and suffering that they went through because of you?

BRIAN: I don't know.

JOHN (to Sarah's parents): How much were the hospital bills?

SARAH'S MOTHER: Ah, $750 with a $300 deductible.

SARAH'S STEPFATHER: If he could repay the deductible, we could call it even.

JOHN: Can you do that?

Brian nods in the affirmative.

JOHN: With your paper-route job, you could pay $50 a month for six months. Is that OK with you?

BRIAN: Yeah, I can do that.

JOHN: Is that OK with everyone else?

All nod agreement. But as John begins to fill out a contract form, Brian's mother speaks:

I think that $50 a month is fair, but I don't think it is enough, given what we are trying to do here and given the amount of personal trauma Brian caused Sarah and her family. I think he should have to do something more personal.

JOHN (addressing Brian): Do you have any ideas?

SARAH (with relaxed smile): He could do my homework for a month.

SARAH'S MOTHER (chuckling): No, that won't be needed, but some help with the yard would certainly be appreciated. And we do want to be good neighbors.

As the mediator writes up the contract, there is some side discussion. The offender's mother talks about how embarrassing all this has been and how she has punished Brian: "There is no more air rifle, ever."

All the parties sign the contract. John thanks everyone for coming and for being so cooperative. The families go out together, and the last comment that John hears comes from Brian's mother: "Now maybe I can go out in the yard again and look across the fence."

One of the most compelling examples of victim-offender reconciliation grew out of the South African Truth and Reconciliation Commission, established in 1995 by then-president Nelson Mandela and headed by Archbishop Desmond Tutu. A member of the commission, the psychologist Pumla Gobodo-Madikizela (2003), spent considerable time interviewing Eugene de Kock, formerly the commanding officer of state-sanctioned apartheid assassination squads, who received a 212-year sentence for crimes against humanity. De Kock—known widely as "Prime Evil"—was considered by many to be the most brutal of the covert police operatives who enforced apartheid.

During his testimony before the Truth and Reconciliation Commission, de Kock asked to meet with, and have the opportunity to apologize to, the widows of several black police officers whose murders he had arranged. Gobodo-Madikizela (2003) describes her powerful encounter with two widows who met with de Kock:

A few days later I met with Mrs. Mgoduka and Mrs. Faku during a weekend of debriefing. "I was profoundly touched by him," Mrs. Faku said of her encounter with de Kock. Both women felt that de Kock had communicated to them something he felt deeply and had acknowledged their pain. "I couldn't control my tears. I could hear him, but I was overwhelmed by emotion, and I was just nodding, as a way of saying yes, I forgive you. I hope that when he sees our tears, he knows that they are not only tears for our husbands, but tears for him as well. . . . I would like to hold him by the hand, and show him that there is a future, and that he can still change." (14–15)

For Gobodo-Madikizela, victims' forgiveness of perpetrators of heinous crimes is not a simple form of letting perpetrators off the hook. Rather, forgiveness—which not all victims can, or should, be expected to offer[1]—can be an empowering gesture:

I doubt that when forgiveness is offered, the gaze is cast on the specifics of the deed. Forgiveness, while not disregarding the act, begins not with it but with the person. Forgiveness recognizes the deed, its impact having been and continuing to be lived by the victim, but transcends it. People who come to the point of forgiveness have lived not only with the pain that trauma and loss bring, but also with the anger and resentment at those who caused the pain. That is their reality—a world of painful emotional wounds, hostility, and resentment at the injustice visited upon them. All these emotions connect them to their loved ones and so are a force that provides continuity and defies death, sustaining their bonds with those they loved who are now dead. The hateful emotions therefore recast the lost loved one as the living dead—"living," through the link maintained by the hateful affect. Paradoxically, these emotions also tie the individual to the one who inflicted the traumatic wounds. . . . Forgiveness is not simply meant to relieve victimizers of their guilt, to make things easy for them. Such an interpretation makes forgiveness a further burden for victims. Forgiveness can also open up a new path toward healing for the victim. . . . When perpetrators express remorse, when they finally acknowledge that they can see what they previously could not see, or did not want to, they are revalidating the victim's pain—in a sense, giving his or her humanity back. Empowered and revalidated, many victims at this point find it natural to extend and deepen the healing process by going a step further: turning around and conferring forgiveness on their torturer. (Gobodo-Madikizela 2003:95–97, 128)

FAMILY GROUP CONFERENCING

Professionals in New Zealand introduced the concept of conferencing in the late 1980s, originally as a way to address deficiencies in the juvenile justice system (Maxwell and Morris 1992, 1993; Umbreit 2000). This restorative justice approach builds on the concept of victim-offender mediation but broadens it to include relevant family members, clergy, social service professionals, law enforcement officials, and attorneys. The principal goal is for the offender to acknowledge the wrongdoing and for the group to reach consensus about what constructive steps the offender can take to make reparations.

To begin family group conferencing, which is typically conducted in a highly structured manner, a facilitator contacts the victim and offender, explains the process, and invites them to participate. The facilitator also asks the victim and offender to identify key people in their lives and important sources of support (for example, family members, close friends), who will also be invited to participate. Everyone's participation must be voluntary. Under family group conferencing the offender must admit to the offense. A trained facilitator then brings the parties together to discuss how they and others have been harmed by the offense and how that harm might be repaired (Umbreit 2000).

A typical family group conference begins with the offender's describing what happened. In response, each victim describes the effect that event had on his or her life. These narrations and descriptions force the offender to deal with the effects on the victim of the offender's behavior, as well as the effects on those who are close to the victim, and the offender's family and friends. The victims have an opportunity to ask the offender questions and express their feelings about the crime.

After thorough discussion the facilitator provides the victim with an opportunity to identify possible outcomes of the conference, thus giving the victim a way to shape the obligations that the offender will be expected to meet. All other participants may contribute ideas as well. The session ends with participants signing an agreement outlining their respective expectations and commitments (Umbreit 2000).

CIRCLES

The concept of circles (of relationships) has a long history in Native American (United States) and First Nation (Canada) cultures (Galaway and

Hudson 1996). These communities use circles to provide offenders with an opportunity to acknowledge their misconduct and to address problems and conflicts between people. The criminal justice system has used circles since the 1980s. Circles usually include diverse participants concerned about the victim and offender (professionals, community leaders, family, neighbors, and so on). In turn, each participant holds the "talking piece" (usually a stick must be handed to a person before someone may speak) and has an opportunity to express his or her views about the crime, the offender, the victim, and opportunities to make reparations.

At first blush one might think that circles would be inappropriate in cases involving offenders who commit heinous crimes. Certainly, this approach would not be appropriate in some instances. Yet circles have been used, with impressive results, in some cases involving heinous crimes. Braithwaite (2002) describes one ambitious use of circles with a group of Canadian sex offenders. The program, Circles of Support and Accountability, brings together volunteers to work with sex offenders, who typically have little family and social support and often significant cognitive impairment. Circle volunteers help offenders solve problems in their lives and address practical challenges related to, for example, finding an apartment or a job. An evaluation of the program found that the recidivism rate for Circles of Support offenders who had been in the community for an average of about two years was significantly lower than for sex offenders in general. Circles of Support and Accountability have since been formed for about fifty-five Canadian offenders, mainly pedophiles and rapists.

RESTITUTION

Restitution programs typically provide offenders with an opportunity to repay their victims for the economic injuries that they have incurred. Individual victims may receive compensation for their property and economic losses, and organizational victims may receive compensation for theft of property or money (for instance, as a result of fraud or embezzlement).

Restitution programs started in earnest in the 1970s. One of the earliest prototypes was the Minnesota Restitution Center, established by the Minnesota Department of Corrections. Under this program offenders were involved in face-to-face negotiations with their victims concerning the amount of damage done by the crime as well as the form and schedule of payments to be made (Hudson and Galaway 1978).

Some restitution plans have a punitive element and some do not. That is, some restitution plans are built into a criminal court sentence and may be combined with a prison term, whereas others are developed entirely out of the voluntary commitment of the offender and victim (Tittle 1978). Further, many restitution plans are designed to have an explicit *therapeutic* purpose. According to Keve (1978), restitution can have a rehabilitative quality when the following conditions are met:

The payment should truly be an extra effort, a sacrifice of time or convenience. That is, the offender should feel as if he or she needs to expend considerable extra effort to make amends. As Keve notes, "Probably no improvement in self-awareness or raising of self-esteem will derive from the writing of a check or any other casual restitutional act that does not interrupt accustomed activities or diminish personal resources in a felt way" (1978:60).

The restitutive effort assigned should be clearly defined, measurable, and, without being easy, achievable. Restitution agreements should not be filled with vague language and expectations; rather they should be as explicit as possible, to minimize the likelihood of misunderstandings. The agreements should include requirements that are challenging, reasonably ambitious, and feasible. The requirements should also be fair. As Keve asserts, "The restitution requirements must be attainable. If the money to be paid is far too much for the client's earning capacity, a realistic compromise sum must be set. If a service is to be performed, it is fine if the service interferes with the client's free time on weekends, but it must not require the person, for example, to get to a distant work site without a car, to lose time from his paid employment, or to compromise essential duties to the family at home" (1978:61).

The restitution effort should be meaningful. Ideally, restitution plans should include options that make a difference. Clearly, direct monetary compensation of victims, and various forms of labor that take advantage of the offender's unique talents and skills (for example, carpentry, automobile mechanics, financial analysis), fall in this category. "Busy work" that has a punitive element and has little redeeming value does not.

The restitutive assignment should be designed to produce rewards. In general, human beings are motivated by activities that lead to rewards. Restitution plans that are oriented toward rewards—such as a special "recognition" ceremony for results achieved, an appreciative acknowledgement from victims and the community—are more likely to be productive than punitive plans.

In their pioneering, comprehensive work on the concept of restitution and models that might work, Abel and Marsh (1984) argue that the judicial parties involved in administering restitution programs must maintain and preserve their neutrality and should be guided by several principles:

- Restitution should be "problem solving" rather than adversarial in method; the court should try to solve the problems born of the crime by sentencing individuals to make monetary compensation to those they have injured.
- In keeping with this problem-solving approach, courts should act as neutral arbiters among conflicting parties; they should address the damage done by an act and not its intrinsic evil, or its possible deterrent effect, or the rehabilitation of offenders.
- In keeping with its role of neutral arbiter, the court should give a hearing to all serious demands pressed by any individual or group involved.
- As neutral arbiter the courts must consider the possibility that the offender may have been forced into the crime (and so mitigate damages) or might have had damage done to his or her rights by the ways and means that officials used in enforcing the law.

COMMUNITY SERVICE

Community service is a popular option in restorative justice programs, especially when the crime had no individual or organizational victims per se. Community service programs provide the offender with an opportunity to "pay back" the community for the misconduct and harm. The service may take the form of teaching (for example, when offenders convicted of killing someone while driving drunk lecture high school students about the dangers of drunk driving), labor (for example, when an offender paints or repairs public buildings, works at a shelter or soup kitchen, cleans public property, or provides carpentry services to nonprofit community agencies), or service (for example, when an offender donates blood or helps a vandalism victim) (Challeen and Heinlen 1978; Keldgord 1978; Macri 1978; Sullivan and Tifft 2001).

In recent years many communities have developed formal community restitution courts in an effort to institutionalize community service as a restorative justice option (Etzioni 1999; Wright 2002):

- The Red Hook Community Justice Center, located in a neighborhood at the southwestern tip of Brooklyn, New York, is overseen by a judge who imposes community restitution sentences to provide opportunities for offenders to pay back the community that they have harmed. Typical dispositions include painting over graffiti, planting trees, maintaining public parks, and stuffing envelopes for local nonprofit agencies.
- The Downtown Austin (Texas) Community Court focuses on offenders who commit crimes in the central city. Community service options have primarily included festival cleanup and litter collection.
- The Atlanta (Georgia) Community Court accepts referrals from the city solicitor, public defender, pretrial services division, and judges. Community services have included cleanup work and general labor at the local humane association, Kiwanis Club, public transportation system, and AIDS Atlanta.
- The Community Court in Multnomah County (Portland), Oregon, started in 1998 and now operates in various sites throughout the metropolitan area. A unique feature of this program is that police can refer individuals directly to the community court.
- The Marion County (Indianapolis) Community Court and Justice Center opened in 2001. This court operates with diverse sources of funding, including the U.S. Department of Justice's "Weed and Seed" program, the Indianapolis Foundation, and the Marion Superior Courts.

It is not realistic to think that offenders who commit heinous crimes will be offered opportunities to perform community service in lieu of prison. For most such offenders a term of incarceration for both retributive and public safety reasons is necessary. However, criminal justice professionals can become much more ambitious and creative in their efforts to incorporate community service as a restorative justice option following the offender's release from prison. For example, recently I conducted a parole hearing for a former banker, Joseph Mollicone Jr., who was sentenced to thirty years following his conviction on twenty-six counts of embezzlement, conspiracy, and violation of banking laws (Mooney 2002). Mollicone was the president of a loan and investment company when bank examiners determined that millions of dollars were missing from the institution. This failure triggered the collapse of forty-four other credit unions and savings institutions that were also covered by a private and vulnerable insurance system. The public was particularly incensed when Mollicone fled the state, became a fugitive, and ended up living on the lam in Utah.

My parole board colleagues and I decided to release Mollicone on parole after he had served ten years of his prison term. As part of the parole plan we required that Mollicone engage in restorative justice efforts beyond the standing court order for Mollicone to begin making monetary restitution payments. Specifically, the parole board required that Mollicone arrange and deliver a series of lectures to high school students and undergraduate and graduate students in college and university business programs about his unwise choices as a senior business executive and about ethical decision making in the business world. Mollicone's lectures have met with an enthusiastic response (Davis 2002).

On occasion there are also opportunities for offenders who are incarcerated for committing heinous crimes to provide community service while behind bars. For example, Dale Simpson, the man who is serving multiple life sentences for killing his best friend, his friend's girlfriend, and the girlfriend's four-year-old daughter (see chapter 1), wrote to me about how pleased he was to have the opportunity to give back to the community he harmed so badly. After nearly a quarter-century in prison Dale had started working in an institutional job that entailed transcribing books for the blind. Dale wrote to me, casually describing his new tasks. Perhaps without realizing it, he slipped in several comments that clearly indicated how pleased he was to have the opportunity to help others: "It feels real good to be able to do something to make someone else's life better. I finally feel like I'm making a contribution."

THEORETICAL UNDERPINNINGS

Braithwaite (2002), clearly one of the restorative justice field's pioneers, argues that a discrete set of theories explains why restorative justice processes tend to be effective: reintegrative shaming, procedural justice, unacknowledged shame, defiance, and self-categorization.

Reintegrative Shaming

The theory of reintegrative shaming grew out of various Asian policing and educational practices, various regulatory practices for responding to corporate crime in Asia and the West, and a number of Western parenting practices. According to this perspective, which is based in part on classic child development theory regarding the importance of moral reasoning, both laissez-faire parenting that fails to confront and disapprove of children's misconduct *and* punitively authoritarian parenting produce many delinquents and, ultimately, adult criminals.

Restorative justice conferences invite victims and their supporters (typically, family members) to meet with the offender and the people who care about the offender and are respected by the offender. This group of people engages in a discussion about the crime, focusing especially on the feelings and experiences of the people who were harmed. The group brainstorms about the ways in which the harm might be repaired and any steps that should be taken to prevent recidivism.

A key feature of the group discussion is the subject of shame, particularly the shame that the offender feels in the eyes of the people she or he cares about and trusts the most: family and friends (rather than law enforcement officials and the media, for example). The concept builds on philosophies that have existed for hundreds of years, such as those of the Maori, the indigenous people of New Zealand. Maori perspectives on *whanau* conferences make frequent references to the words for *shame* (*whakama*) and *healing* or *embrace*. In Maori tradition what is most important is the shame involved in disappointing one's extended family (Braithwaite 1989, 2002).

Some offenders who commit heinous crimes feel deep shame for their actions, although in prison settings they may be loathe to admit it for fear of showing any sign of "weakness." This was brought home to me by Dale Simpson, the inmate serving multiple life sentences, in one of his letters about the night he murdered three people: "I wasn't saying I don't ever think about my past life or that one night. I do, but I usually try to push it out again as quickly as possible. It is painful for me to think about it. I hate myself a lot for that night for many reasons. I am certainly not proud of what I did. I've felt nothing but shame since it happened. I cannot look someone in the eye and discuss it, even someone who has done the same thing."

Procedural Justice

A major goal of restorative justice is to promote fairness and avoid the biased, discriminatory administration of justice. The aim is to include people—family, friends, acquaintances, clergy, employers, and so on—who are supportive and are not out to persecute the offender (which is not to say that participants do not express their anger and indignation). Research evidence suggests that individuals who participate in restorative justice conferences are more likely to understand what goes on there than during criminal court proceedings, feel more empowered to express their opinions and feelings, have more time to do so, are more likely to feel that their rights are respected, that they have an opportunity to correct errors of fact, that they are treated with respect, and are less likely to feel that they are disadvantaged because of age, income, sex, race, sexual orientation, and so on (Braithwaite 2002).

Unacknowledged Shame

Many scholars believe that the shame that many offenders experience can, if left unresolved, be a destructive emotion that leads offenders to attack others, purposely harm themselves physically, avoid people, or withdraw from people who are important in their lives. That is, some offenders internalize their shame in a way that exacerbates their self-esteem problems, depression, and interpersonal conflict (Moore and Forsythe 1995; Nathanson 1992). What restorative justice requires is a process of "constructive conflict" that enables offenders to deal constructively with and confront the shame they experience when they commit a serious crime. Offenders must be provided with

> rituals of disapproval and acknowledged shame of the dominating behavior, rituals that avert disapproval-unacknowledged shame sequences . . . [and] institutionalize pride and acknowledged shame that heals damaged social bonds. Circles in this formulation are ceremonies of constructive conflict. When hurt is communicated, shame acknowledged by the person or persons who caused it, respect shown for the victim's reasons for communicating the hurt, and respect reciprocated by the victim, constructive conflict has occurred between victim and offender. It may be that in the "abused spouse syndrome," for example, shame is bypassed and destructive, as a relationship iterates through a cycle of abuse, manipulative contrition, peace, perceived provocation, and renewed abuse. (Braithwaite 2002:80)

In a fascinating assessment of the effects of constructive conflict facilitated by the use of group conferences in New Zealand, researchers found that the minority of offenders who failed to apologize during conferences were three times more likely to reoffend than those who had apologized (Braithwaite 2002).

Defiance

Some offenders have a chronic history of defying authority. A key goal of restorative justice is to reduce such defiance and enhance compliance with authority. The theory of defiance (Sherman 1993, cited in Braithwaite 2002:82) rests on three propositions:

1. Sanctions provoke future defiance of the law (persistent, more frequent, or more serious violations) to the extent that offenders experience sanctions as illegitimate, that offenders have weak bonds to the sanctioning agent and community, and that offenders deny their shame and become proud of their isolation from the sanctioning community.
2. Sanctions produce future deterrence of lawbreaking (desistance, less frequent, or less serious violations) to the extent that offenders experience sanctions as legitimate, that offenders have strong bonds to the sanctioning agent and community, and that offenders accept their shame and remain proud of solidarity with the community.
3. Sanctions become irrelevant to future lawbreaking (no effect) to the extent that the factors encouraging defiance or deterrence are fairly evenly counterbalanced.

Lawrence Sherman argues that restorative justice options are much more likely to promote deterrence (proposition 2) than are punitive sanctions. Braithwaite (2002) offers this illustrative and compelling example of the use of restorative justice and group conferencing in a case involving a very serious crime:

> One man assaulted another very seriously; the victim was left lying in a liter and a half of his own blood and required $3,000 in dental work. The outcome of the conference was simply an agreement for the offender never to go within an agreed distance of the victim. On the face of it, this seems a totally inadequate remedy for a life-threatening assault; a court would likely have imposed prison time for it. But the participants in the conference would have seen such a court outcome as less just.
>
> The victim asked for compensation for his dental bills from the offender. The offender had no money and no job, so he felt he could not agree to this. He had just come out of prison for another offense and was about to go back to prison for a third matter. A court, given his record, would likely have extended this sentence for such a serious assault. During his last prison term, the offender cultivated a spiral of rage against the victim of the assault. He

believed the victim had raped his fiancée. The fiancée did not want to press charges, partly because all involved were part of a heroin subculture in which one simply did not press charges against others. Second, the circumstances of the alleged rape were that the rape victim had been having sex with another friend of her fiancée, which her alleged rapist took to be a signal that it was okay for him to do the same. It seemed plausible to our observer and to the police that this rape had occurred, especially when the assault victim said during the conference, "I didn't go out of my way to rape her." However, others at the conference did not believe that the rape had occurred.

It seemed to be the case that the victim and offender were thrown into regular contact because they purchased heroin from the same place, though this was never explicitly said. The victim was terrified that the offender would get angry again back in prison, come out, and kill him the next time. If the offender got an extra few months in jail for the assault, this would make such rage even more likely. So the victim and his supporters were well pleased with an outcome that guaranteed him a secure distance from the offender. The offender never rationally planned to do such damage to the victim. He had "lost it" and knew he was strong enough to kill the victim if he did the same again. He and his supporters wanted to secure him against a shame-rage spiral that would put him back in prison for a third term. While the conference failed to restore harmony, it did restore peace in a way that both sides saw as just in the circumstances. My hypothesis is that the participants are right; this was better justice than the court would have delivered, and a justice that may have prevented a murder by defusing defiance and putting in place a permanent voluntary segregation regime that was more effective incapacitation than the temporary compulsory segregation of a prison. In the four years since the conference, neither the victim nor the offender has been arrested for anything. (83)

Self-Categorization

According to self-categorization theory (Turner et al. 1987), individuals' self-concept and identity directly influence their behavior. With respect to restorative justice, self-categorization theory posits that procedural fairness increases cooperative behavior by giving people who are treated fairly the message that the group respects them. This increases their pride in or identity with the group and therefore increases their willingness to cooperate with the group's expectations (Braithwaite 2002; Tyler and Blader 2000). Braithwaite (2002) argues that offenders often arrive indirectly at positive self-categorization in the context of group conferences:

Restorative justice conferences may prevent crime by facilitating a drift back to law-supportive identities from law-neutralizing ones. How might they accomplish this? At a victim-offender mediation or conference when the victim is present, it is hard to sustain *denial of victim* and *denial of injury*. In contrast, these techniques of neutralization are fostered by criminal justice institutions that sustain separation of victims and offenders. Admittedly, victims often do not convince the offender in a conference that they were hurt in a way they could ill afford. Yet when this occurs, victim supporters will often move offenders through the communicative power, the authenticity, that comes from their love of the victim. An upset daughter explaining how frightened her mother now is in her own house can have a more powerful impact on the offender than direct expressions of concern by the victim. . . .

Criminal offenders are criminal offenders partly because they are good at denial. When shame is projected across the room from victim to offender, the offender may have a shield that deflects the shame, only to find the deflected shame spears through the heart of his mother who sobs quietly beside him. What I have observed in many conferences is that it may be the shame of the offender's mother, father, or sister that gets behind the shield of his denial. This only happens when he loves one of these intimates. (85, 86)

EVIDENCE OF EFFECTIVENESS

In recent years a substantial body of empirical evidence has emerged suggesting that restorative justice processes can be very effective (Braithwaite 2002; Umbreit and Coates 1992; Umbreit, Coates, and Kalanj 1994). The evidence shows that restorative justice restores and satisfies victims, offenders, and the community at large better than existing criminal justice practices. Various studies demonstrate relatively high victim *and* offender approval of their restorative justice experiences, although victims tend to be somewhat less satisfied than other participants. Further, there is encouraging evidence that offenders who participate in restorative justice processes have lower recidivism rates than their peers who do not (Braithwaite 2002; Latimer, Dowden, and Muise 2001; Moore and Forsythe 1995; Umbreit 1994; Walgrave and Bazemore 1998).

Based on his exhaustive review of available research data, Braithwaite (2002) concludes that restorative justice programs are effective for five principal reasons. For Braithwaite restorative justice can

- Build motivation
- Mobilize resources
- Reinforce the social cognitive principles that have been shown to be hallmarks of effective rehabilitation programs
- Foster comprehensive interventions
- Improve offenders' follow-through with their commitments and obligations

Building Motivation

Personal crises often precipitate motivation to change. Consider the well-known adage in the substance abuse field, that many alcoholics will not begin to take recovery seriously until they have hit bottom. That is, many people need to experience overwhelming circumstances in their lives, where they feel desperate to change and sufficiently hopeful to take steps in that direction, in order to go into rehabilitation. Restorative justice processes, which take place in a hopeful context rather than an adversarial and punitive court environment, often provide offenders with the climate they need to feel motivation to change destructive aspects of their lives.

Mobilizing Resources

Restorative justice provides a practical mechanism for marshalling the resources needed to make a difference in offenders' lives. With careful orchestration relatives of victims and offenders, offenders themselves, social service and law enforcement professionals, neighbors, and other people who matter to victims and offenders can be brought under the same roof in a concerted effort to address the harm caused by the offender and to think together about creative acts of reparation (for example, genuine apologies, restitution, community service).

Reinforcing Social Cognitive Principles

A very significant percentage of offenders have weak cognitive skills that affect their ability to exercise good judgment and resist destructive temptation. By now empirical evidence is ample that cognitive-behavioral interventions can have a positive effect on offenders who have weak cognitive skills and tend to engage in "criminal thinking" (see chapter 5). In this regard, Braithwaite (2002) observes,

Restorative justice aspires to confront wrongdoing, to communicate understanding about why it is wrong through a discussion of its consequences and to discuss the pro-social alternative courses of conduct. And it is about nurturing loved ones to take responsibility for such communication. It can also create a space where loved ones can appeal for professional help in meeting these responsibilities. So restorative justice can and should be designed to reinforce both social cognitive processes for pro-social learning within communities of care and to call up professional help with social cognitive skill development. The restorative theory of rehabilitation predicts that a combination of reinforcing pro-social learning among loved ones and seeking professional help in the community will be more effective than the demonstrated effectiveness of professional help of that kind in a correctional institution. (99)

Fostering Comprehensive Interventions

Traditional responses to crime often involve identifying a single intervention or program in an effort to deal with the offender. The restorative justice perspective is that "plural understandings of a crime problem are needed to stimulate a disparate range of action possibilities that can be integrated into a hedged, mutually reinforcing package of preventive policies" (Braithwaite 2002:99–100). In any one case the most appropriate response may be multifaceted, for example, arranging for the offender to have an opportunity to apologize to victims, facilitating a restitution payment plan, organizing community service restitution, arranging a meeting between the offender and police in the community where he will live after his release from prison, and enrolling the offender in a substance abuse treatment program and vocational education workshop.

Improving Follow-through

Many experienced professionals believe that agreements reached in the context of restorative justice are more likely to be implemented than orders handed down by courts of law and other law enforcement officials. The reason, presumably, is that "voluntary commitment works better than state orders, that the open discussion of consequences that need to be put right motivates that commitment, and that when aunts and uncles offer to monitor implementation of an agreement they are generally more capable of doing so than the police" (Braithwaite 2002:102). Braithwaite (2002) offers a useful example of how circles can produce effective follow-through; it is drawn from the fieldwork notes of a researcher who was investigating the use of restorative justice with juvenile offenders:

> A difference of the north Minneapolis African American circles (run by the northside community justice committee) from other restorative justice programs is that a series of circles are held for each offender. The first is the interview circle at which the offender and his or her parents or guardian meet the circle volunteers and decide whether they wish to participate in the program. The program is described in some detail so as to allow the young person to make an informed choice. The crime itself is not mentioned in this meeting. At this meeting the young person's needs and interests are also considered so that individual members of the circle can begin to act as mentors. So, for instance, in a circle I attended, it was established that the young person was a keen basketballer. Some of the male members of the group were also keen basketballers and said they would come and watch the young offender play. The circle also identified that the young person had a problem with math. Another volunteer said she would assist the young person with his math. If the young person agrees to participate in the program, and the volunteers agree to accept the case, a second circle is held in which the crime is discussed, and a social compact developed (which involves a number of commitments by the young offender). Another circle is held for the victim. A fourth circle is held for the victim and offender—a healing circle. Other circles are then held to monitor completion of the social compact the young person makes, culminating in a celebration circle where the group celebrates the young person's completion of his agreement. (103)

THE RISKS OF RESTORATIVE JUSTICE

The restorative justice movement certainly has many virtues and has a number of potential applications with regard to heinous crime. The movement's emphasis on empowering victims and the community, offender accountability, humane dispositions, dignity, fairness, and due process is impressive. However, we should be mindful of the model's limitations and several potential risks (Braithwaite 2002; Kurki 2000; Umbreit 2000; Umbreit and Coates 2000):

Revictimization. Restorative justice processes have the potential to revictimize victims. Victims might feel pressured to participate in restorative justice options before they are emotionally ready to do so. Prosecutors and defense attorneys may subtly manipulate victims into agreeing to participate in order to work out an alternative to formal court adjudication.

Insensitivity to victims and coercion. Some restorative justice programs fail to pay primary attention to victims. Inadvertently or otherwise, staffers may behave in a way that communicates that offenders' interests prevail over victims' interests. For example, at family group conferences staffers may seat the offender's group first, thus limiting the choices available to the victim's family and supporters, or staffers may begin with the offender's story rather than the victim's. This would undermine one of the restorative justice movement's main goals: to enhance sensitivity to victims' emotional needs.

Lack of neutrality. One of the restorative justice movement's greatest assets is trust and participants' perception that program staffers are neutral. Especially when public officials participate in the process—for example, police, probation officers, and parole officers—one risk is that these individuals will revert to their "official" authoritarian role and abandon their neutrality. Authoritarian behavior can exacerbate destructive, counterproductive shaming rather than promote constructive "reintegrative shaming" (Braithwaite 2002).

Insensitivity and assumed cultural neutrality of the process. Restorative justice processes are being implemented in diverse cultures, such as Canada, South Africa, European countries, the United States, New Zealand, and Australia. It is naive to think that a "one size fits all" curriculum or script is appropriate for all cultural contexts. In fact, variation in cultural norms with respect to communication styles (both verbal and nonverbal), the role of authority, privacy and confidentiality, and mediation requires careful tailoring of restorative justice programs to ensure sensitivity to local cultural norms. Some cultural groups tend to prefer understated and indirect communication, whereas others value more direct messages. Some cultural groups are more comfortable with conversations in which participants interrupt each other. Some cultural groups place much more emphasis on the family and community, whereas others tend to be much more oriented toward individuals.

Inadequate procedural safeguards. Restorative justice programs do not always provide adequate procedural safeguards. Some participants may feel intimidated by the process and do not have an attorney to speak on their behalf or to protect them against exploitation and power imbalances.

Broad discretion. The absence of strict restorative justice standards with regard to appropriate dispositions—comparable to sentencing guidelines—can result in inconsistent results. Some argue that the broad range of discretion exercised by restorative justice staffers is one of the model's principal virtues; others worry that apparent inconsistencies in outcome could undermine actual and potential participants' trust in the process.

Inadequate preparation. Many professionals who administer restorative justice programs prepare diligently. They meet with relevant parties in advance of conferences and build rapport and trust in the process. Some program staffers, however, do not take the time to engage in this essential "prep" work, and participants have left the process feeling frustrated and angry.

——

These concerns and potential risks should not dampen enthusiastic attempts to incorporate restorative justice options in our dealings with offenders who commit heinous crimes. Rather, they should serve as cautionary signals that alert us to potential pitfalls and thus help us shape restorative justice constructively, prudently, and sensitively.

I have learned a great deal during the years I have worked in the criminal justice system. Many ideas that I have today about how best to respond to offenders who commit heinous crimes are similar to those I held at the start of my career. And, not surprisingly, some other ideas have changed over time.

But why the change? For one thing, years and years of reading and hearing media accounts and reviewing police reports, court transcripts, prison inmates' social histories completed by counselors, and victims' testimony and letters describing heinous crimes have a cumulative effect, as I suspect they would for any thoughtful citizen. One by-product of the passage of time and accumulated experience is increased opportunity to hear bad news, and over time one cannot help but notice the growing collection of bad stories. I am not the first person to find that his threshold of tolerance for bad behavior—especially heinous behavior—has gotten lower over time.

Ironically, however, as my tolerance for bad behavior has decreased, my understanding of the reasons why some people behave very badly has grown. Earlier in my career I had a reasonably good intellectual grasp of diverse etiological theories and debates about why people commit crime. Many turns of the clock later I have supplemented this intellectual understanding with the valuable insights one can gain only from extensive experience. In my case that experience is the result of thousands and thousands of conversations with offenders, victims, and their respective family members and loved ones.

When I blend the elements of all that I have learned, and boil the mix down to its essence, I come to several core conclusions. The conclusions themselves are not complicated, although, as this book shows, the paths leading to them are:

- Heinous crimes and the people who commit them come in all shapes and sizes. Offenders include people from every socioeconomic level, racial and ethnic group, national origin, gender, sexual orientation, educational level, and religion. Stereotypes of offenders who commit heinous crimes are very misleading, although some subtypes of heinous crime are correlated with some offender attributes.

- No simple, one-stop-shopping theories explain why people commit heinous crimes. Important factors include the nature of people's desperate circumstances in life (economic and personal); ability to manage anger and control impulses; tendency toward greed, opportunism, and exploitation; ability to avoid harmful and reckless frolic; addictions (drugs, alcohol, and gambling); and level of mental functioning and competence. Variables related to, for example, family circumstances and values, personality, economic resources, discrimination (ethnic, racial, sexual), community, biochemistry, genetics, and education also make a difference.

- How we respond to people who commit heinous crimes should be a function of the circumstances that led to the crimes. People who commit heinous crimes because of their addictions or mental illness warrant a different response than people who commit heinous crimes because of their greed, lack of remorse or insight, or tendency toward reckless frolic. Our use of punishment, imprisonment, rehabilitation, and restorative justice should be selective and tailored to the individual needs of each offender and victim. Adjustments should be made over time as each individual's circumstances change.

- A wish for retribution is an understandable, legitimate human response to a heinous crime. Individual victims, families, and communities have a right to convey the depth of their despair, resentment, indignation, and anger toward the offender. These messages are best delivered in the context of civilized, constructive, and supervised discourse that allows victims to express their feelings fully and provides offenders with an opportunity to apologize and, when feasible, take steps toward reparation. We should avoid vigilante justice at all costs.

- Offenders who commit heinous crimes should be incarcerated. The length of incarceration should depend upon the degree of retribution and punishment warranted by the offense, the circumstances that led to the offense, the offender's remorse and insight, and the likelihood that the offender will recidivate (based on his or her pattern of criminal behavior, psychosocial profile, participation in rehabilitation programs, and so on). Our ability to predict who will and will not reoffend is limited; we do the best we can with the information available to us.

• Rehabilitation can work. Rehabilitation programs will not work in every instance or with every offender. High-quality services delivered by competent professionals to motivated offenders can make an enormous difference. Low-quality services delivered by less-than-competent staff to unmotivated offenders are a waste of time and money.

• Restorative justice is a critical element in the administration of justice. Restorative justice options—such as victim-offender mediation, family group conferencing, community service, and so on—can humanize an otherwise toxic and intimidating process, empower victims and other parties, and achieve a greater degree of fairness than formal criminal justice proceedings tend to yield. Restorative options are not always appropriate in cases involving heinous crime. But restorative justice can be pursued creatively in many cases involving heinous crime.

• Opportunities should be created to enable offenders to feel shame for heinous crimes over which they had considerable control (as opposed to offenders whose crimes are a direct result of their psychiatric illness, for example). The goal of shaming offenders should be to help them accept responsibility, examine their conduct in a constructively critical way, and begin the process of restorative justice. The purpose of shaming should not be destructive.

• Achieving justice in cases involving heinous crime is very hard, especially when the victims, the community, and criminal justice professionals are filled with shock and rage.

My efforts to respond to offenders who commit heinous crimes, and to their victims, have forced me to struggle with many of life's most difficult questions about the value of a life, cruelty, and goodness. Some years ago I stumbled across a book, *Lest Innocent Blood Be Shed*, that taught me that out of the depths of life's worst cruelties one can find veins of goodness. The book's author, a moral philosopher named Philip Hallie, writes about how his preoccupation with the horrors of the Holocaust—the epitome of heinous crimes if there ever was one—led him, inadvertently, to the discovery of remarkable goodness, in the form of a group of non-Jewish villagers in Le Chambon-sur-Lignon in southern France. The villagers, a group of extraordinary altruists, risked their lives to save and protect Jews fleeing Nazi Germany and the Vichy government of France. Hallie (1979) writes about how he felt compelled to explore the goodness in that village, which was surrounded by unspeakable horror:

> I knew that always a certain region of my mind contained an awareness of men and women in bloody white coats breaking and rebreaking the bones of six- or seven- or eight-year-old Jewish children in order, the Nazis said, to study the processes of natural healing in young bodies. All of this I knew. But why not know joy? Why not leave root room for comfort? Why add myself to the millions of victims? Why must life be for me that vision of those children lying there with their children's eyes looking up at the adults who were breaking a leg for the second time, a rib cage for the third time? Something had happened, had happened for years in that mountain village. Why should I be afraid of it? (3–4)

My preoccupation with heinous crime has also led me to some encounters with remarkable goodness. In my case it has been in the form of a relatively small group of truly remarkable offenders who have the ability to apologize sincerely for the horror that they have caused in other people's lives, victims who are somehow able to muster whatever it takes to accept apologies and forgive people who have harmed them terribly, and professionals who have a sensitive, mature commitment to the important work that they do to promote justice.

Without question, laboring in the fields of heinous crime takes its toll. The work can be very depressing, enraging, discouraging, and frustrating. In the midst of it all, however, is a potential for goodness that can be inspirational. Spending years working inside prisons is, I suspect, something like working in a large-city hospital emergency room. One can expect that lots of bad things are going to come through the front door—a steady stream of bad things. Fortunately, some events that appear to loom large turn out to be relative nuisances, like the chest and arm pain, caused by a pinched cervical disk, that masquerades as a heart attack. One deals with the scare, learns how to prevent a recurrence, and moves on. Likewise, a short jail sentence for assaulting an acquaintance while under the influence of alcohol can serve as a much-needed wake-up call for the person who needs to address his serious drinking problem in order to move on with his life.

Sometimes, however, the crisis is much more severe. The severe prison sentence for first-degree homicide is akin to the catastrophic, massive coronary; this thing is not going to go away anytime soon, and it is likely to involve a long haul. In the worst cases the penalty is death.

The wisest emergency room staffers are those who leave at the end of every shift, taking nothing in life for granted and with fresh appreciation of what matters most. So too with prison work involving people who commit heinous crimes. Heinous crime is full of pathos and tragedy. If we are fortunate and wise, contact with heinous crime will teach us about what matters most. And that is the gift that is sometimes embedded in evil.

Notes

1. The Nature of Heinous Crime

1. The inmate to whom I refer here, "Dale Simpson," has authorized this disclosure of details about his crimes and life circumstances. He has asked me to use pseudonyms in order to protect the privacy of his children and former wife.

2. I have edited the syntax, grammar, and punctuation of Dale's letters only slightly to enhance readability.

3. I report the most recent, valid, and reliable data available. For decades scholars have noted the strengths and limitations of various crime data sources. Researchers typically report arrest data—usually using data reported to the FBI by local police departments—while recognizing that not all crimes come to the attention of the police and, further, that police departments do not always report crime data accurately. Well-known differences among police departments can affect the data they report, for example, differences in investigative resources and techniques, police force size, and community tolerance for various crimes. Data obtained from a cross-section of victims provide a useful check; however, victim surveys have their own limitations. Victims do not always recall or report incidents accurately. So-called victimless crimes (for example, drug use, prostitution) are not represented, and murder victims obviously cannot participate.

4. Widespread publicity in recent years about sexual abuse of children by priests and other authority figures has enhanced the public's understanding of sexual molestation of children. Prominent examples include the cases of James R. Porter, John Geoghan, and Louis E. Miller, former Catholic priests who were convicted of abusing children (Robinson 2002).

5. These case examples and many other cases that I present throughout the book are drawn from my work with inmates in several correctional facilities. I have served as a group worker and social worker in a U.S. Bureau of Prisons institution (the Metropolitan Correctional Center in Chicago), a maximum-security state penitentiary in Jefferson City, Missouri, and the forensic unit of the state psychiatric hospital in Rhode Island. Since 1992 I have served on the Rhode Island Parole Board. I have disguised names and other identifying information to ensure anonymity and to protect victims' privacy.

2. Heinous Crime

1. Portions of this discussion of etiological theory are adapted from Reamer (2003a).

2. This typology is based on my direct involvement with more than thirteen thousand cases in my capacity as a member of the Rhode Island Parole Board and my work with offenders in the Metropolitan Correctional Center (U.S. Department of Justice, Federal Bureau of Prisons, Chicago), the Missouri State Penitentiary, and the forensic unit of the Rhode Island Department of Mental Health, Retardation and Hospitals. My analysis uses widely accepted qualitative research methods. The steps included (1) logging data about the criminal offense and the circumstances leading up to it (e.g., murder committed while the offender was under the influence of drugs, marital rape committed in the context of a bitter dispute, robbery committed to obtain money to feed the offender's heroin addiction, arson committed as a vengeful act against a former employer); (2) developing a code book; (3) conducting first-level coding, based on identifying initial conceptual units and placing them in categories; (4) conducting second-level coding, during which I created broader conceptual categories; and (5) looking for meaning and relationships in the data (Holosko 2001; Reamer 1998b; Sherman and Reid 1994; Unrau and Coleman 1997). I have disguised the identities of offenders and victims in most of the case examples that follow to ensure anonymity and to respect privacy. In several instances I report actual names and circumstances that are a matter of public record. Some case examples are based on composite information drawn from more than one case. All case examples are based on actual circumstances.

3. Retribution and Revenge

1. Historically, moral and political philosophers have espoused three different views on the concept of punishment: The retributivist view—often known as the deontological view—reflects the widespread belief that wrongdoers should be punished for punishment's sake and to convey the community's anger, indignation, and resentment. The teleological view (from the Greek *teleios*, "brought to its end or purpose") holds that the purpose of punishment is to bring about a desirable consequence, such as rehabilitation or prevention of future crime. The teleological-retributivist perspective acknowledges the legitimate right of the community to express its indignation and resentment toward those offenders who have the ability to exercise some measure of control over their behavior; further, punishment should serve a constructive purpose beyond retribution, such as public safety, deterrence, and rehabilitation (Ezorsky 1972).

2. As a member of the Rhode Island Parole Board I have met with hundreds and hundreds of victims, who have the opportunity to meet board members in person before an inmate's parole hearing. During these meetings we invite victims to share with us any feelings or opinions they have about the crime, the inmate, and the possibility of parole. I have paraphrased and edited victims' comments to ensure anonymity and to enhance readability. (Several quotations reflect conversations I had with victims during my work in Missouri prisons.)

3. Professional literature on addictions distinguishes between substance dependence and substance abuse. Substance dependence is "a cluster of cognitive, behavioral, and physiological symptoms indicating that the individual continues use of the substance despite significant substance-related problems. There is a pattern of repeated self-administration that can result in tolerance, withdrawal, and compulsive drug-taking behavior" (American Psychiatric Association 2000:192). Substance abuse is "a maladaptive pattern of substance

use manifested by recurrent and significant adverse consequences related to the repeated use of substances. . . . Unlike the criteria for Substance Dependence, the criteria for Substance Abuse do not include tolerance, withdrawal, or a pattern of compulsive use and instead include only the harmful consequences of repeated use" (American Psychiatric Association 2000:198).

4. I distinguish between major mental disorders over which offenders have no or very little control and psychological conditions that are less disabling and over which individuals can reasonably be expected to exercise significant degrees of control. Major mental illnesses primarily include various forms of psychosis, such as schizophrenia and dissociative disorders, where there is evidence of delusions (grossly distorted thinking and cognition, for example, paranoid ideation) or prominent hallucinations (hearing voices, for example). Other psychiatric disorders—such as bipolar disorder—can also be severely disabling and may limit an individual's ability to control his or her behavior. For example, I have spent time with prison inmates in the midst of a manic phase (a feature of bipolar disorder) where it was clear that the inmate had virtually no insight into his manic behavior or ability to control it.

4. Imprisonment

1. In 1998 the FBI began to use the term *criminal homicide* to include all acts of murder (the willful killing of one human being by another) and manslaughter by negligence (the killing of another person through gross negligence). Examples of manslaughter by negligence might include a death that results when a drunk driver plows into a child playing on the sidewalk; a doctor who ignores a patient's serious medical condition; and a parent who neglects an impaired child.

5. Treatment and Rehabilitation

1. To be included in a meta-analysis, a study must include enough information to calculate an effect size. An effect size is a standardized mathematical indicator of the treatment effect of an intervention that takes into account the different methodological approaches of different studies (i.e., samples are weighted according to their size) and such factors as treatment type and client population (Cooper and Hedges 1994; Gaes et al. 1999).

2. For a discussion of the need to assess and monitor offenders' readiness to address issues in their lives, see Reamer (2003a) and Prochaska, Norcross, and DiClemente (1995). Prochaska and his colleagues have developed a useful "stages of change" model that is highly relevant to work with offenders. The model, which is based on extensive empirical research, describes how people modify a problem behavior or engage in positive or desirable behavior. The approach focuses on the individual's emotions, cognitions (ways of thinking), and behaviors and focuses on intentional change. The process involves five specific stages: precontemplation, contemplation, preparation, action, and maintenance. Interventions should be based on realistic assessments of individuals' readiness and motivation to change. Interventions introduced when offenders are not eager or ready to change are not likely to be productive.

3. I am a strong supporter of discretionary parole. Having said this, I think it is important to acknowledge how difficult criminal justice professionals find their attempts to predict which inmates are likely to engage in violent behavior in the future. Multiple studies demonstrate the inaccuracy of such forecasts (Monahan 1981; Monahan and Steadman 1994).

4. Ideally, offenders who are released from prison would experience a gradual transition under strict, extensive parole supervision. However, in some instances release on parole may not be feasible or appropriate, for example, when an inmate's disciplinary record in prison or refusal to participate in rehabilitation programs prohibits parole release. Typically, inmates who serve their entire sentence are released to probation, as opposed to parole, supervision. Ordinarily, the length of probation supervision will coincide with the portion of the offender's sentence that was suspended. In these instances the spirit of recommendations 7–12, which pertain to parole supervision, should be extended to probation supervision.

5. See my discussion of the concepts of calibration and recalibration (Reamer 2003a). I argue that we should initially assess each offender's unique social service, educational, and vocational needs and create conditions designed to help the offender achieve realistic goals, a process that I call calibration. As the offender's circumstances change—for example, as a result of personal or family crises, job loss, substance abuse relapse, commission of a new crime, or any number of positive achievements—we should recalibrate parole conditions. In some instances recalibration will entail shortening the leash with new expectations and requirements (e.g., more frequent meetings with the parole officer, placing the offender on electronic monitoring, requiring more frequent drug screens), and in some instances recalibration will permit lengthening the leash (e.g., reducing the frequency of visits to the parole officer, removing the electronic bracelet, extending the offender's curfew).

6. Restorative, Reparative, and Community Justice

1. Gobodo-Madikizela clearly recognizes that some victims of heinous crimes cannot bring themselves to forgive the perpetrators: "There are many people who find it hard to embrace the idea of forgiveness. And it is easy to see why. In order to maintain some sort of moral compass, to hold on to some sort of clear distinction between what is depraved but conceivable and what is simply off the scale of human acceptability, we feel an inward emotional and mental pressure *not* to forgive, since forgiveness can signal acceptability, and acceptability signals some amount, however small, of condoning" (2003:103). Gobodo-Madikizela goes on to say that "feelings of anger and revenge against those who commit gross abuses are, understandably, easier to develop and to sustain than an attitude that seeks engagement and dialogue. One reason we distance ourselves through anger from those who have hurt us or others we know is the fear that if we engage them as real people, we will be compromising our moral stance and lowering the entry requirements into the human community" (2003:120).

References

Abadinsky, Howard. 2003. *Organized Crime.* 7th ed. Belmont, Calif.: Wadsworth.

Abbott, Jack H. 1981. *In the Belly of the Beast: Letters from Prison.* New York: Random House.

Abel, Charles F., and Frank H. Marsh. 1984. *Punishment and Restitution: A Restitutionary Approach to Crime and the Criminal.* Westport, Conn.: Greenwood.

Abma, Joyce, et al. 1997. "Fertility, Family Planning, and Women's Health: New Data from the 1995 National Survey of Family Growth." *Vital and Health Statistics,* May 1997. National Center for Health Statistics, Centers for Disease Control and Prevention. Available at: http://www.cdc.gov/nchs/data/series/sr_23/sr23_019.pdf (February 4, 2004).

Abrahamsen, David. 1960. *The Psychology of Crime.* New York: Columbia University Press.

Abrams, Karen M. and Gail Erlick Robinson. 2002. "Occupational Effects of Stalking." *Canadian Journal of Psychiatry* 47:168–72.

Albanese, Jay S. 1989. *Organized Crime in America.* 2d ed. Cincinnati: Anderson.

American Psychiatric Association. 1989. *Psychiatric Services in Jails and Prisons.* Task Force Report No. 29. Washington, D.C.: American Psychiatric Association.

———. 2000. *DSM-IV-TR: Diagnostic and Statistical Manual of Mental Disorders.* 4th ed. Washington, D.C.: American Psychiatric Association.

Amir, Menachem. 1971. *Patterns in Forcible Rape.* Chicago: University of Chicago Press.

Anderson v. County of Kern, 45 F.3d 1310 (9th Cir. 1995).

Andrews, D. A., and James Bonta. 1995. *The Level of Service Inventory-Revised.* Toronto: Multi-Health Systems.

———. 1998. *The Psychology of Criminal Conduct.* 2d ed. Cincinnati: Anderson.

Andrews, D. A., et al. 1990. "Does Correctional Treatment Work? A Psychologically Informed Meta-Analysis." *Criminology* 28:369–404.

Annis, Helen M. 1998. "Effective Treatment for Drug and Alcohol Problems: What Do We Know?" In Timothy J. Flanagan, James M. Marquart, and Kenneth G. Adams, eds., *Incarcerating Criminals: Prisons and Jails in Social and Organizational Context,* 174–83. New York: Oxford University Press.

Antonowicz, David, and Robert R. Ross. 1994. "Essential Components of Successful Rehabilitation Programs for Offenders." *International Journal of Offender Therapy and Comparative Criminology* 38:97–104.

Arizona v. Noble, 829 P.2d 1217 (Ariz. 1992).

Arkin, Steven D. 1980. "Discrimination and Arbitrariness in Capital Punishment: An Analysis of Post-*Furman* Murder Cases in Dade County, Florida, 1973–1976." *Stanford Law Review* 33:75–101.

Asch, Solomon E. 1951. "Effects of Group Pressures upon the Modification and Distortion of Judgment." In Harold Guetzkow, ed., *Groups, Leadership, and Man*, 177–90. Pittsburgh: Carnegie Press.

Avi-Itzhak, Benjamin, and Reuel Shinnar. 1973. "Quantitative Models in Crime Control." *Journal of Criminal Justice* 1:185–217.

Bahrenfus v. Bachik, 806 P.2d 170 (Or. Ct. App. 1991).

Bailey, William C., and Ruth D. Peterson. 1999. "Capital Punishment, Homicide, and Deterrence: An Assessment of the Evidence and Extension to Female Homicide." In M. Dwayne Smith and Margaret A. Zahn, eds., *Homicide: A Sourcebook of Social Research*, 257–76. Thousand Oaks, Calif.: Sage.

Baird, Robert M., and Stuart E. Rosenbaum, eds. 1995. *Punishment and the Death Penalty: The Current Debate*. Amherst, N.Y.: Prometheus.

Baldus, David, Charles Pulaski, and George Woodworth. 1983. "Comparative Review of Death Sentences: An Empirical Study of the Georgia Experience." *Journal of Criminal Law and Criminology* 74:661–753.

———. 1985. "Monitoring and Evaluating Contemporary Death Sentencing Systems: Lessons from Georgia." *University of California Davis Law Review* 18:1375–1407.

Baldus, David, George Woodworth, and Charles Pulaski. 1990. *Equal Justice and the Death Penalty*. Boston: Northeastern University Press.

Ball, John, Lawrence Rosen, John Flueck, and David N. Narco. 1982. "Lifetime Criminality of Heroin Addicts in the United States." *Journal of Drug Issues* 12:225–39.

Barbaree, Howard E., and William L. Marshall. 1998. "Treatment of the Sexual Offender." In Robert M. Wettstein, ed., *Treatment of Offenders with Mental Disorders*, 265–328. New York: Guilford.

Barkan, Steven. 2000. *Criminology: A Sociological Understanding*. Englewood Cliffs, N.J.: Prentice-Hall.

Barnhill, Sandra. 1996. "Three Generations at Risk: Imprisoned Women, Their Children, and Grandmother Caregivers." *Generations* 20:39–40.

Baunach, Phyllis Jo. 1985. *Mothers in Prison*. New Brunswick, N.J.: Transaction Books.

Baxstrom v. Herold, 383 U.S. 107 (1966).

Bazemore, Gordon, and Lode Walgrave, eds. 1999. *Restorative Juvenile Justice: Repairing the Harm of Youth Crime*. Monsey, N.Y.: Criminal Justice Press.

Bean, Philip. 1981. *Punishment: A Philosophical and Criminological Inquiry*. Oxford: Robertson.

Beccaria, Cesare. 1963. *On Crimes and Punishments*. Translated by Henry Paolucci. 1764. Reprint. Indianapolis: Bobbs-Merrill.

Beck, Allen J. 2000. *State and Federal Prisoners Returning to the Community: Findings from the Bureau of Justice Statistics*. Washington, D.C.: Department of Justice, Bureau of Justice Statistics.

Beck, Allen J., and Paige M. Harrison. 2001. "Prisoners in 2000." *Bureau of Justice Statistics Bulletin*, August, 1–66.

Becker, Howard. 1963. *Outsiders: Studies in the Sociology of Deviance*. New York: Free Press.

———, ed. 1964. *The Other Side: Perspectives on Deviance*. New York: Free Press.

Beirne-Smith, Mary, James R. Patton, and Richard F. Ittenbach. 2001. *Mental Retardation.* Englewood Cliffs, N.J.: Prentice-Hall.

Bentham, Jeremy. 1973. *An Introduction to the Principles of Morals and Legislation.* 1789. Reprint. New York: Anchor.

Bequai, August. 1979. *Organized Crime: The Fifth Estate.* Lexington, Mass.: Heath.

Bernard, Thomas J., George B. Vold, and Jeffrey B. Snipes. 2002. *Theoretical Criminology.* 2d ed. New York: Oxford University Press.

Bidinotto, Robert J. 1998. "Capital Punishment Is Moral." In Mary E. Williams, ed., *Capital Punishment,* 18–24. San Diego: Greenhaven.

Bies, Robert J., and Thomas M. Tripp. 1996. "Beyond Distrust: 'Getting Even' and the Need for Revenge." In Roderick M. Kramer and Tom T. Tyler, eds., *Trust in Organizations: Frontiers of Theory and Research,* 246–60. Thousand Oaks, Calif.: Sage.

Bies, Robert J., Thomas M. Tripp, and Roderick M. Kramer. 1997. "At the Breaking Point: Cognitive and Social Dynamics of Revenge in Organizations." In Robert A. Giacalone and Jerald Greenberg, eds., *Antisocial Behavior in Organizations,* 18–36. Thousand Oaks, Calif.: Sage.

Black, Lisa, and Rex W. Huppke. 2003. "District Expels 31 for Hazing." *Chicago Tribune,* May 27. Available at: http://www.chicagotribune.com/news/local/chi-0305270217may27,1,6137057.story?coll=chi%2Dnews%2Dhed (January 26, 2004).

Blanshard, Brand. 1968. "Retribution Revisited." In Edward H. Madden, Rollo Handy, and Marvin Farber, eds., *Philosophical Perspectives on Punishment,* 59–89. Springfield, Ill.: Thomas.

Blaszczynski, Alex, and Derrick Silove. 1995. "Cognitive and Behavioral Therapies for Pathological Gambling." *Journal of Gambling Studies* 11:195–200.

Bloch, Herbert A., and Gilbert Geis. 1970. *Man, Crime, and Society.* 2d ed. New York: Random House.

Blomberg, Thomas G., and Stanley Cohen. 1995. *Punishment and Social Control.* Hawthorne, N.Y.: Aldine de Gruyter.

Bloom, Barbara, and David Steinhart. 1993. *Why Punish the Children? A Reappraisal of the Children of Incarcerated Mothers in America.* San Francisco: National Council on Crime and Delinquency.

Bloom, Joseph D., and William H. Wilson. 2000. "Offenders with Schizophrenia." In Sheilagh Hodgins and Rudiger Muller-Isberner, eds., *Violence, Crime, and Mentally Disordered Offenders: Concepts and Methods for Effective Treatment and Prevention,* 113–30. Chichester, Eng.: Wiley.

Blume, Sheila. 1995. "Pathological Gambling." *British Medical Journal* 311:522–23.

Blumstein, Alfred, and Allen J. Beck. 1999. "Population Growth in U.S. Prisons, 1980–1996." In Michael Tonry and Joan Petersilia, eds., *Prisons,* 17–62. Chicago: University of Chicago Press.

Blumstein, Alfred, and Richard Rosenfeld. 1998. "Explaining Recent Trends in U.S. Homicide Rates." *Journal of Criminal Law and Criminology* 88:1175–1216.

Blumstein, Alfred, Jacqueline Cohen, Jeffrey Roth, and Christy Visher, eds. 1986. *Criminal Careers and "Career Criminals."* Report of the National Academy of Sciences Panel on Research on Criminal Careers. Washington, D.C.: National Academy Press.

Bonger, Willem. 1969. *Criminality and Economic Conditions.* 1910. Reprint. Bloomington: Indiana University Press.

Booth, Stephanie. 2001. "I Was Raped." In Mary E. Williams, ed., *Rape*, 120–22. San Diego: Greenhaven.

Bottoms, Anthony E. 1999. "Interpersonal Violence and Social Order in Prison." In Michael Tonry and Joan Petersilia, eds., *Prisons*, 205–81. Chicago: University of Chicago Press.

Bowers, William. 1983. "The Pervasiveness of Arbitrariness and Discrimination Under Post-*Furman* Capital Statutes." *Journal of Criminal Law and Criminology* 74:1067–1100.

Bowers, William, and Glenn Pierce. 1980. "Arbitrariness and Discrimination Under Post-*Furman* Capital Statutes." *Crime and Delinquency* 26:563–75.

Bowker, Lee H. 1982. "Victimizers and Victims in American Correctional Institutions." In Robert Johnson and Hans Toch, eds., *The Pains of Imprisonment*, 63–76. Beverly Hills, Calif.: Sage.

Bradford, John M. 1982. "Arson: A Clinical Study." *Canadian Journal of Psychiatry* 27:188–93.

Bradley, Francis H. 1927. *Ethical Studies*. 2d ed. London: Oxford University Press.

Braithwaite, John. 1989. *Crime, Shame, and Reintegration*. New York: Cambridge University Press.

———. 1998. "Restorative Justice." In Michael Tonry, ed., *The Handbook of Crime and Punishment*, 323–44. New York: Oxford University Press.

———. 1999. "Restorative Justice: Assessing Optimistic and Pessimistic Accounts." In Michael Tonry, ed., *Crime and Justice: A Review of Research*, 25:1–127. Chicago: University of Chicago Press.

———. 2002. *Restorative Justice and Responsive Regulation*. New York: Oxford University Press.

Brettschneider, Corey L. 2001. *Punishment, Property, and Justice*. Aldershot, Eng.: Ashgate.

Brewer, Ann M. 2000. "Road Rage: What, Who, When, Where, and How?" *Transport Reviews* 20:49–64.

Brown, Angela K. 2003. "Driver Guilty of Murder in Windshield Death." *Providence (R.I.) Journal*, June 17, A-3.

Browne, Angela, Kirk R. Williams, and Donald G. Dutton. 1999. "Homicide Between Intimate Partners." In M. Dwayne Smith and Margaret A. Zahn, eds., *Studying and Preventing Homicide*, 55–78. Thousand Oaks, Calif.: Sage.

Browne, Dorothy. 1989. "Incarcerated Mothers and Parenting." *Journal of Family Violence* 4:211–21.

Bullough, Vern L. 1973. *The Subordinate Sex: A History of Attitudes Toward Women*. Urbana: University of Illinois Press.

Bureau of Justice Statistics. 2003a. *Criminal Victimization in the United States—Statistical Tables*. National Crime Victimization Survey. Available at: http://www.ojp.usdoj.gov/bjs/abstract/cvusst.htm (January 19, 2004).

———. 2003b. *Prison Statistics: Summary Findings*. Available at: http://www.ojp.usdoj.gov/bjs/prisons.htm (January 19, 2004).

———. 2003c. "Persons Under Correctional Supervision," sec. 6. In *Sourcebook of Criminal Justice Statistics Online*. Available at: http://www.albany.edu/sourcebook/section6.pdf (June 17, 2003).

———. 2004. "Sexual Assault of Young Children as Reported to Law Enforcement: Victim, Incident, and Offender Characteristics." In *Incidence-based Statistics*. Available at: http://www.ojp.usdoj.gov/bjs/abstract/saycrle.htm (January 19, 2004).

Burgess, Ernest W. 1925. "The Growth of the City." In Robert E. Park, Ernest W. Burgess, and Robert D. McKenzie, eds., *The City*, 47–62. Chicago: University of Chicago Press.

Bushway, Shawn, and Peter Reuter. 2002. "Labor Markets and Crime." In James Q. Wilson and Joan Petersilia, eds., *Crime: Public Policies for Crime Control*, 191–224. San Francisco: ICS Press.

Callahan, Sidney. 1997. "Oh, Behave!" *Commonweal* 126:8–9.

Campbell, Bruce A. 1980. "A Theoretical Approach to Peer Influence in Adolescent Socialization." *American Journal of Political Science* 24:324–44.

Canterino v. Wilson, 546 F. Supp. 174 (W.D. Ky. 1982).

Caplow, Theodore, and Jonathan Simon. 1999. "Understanding Prison Policy and Population Trends." In Michael Tonry and Joan Petersilia, eds., *Prisons*, 63–120. Chicago: University of Chicago Press.

Carlson, Bonnie, and Neil Cervera. 1991. "Inmates and Their Families." *Criminal Justice and Behavior* 18:318–31.

Carpenter, William A., and Edwin P. Hollander. 1982. "Overcoming Hurdles to Independence in Groups." *Journal of Social Psychology* 117:237–41.

Carter, Madeline M., and Ann Ley. 2001. "Making It Work: Developing Tools to Carry Out the Policy." In Madeline M. Carter, ed., *Responding to Parole and Probation Violations*, 51–71. Silver Spring, Md.: Center for Effective Public Policy.

Casey v. Lewis, 834 F. Supp. 1477 (D. Ariz. 1993).

Cavanaugh, James, and Orest Wasyliw. 1985. "Adjustment of the Not Guilty by Reason of Insanity (NGRI) Outpatient: An Initial Report." *Journal of Forensic Sciences* 30:24–30.

Challeen, Dennis A., and James H. Heinlen. 1978. "The Win-onus Restitution Program." In Burt Galaway and Joe Hudson, eds., *Offender Restitution in Theory and Action*, 151–59. Lexington, Mass.: Lexington.

Chambliss, William J. 1975. "Toward a Political Economy of Crime." *Theory and Society* 2:152–53.

Clemmer, Donald. 1940. *The Prison Community*. Boston: Christopher.

Clinard, Marshall B., and Richard Quinney. 1973. *Criminal Behavior Systems: A Typology*. 2d ed. New York: Holt, Rinehart and Winston.

Clinard, Marshall B., Richard Quinney, and John Wildeman. 1994. *Criminal Behavior Systems: A Typology*. 3d ed. Cincinnati: Anderson.

Cloward, Richard, and Lloyd Ohlin. 1960. *Delinquency and Opportunity: A Theory of Delinquent Gangs*. New York: Free Press.

Cohen, Albert K. 1955. *Delinquent Boys*. New York: Free Press.

Cohen, Stanley, and Laurie Taylor. 1972. *Psychological Survival: The Experience of Long-Term Imprisonment*. New York: Vintage.

Coleman v. Wilson, 912 F. Supp. 1282 (E.D. Cal. 1995).

Commonwealth v. Davis, 551 N.E.2d 39 (Mass. 1990).

Commonwealth v. Wiseman, 249 N.E.2d 610 (Mass. 1969).

Consedine, Jim. 1995. *Restorative Justice: Healing the Effects of Crime*. Lyttleton, N.Z.: Ploughshares.

Cooke, David J. 1998. "Prison Violence: A Scottish Perspective." In Timothy J. Flanagan, James M. Marquart, and Kenneth G. Adams, eds., *Incarcerating Criminals: Prisons and Jails in Social and Organizational Context*, 106–17. New York: Oxford University Press.

Cooper, Harris, and Larry V. Hedges, eds. 1994. *The Handbook of Research Synthesis.* New York: Russell Sage Foundation.

Costanzo, Mark. 1998. "Capital Punishment Is Not Morally Justified." In Mary E. Williams, ed., *Capital Punishment,* 35–41. San Diego: Greenhaven.

Crocker, Anne G., and Shielagh Hodgins. 1997. "The Criminality of Noninstitutionalized Mentally Retarded Persons: Evidence from a Birth Cohort Followed to Age 30." *Criminal Justice and Behavior* 24:432–54.

Crutchfield, Robert D., Charles Kubrin, and George S. Bridges, eds. 2000. *Crime.* Thousand Oaks, Calif.: Pine Forge Press.

Cullen, Francis T., and Paul Gendreau. 1989. "The Effectiveness of Correctional Rehabilitation: Reconsidering the 'Nothing Works' Debate." In Lynne Goodstein and Doris Layton MacKenzie, eds., *The American Prison: Issues in Research and Policy,* 23–44. New York: Plenum.

Cullen, Francis T., Bonnie S. Fisher, and Brandon K. Applegate. 2000. "Public Opinion About Punishment and Corrections." In Michael Tonry, ed., *Crime and Justice: A Review of Research,* 27:1–79. Chicago: University of Chicago Press.

Custer, Robert L., and Harry Milt. 1985. *When Luck Runs Out: Help for Compulsive Gamblers and Their Families.* New York: Warner.

Dagger, Richard. 1995. "Playing Fair with Punishment." In Robert M. Baird and Stuart E. Rosenbaum, eds., *Punishment and the Death Penalty: The Current Debate,* 77–92. Amherst, N.Y.: Prometheus.

Daro, Deborah. 1995. "Current Trends in Child Abuse Reporting and Fatalities: NCPCAs 1994 Annual Fifty State Survey." *APSAC Advisor* 8: 5–6.

Darwin, Charles. 1963. *On the Origin of Species by Means of Natural Selection.* 1859. Reprint. New York: Heritage.

Davis, Marion. 2002. "Mollicone: Pride, Vanity, Greed Took Over." *Providence (R.I.) Journal,* September 19, B-1.

Dickerson, Mary, and Ellen Baron. 2000. "Contemporary Issues and Future Directions for Research into Pathological Gambling." *Addiction* 95:1145–59.

Dietz, Park E. 1986. "Mass, Serial, and Sensational Homicides." *Bulletin of the New York Academy of Medicine* 62:477–91.

Ditton, Paula M. 1999. *Mental Health and Treatment of Inmates and Probationers.* Washington, D.C.: Department of Justice, Bureau of Justice Statistics.

Doe v. Gainer, 642 N.E.2d 114 (Ill. 1994).

Doe v. Gaughan, 808 F.2d 871 (1st Cir. 1986).

Doe v. Poritz, 662 A.2d 367 (N.J. 1995).

Douglas, John E., Ann W. Burgess, Allen G. Burgess, and Robert K. Ressler. 1997. *Crime Classification Manual: A Standard System for Investigating and Classifying Violent Crimes.* San Francisco: Jossey-Bass.

Douglas, Scott C., and Mark J. Martinko. 2001. "Exploring the Role of Individual Differences in the Prediction of Workplace Aggression." *Journal of Applied Psychology* 86:547–59.

Draper, Robert. 2003. "The Toxic Pharmacist." *New York Times Magazine,* June 8, 83–86.

Dugdale, Robert. 1877. *The Jukes: A Study in Crime, Pauperism, and Heredity.* New York: Putnam.

Dukes, Richard L., Stephanie L. Clayton, Lessie T. Jenkins, Thomas L. Miller, and Susan E. Rodgers. 2001. "Effects of Aggressive Driving and Driver Characteristics on Road Rage." *Social Science Journal* 38:323–31.

Durkheim, Emile. 1951. *Suicide*. New York: Free Press.

———. 1964. *The Division of Labor in Society*. New York: Free Press.

Dvoskin, Joel A. and Raymond F. Patterson. 1998. "Administration of Treatment Programs for Offenders with Mental Disorders." In Robert M. Wettstein, ed., *Treatment of Offenders with Mental Disorders*, 1–43. New York: Guilford.

Edelhertz, Herbert. 1970. *The Nature, Impact, and Prosecution of White-Collar Crime*. Report prepared for the National Institute of Law Enforcement and Criminal Justice. Washington, D.C.: Government Printing Office.

Ehrlich, Isaac. 1975. "The Deterrent Effect of Capital Punishment: A Question of Life and Death." *American Economic Review* 65:397–417.

Ellison, Patricia A., John McGovern, Herbert L. Petri, and Michael H. Figler. 1995. "Anonymity and Aggressive Driving Behavior: A Field Study." *Journal of Social Behavior and Personality* 10:265–72.

Etzioni, Amitai. 1999. "Shaming Criminals: An Alternative Punishment." *Current*, November 1, 7–11.

Ezorsky, Gertrude, ed. 1972. *Philosophical Perspectives on Punishment*. Albany: State University of New York Press.

Farrington, David P. 1998. "Individual Differences and Offending." In Michael Tonry, ed., *The Handbook of Crime and Punishment*, 241–68. New York: Oxford University Press.

"Father Accused of Murder Attempt." 2003. *Providence (R.I.) Journal*, June 24, A-3.

FBI. 2003. *Crime in the United States, 2002: Uniform Crime Reports*. Available at: http://www.fbi.gov/ucr/cius_02/pdf/ofront.pdf (January 19, 2004).

Feierman, Jay R. 1990. *Pedophilia: Biosocial Dimensions*. New York: Springer.

Feinberg, Joel. 1965. "The Expressive Function of Punishment." *Monist* 49:397–408.

———. 1970. *Doing and Deserving: Essays on the Theory of Responsibility*. Princeton, N.J.: Princeton University Press.

Ferraro, Kathleen, John Johnson, Stephen Jorgenson, and F. G. Bolton. 1983. "Problems of Prisoners' Families: The Hidden Costs of Imprisonment." *Journal of Family Issues* 4:575–91.

Festinger, Leon, Stanley Schachter, and Kurt Bach. 1950. *Social Pressures in Informal Groups*. New York: Harper.

Finkelhor, David, and Kersti Yilo. 1995. "Types of Marital Rape." In Patricia Searles and Ronald J. Berger, eds., *Rape and Society: Readings on the Problem of Sexual Assault*, 152–59. Boulder, Colo.: Westview.

Finkelhor, David, Gerald T. Hotaling, I. A. Lewis, and Christine Smith. 1990. "Sexual Abuse in a National Survey of Adult Men and Women: Prevalence, Characteristics, and Risk Factors." *Child Abuse and Neglect* 14:19–28.

Fishman, Laura T. 1990. *Women at the Wall: A Study of Prisoners' Wives Doing Time on the Outside*. Albany: State University of New York Press.

Flanagan, Timothy J., James M. Marquart, and Kenneth G. Adams, eds. 1998. *Incarcerating Criminals: Prisons and Jails in Social and Organizational Context*. New York: Oxford University Press.

Florida DHRS v. Schreiber, 561 So. 2d 1236 (Fla. Dist. Ct. App. 1990).

Fox, James. 1982. "Women in Prison: A Case Study in the Social Reality of Stress." In Robert Johnson and Hans Toch, eds., *The Pains of Imprisonment*, 205–20. Beverly Hills, Calif.: Sage.

Fox, James A., and Jack Levin. 1998. "Multiple Homicide: Patterns of Serial and Mass Murder." In Michael Tonry, ed., *Crime and Justice: A Review of Research*, 23:407–55. Chicago: University of Chicago Press.

———. 1999. "Serial Murder: Myths and Realities." In M. Dwayne Smith and Margaret A. Zahn, eds., *Studying and Preventing Homicide*, 79–96. Thousand Oaks, Calif.: Sage.

Fox, James A., and Marianne W. Zawitz. 2002. "Homicide Trends in the United States." Department of Justice, Bureau of Justice Statistics. Available at: http://www.ojp.usdoj.gov/bjs/homicide/homtrnd.htm (January 19, 2004).

———. 2003. *Crime Data Brief: Homicide Trends in the United States: 2000 Update*. Washington, D.C.: Department of Justice, Bureau of Justice Statistics.

Frankel, Marvin E. 1973. *Criminal Sentences: Law Without Order*. New York: Hill and Wang.

Frankfurt, Harry. 1973. "Coercion and Moral Responsibility." In Ted Honderich, ed., *Essays on Freedom of Action*, 63–86. London: Routledge and Kegan Paul.

Frazier, Shervert H., and Arthur C. Carr. 1974. *Introduction to Psychopathology*. New York: Aronson.

Friedken, Noah E., and Karen S. Cook. 1990. "Peer Group Influence." *Sociological Methods and Research* 19:122–43.

Gabel, Katherine, and Denise Johnston, eds. 1995. *Children of Incarcerated Parents*. New York: Lexington.

Gaes, Gerald G. 1998. "Correctional Treatment." In Michael Tonry, ed., *The Handbook of Crime and Punishment*, 712–38. New York: Oxford University Press.

Gaes, Gerald G., Timothy J. Flanagan, Laurence L. Motiuk, and Lynn Stewart. 1999. "Adult Correctional Treatment." In Michael Tonry and Joan Petersilia, eds., *Prisons*, 361–426. Chicago: University of Chicago Press.

Galaway, Burt, and Joe Hudson, eds. 1978. *Offender Restitution in Theory and Action*. Lexington, Mass.: Lexington.

———. 1996. *Restorative Justice: International Perspectives*. Monsey, N.Y.: Criminal Justice Press.

Gardner, William I., Janice L. Graeber, and Susan J. Machkovitz. 1998. "Treatment of Offenders with Mental Retardation." In Robert M. Wettstein, ed., *Treatment of Offenders with Mental Disorders*, 329–64. New York: Guilford.

Gaylin, Willard. 1982. *The Killing of Bonnie Garland*. New York: Simon and Schuster.

Gelernter, David. 1998. "Capital Punishment Is Reasonable." In Mary E. Williams, ed., *Capital Punishment*, 25–30. San Diego: Greenhaven.

Gelles, Richard J. 1998. "Family Violence." In Michael Tonry, ed., *The Handbook of Crime and Punishment*, 178–206. New York: Oxford University Press.

Gelles, Richard J., and Murray Straus. 1987. "Is Violence Towards Children Increasing? A Comparison of 1975 and 1985 National Survey Rates." *Journal of Interpersonal Violence* 2:212–22.

Gendreau, Paul, and Robert R. Ross. 1987. "Revivification of Rehabilitation: Evidence from the 1980s." *Justice Quarterly* 4:349–407.

General Accounting Office. 1990. *Death Penalty Sentencing: Research Indicates Pattern of Racial Disparities*. Washington, D.C.: Government Printing Office.

Gibbons, Don C. 1982. *Society, Crime, and Criminal Behavior*. 4th ed. Englewood Cliffs, N.J.: Prentice-Hall.

Gifis, Steven H. 1991. *Law Dictionary*. 3d ed. Hauppauge, N.Y.: Barron's.

Ginet, Carl. 1962. "Can the Will Be Caused?" *Philosophical Review* 71:49–55.

Glaser, Daniel. 1978. *Crime in Our Changing Society*. New York: Holt, Rinehart and Winston.

Glatz v. Kort, 807 F.2d 1514 (10th Cir. 1986).

Glueck, Sheldon, and Eleanor Glueck. 1956. *Physique and Delinquency.* New York: Harper & Row.

Gobodo-Madikizela, Pumla. 2003. *A Human Being Died That Night: A South African Story of Forgiveness.* Boston: Houghton Mifflin.

Goddard, Henry H. 1912. *The Kallikak Family.* New York: Macmillan.

Goldstein, Paul. 1985. "The Drug/Violence Nexus: A Tripartite Concept Framework." *Journal of Drug Issues* 14:493–506.

Goldstein, Paul, Henry Brownstein, and Patrick Ryan. 1992. "Drug-Related Homicide in New York: 1984 and 1988." *Crime and Delinquency* 38:459–76.

Goring, Charles. 1913. *The English Convict.* London: His Majesty's Stationery Office.

Gottfredson, Michael R., and Travis Hirschi. 1990. *A General Theory of Crime.* Stanford, Calif.: Stanford University Press.

Green v. Baron, 879 F.2d 305 (8th Cir. 1989).

Greenfeld, Lawrence A. 1998. *Alcohol and Crime.* Washington, D.C.: Department of Justice, Bureau of Justice Statistics.

Greenfield, Lawrence A., and Tracy L. Snell. 1999. *Women Offenders.* Washington, D.C.: Department of Justice, Bureau of Justice Statistics.

Gross, Samuel R., and Robert Mauro. 1984. "Patterns of Death: An Analysis of Racial Disparities in Capital Sentencing and Homicide Victimization." *Stanford Law Review* 37:27–153.

———. 1989. *Death and Discrimination: Racial Disparities in Capital Sentencing.* Boston: Northeastern University Press.

Guy, Edward, Jerome Platt, Israel Zwerling, and Samuel Bullock. 1985. "Mental Health Status of Prisoners in an Urban Jail." *Criminal Justice and Behavior* 12:29–53.

Hacker, Frederick. 1976. *Crusaders, Criminals, and Crazies.* New York: Norton.

Hafemeister, Thomas L. 1998. "Legal Aspects of the Treatment of Offenders with Mental Disorders." In Robert M. Wettstein, ed., *Treatment of Offenders with Mental Disorders,* 44–125. New York: Guilford.

Hagan, Frank E. 1990. *Introduction to Criminology.* 2d ed. Chicago: Nelson-Hall.

Hagan, John. 1994. *Crime and Disrepute.* Thousand Oaks, Calif.: Pine Forge Press.

Hagan, John, and Ronit Dinovitzer. 1999. "Collateral Consequences of Imprisonment for Children, Communities, and Prisoners." In Michael Tonry and Joan Petersilia, eds., *Prisons,* 121–62. Chicago: University of Chicago Press.

Hagan, Michele P., Robert P. King and Ronald L. Patros. 1994. "The Efficacy of a Serious Sex Offenders Treatment Program for Adolescent Rapists." *International Journal of Offender Therapy and Comparative Criminology* 38:141–50.

Hairston, Creasie Finney. 1989. "Men in Prison: Family Characteristics and Parenting Views." *Journal of Offender Counseling, Services and Rehabilitation* 14:23–30.

———. 1991. "Family Ties During Imprisonment: Important to Whom and for What?" *Journal of Sociology and Social Welfare* 18:87–104.

———. 1998. "The Forgotten Parent: Understanding the Forces that Influence Incarcerated Fathers' Relationships with Their Children." *Child Welfare* 77:617–39.

Hale, Donna C. 1988. "The Impact of Mothers' Incarceration on the Family System: Research and Recommendations." *Marriage and Family Review* 2:143–54.

Hallie, Philip P. 1979. *Lest Innocent Blood Be Shed: The Story of the Village of Le Chambon and How Goodness Happened There.* New York: Harper & Row.

Hancock, Roger N. 1974. *Twentieth Century Ethics.* New York: Columbia University Press.

Harmes, Roberta. 1999. "Marital Rape: A Selected Bibliography." *Violence Against Women* 5:1082–83.

Harris, Patricia M. 1994. "Client Management Classification and Prediction of Probation Outcome." *Crime and Delinquency* 40:154–74.

Harrison, Lana, and Joseph Gfroerer. 1992. "The Intersection of Drug Use and Criminal Behavior: Results from the National Household Survey on Drug Abuse." *Crime and Delinquency* 38:422–43.

Harrison, Paige M., and Jennifer C. Karberg. 2003. *Prison and Jail Inmates at Midyear 2002*. Washington, D.C.: Department of Justice, Bureau of Justice Statistics.

Hart, H. L. A. 1968. *Punishment and Responsibility: Essays in the Philosophy of Law*. New York: Oxford University Press.

Heide, Kathleen M. 1999. "Youth Homicide." In M. Dwayne Smith and Margaret A. Zahn, eds., *Studying and Preventing Homicide*, 175–96. Thousand Oaks, Calif.: Sage.

Heilbrun, Kirk, and Patricia A. Griffin. 1998. "Community-Based Forensic Treatment." In Robert M. Wettstein, ed., *Treatment of Offenders with Mental Disorders*, 168–210. New York: Guilford.

Henberg, Marvin. 1990. *Retribution: Evil for Evil in Ethics, Law, and Literature*. Philadelphia: Temple University Press.

Hirschi, Travis. 1969. *Causes of Delinquency*. Berkeley: University of California Press.

Hodgins, Sheilagh, and Rudiger Muller-Isberner, eds. 2000. *Violence, Crime, and Mentally Disordered Offenders: Concepts and Methods for Effective Treatment and Prevention*. Chichester, Eng.: Wiley.

Holmes, Ronald M., and James DeBurger. 1988. *Serial Murder*. Newbury Park, Calif.: Sage.

Holmes, Ronald M., and Stephen T. Holmes. 1994. *Murder in America*. Thousand Oaks, Calif.: Sage.

Holosko, Michael J. 2001. "Overview of Qualitative Research Methods." In Bruce Thyer, ed., *The Handbook of Social Work Research Methods*, 263–72. Thousand Oaks, Calif.: Sage.

Hood, Roger. 1998. "Capital Punishment." In Michael Tonry, ed., *The Handbook of Crime and Punishment*, 739–76. New York: Oxford University Press.

Hoptowit v. Ray, 682 F.2d 1237 (9th Cir. 1982).

Hospers, John. 1966. "What Means This Freedom?" In Bernard Berofsky, ed., *Free Will and Determinism*, 54–63. New York: Harper & Row.

Hudson, Joe, and Burt Galaway. 1978. Introduction to Burt Galaway and Joe Hudson, eds., *Offender Restitution in Theory and Action*, 1–11. Lexington, Mass.: Lexington.

Idaho v. Hargis, 889 P.2d 1117 (Idaho Ct. App. 1995).

Information Plus. 1995. "A General History of Capital Punishment in the United States." In Robert M. Baird and Stuart E. Rosenbaum, eds., *Punishment and the Death Penalty: The Current Debate*, 103–10. Amherst, N.Y.: Prometheus.

In re Blodgett, 510 N.W.2d 910 (Minn. 1994).

In re G. S., 551 N.E.2d 337 (Ill. App. Ct. 1990).

In re Martin B., 525 N.Y.S.2d 469 (N.Y. Sup. Ct. 1987).

Jackson v. Indiana, 406 U.S. 715 (1972).

Jacobs, James B. 1977. *Stateville: The Penitentiary in Mass Society*. Chicago: University of Chicago Press.

Jacobs, James B., and Christopher Panarella. 1998. "Organized Crime." In Michael Tonry, ed., *The Handbook of Crime and Punishment,* 159–77. New York: Oxford University Press.

Janis, Irving. 1972. *Victims of Groupthink.* Boston: Houghton Mifflin.

Johnson, Robert. 1982. "Life Under Sentence of Death." In Robert Johnson and Hans Toch, eds., *The Pains of Imprisonment,* 129–45. Beverly Hills, Calif.: Sage.

———. 1987. *Hard Time: Understanding and Reforming the Prison.* Pacific Grove, Calif.: Brooks/Cole.

———. 1998. "Execution Is Inhumane." In Mary E. Williams, ed., *Capital Punishment,* 42–49. San Diego: Greenhaven.

Johnson, Robert, and Hans Toch, eds. 1982. *The Pains of Imprisonment.* Beverly Hills, Calif.: Sage.

Jones v. Murray, 962 F.2d 302 (4th Cir. 1992).

Jones v. United States, 463 U.S. 354 (1983).

Kansas v. Hendricks, 117 S. Ct. 2072 (1997).

Kant, Immanuel. 1887. *The Philosophy of Law.* Translated by W. Hastie. Edinburgh: Clark.

Karter, Michael, Jr. 2001. *Fire Loss in the United States During 2000.* Quincy, Mass.: National Fire Protection Association.

Keldgord, Robert. 1978. "Community Restitution Comes to Arizona." In Burt Galaway and Joe Hudson, eds., *Offender Restitution in Theory and Action,* 161–66. Lexington, Mass.: Lexington.

Kercher, Glen A., and Marilyn McShane. 1984. "The Prevalence of Child Sexual Abuse Victimization in an Adult Sample of Texas Residents." *Child Abuse and Neglect* 8:495–501.

Kessler, Ronald, Amanda Sonnega, Evelyn Bromet, and Michael Hughes. 1995. "Posttraumatic Stress Disorder in the National Comorbidity Survey." *Archives of General Psychiatry* 52:1048–60.

Keve, Paul. 1978. "The Therapeutic Uses of Restitution." In Burt Galaway and Joe Hudson, eds., *Offender Restitution in Theory and Action,* 59–64. Lexington, Mass.: Lexington.

Kilpatrick, Dean, Christine N. Edmunds, and Anne Seymour. 1992. *Rape in America: A Report to the Nation.* Arlington, Va.: National Victim Center.

Kilpatrick, Dean G., et al. 1985. "Mental Health Correlates of Criminal Victimization: A Random Community Survey." *Journal of Consulting and Clinical Psychology* 53:866–73.

Kim, Sung Hee, and Richard H. Smith. 1993. "Revenge and Conflict Escalation." *Negotiation Journal* 9:37–43.

King, Anthony. 1993. "The Impact of Incarceration on African American Families: Implications for Practice." *Families in Society* 74:145–53.

King, Roy D. 1998. "Prisons." In Michael Tonry, ed., *The Handbook of Crime and Punishment,* 589–625. New York: Oxford University Press.

Klein, Lawrence, Brian E. Forst, and Victor Filatov. 1978. "The Deterrent Effect of Capital Punishment: An Assessment of the Estimates." In Alfred Blumstein, Jacqueline Cohen, and Daniel Nagin, eds., *Deterrence and Incapacitation: Estimating the Effects of Criminal Sanctions on Crime Rates,* 336–60. Washington, D.C.: National Academy of Sciences.

Klein, Malcolm. 1998. "Street Gangs." In Michael Tonry, ed., *The Handbook of Crime and Punishment,* 111–32. New York: Oxford University Press.

Kluft, Richard P., and Catherine G. Fine, eds. 1993. *Clinical Perspectives on Multiple Personality Disorder.* Washington, D.C.: American Psychiatric Press.

Knecht v. Gillman, 488 F.2d 1136 (8th Cir. 1973).

Knight v. Mills, 836 F.2d 659 (1st Cir. 1987).

Kretschmer, Ernst. 1926. *Physique and Character.* Translated by W. J. H. Sprott. New York: Harcourt, Brace.

Kulow v. Nix, 28 F.3d 855 (8th Cir. 1994).

Kupers, Terry. 1999. *Prison Madness: The Mental Health Crisis Behind Bars and What We Must Do About It.* San Francisco: Jossey-Bass.

Kurki, Leena. 2000. "Restorative and Community Justice in the United States." In Michael Tonry, ed., *Crime and Justice: A Review of Research*, 27:235–303. Chicago: University of Chicago Press.

Landesman, Peter. 2004. "The Girls Next Door." *New York Times Magazine*, January 25, 30–39, 66–67, 72–75.

Lane, Roger. 1997. *Murder in America: A History.* Columbus: Ohio State University Press.

Langan, Patrick, and David Levin. 2002. *Recidivism of Prisoners Released in 1994.* Washington, D.C.: Department of Justice, Bureau of Justice Statistics.

Langbein, John H. 1998. "The Historical Origins of the Sanction of Imprisonment for Serious Crime." In Timothy J. Flanagan, James M. Marquart, and Kenneth G. Adams, eds., *Incarcerating Criminals: Prisons and Jails in Social and Organizational Context*, 10–15. New York: Oxford University Press.

Lanier, Charles S. 1993. "Affective States of Fathers in Prison." *Justice Quarterly* 10:49–66.

Latimer, Jeff, Craig Dowden, and Danielle Muise. 2001. *The Effectiveness of Restorative Justice Practices: A Meta-Analysis.* Ottawa: Department of Justice.

Lemert, Edwin. 1951. *Social Pathology.* New York: McGraw-Hill.

———. 1967. *Human Deviance: Social Problems and Social Control.* New York: Prentice-Hall.

Lerner, Kenneth, Gary Arling, and S. Christopher Baird. 1986. "Client Management Classification Strategies for Case Supervision." *Crime and Delinquency* 32:254–71.

Levitt, Steven. 1996. "The Effect of Prison Population Size on Crime Rates: Evidence from Prison Overcrowding Litigation." *Quarterly Journal of Economics* 111:319–52.

Liebling, Alison. 1999. "Prison Suicide and Prisoner Coping." In Michael Tonry and Joan Petersilia, ed., *Prisons*, 283–359. Chicago: University of Chicago Press.

Light, Stephen C. 1991. "Assaults on Prison Officers: Interactional Themes." *Justice Quarterly* 8:243–61.

Linch v. Thomas-Davis Med. Centers, 925 P.2d 686 (Ariz. Ct. App. 1996).

Lipsey, Mark W. 1995. "What Do We Learn from 400 Research Studies on the Effectiveness of Treatment with Juvenile Delinquents?" In James McGuire, ed., *What Works? Reducing Reoffending*, 63–78. Chichester, Eng.: Wiley.

Lipsey, Mark W., and David B. Wilson. 1993. "The Efficacy of Psychological, Educational, and Behavioral Treatment." *American Psychologist* 48:1181–1209.

Lipton, Douglas, Robert Martinson, and Judith Wilks. 1975. *The Effectiveness of Correctional Treatment: A Survey of Correctional Treatment Evaluations.* New York: Praeger.

Lockwood, Daniel. 1982. "Reducing Prison Sexual Violence." In Robert Johnson and Hans Toch, eds., *The Pains of Imprisonment*, 257–65. Beverly Hills, Calif.: Sage.

Loesel, Friedrich. 1996. "Effective Correctional Programming: What Empirical Research Tells and What It Doesn't." *Forum on Corrections Research* 8:33–37.

Lombroso, Cesare. 1911. *Criminal Man: According to the Classification of Cesare Lombroso.* Edited by Gina Lombroso-Ferrero. 1876. Reprint. New York: Putnam.

Lombroso, Cesare, and William Ferrero. 1895. *The Female Offender.* London: Fisher and Unwin.

Louisiana v. Sorrell, 656 So. 2d 1045 (La. Ct. App. 1995).

Lovell v. Brennan, 566 F. Supp. 672 (D. Me. 1983), *aff'd* 728 F.2d 560 (1st Cir. 1984).

MacCoun, Robert, and Peter Reuter. 1998. "Drug Control." In Michael Tonry, ed., *The Handbook of Crime and Punishment,* 207–38. New York: Oxford University Press.

MacDonald v. Clinger, 446 N.Y.S.2d 801 (N.Y. App. Div. 1982).

Mackey v. Procunier, 477 F.2d 877 (9th Cir. 1973).

Macri, Anthony. 1978. "Off Days Sentencing Program." In Burt Galaway and Joe Hudson, eds., *Offender Restitution in Theory and Action,* 167–70. Lexington, Mass.: Lexington.

Madigan, Nick. 2003. "Woman Who Killed Spouse with Car Is Guilty of Murder." *New York Times,* February 14. Available at: www.nytimes.com/2003/02/14/national/14SLAY.html (June 10, 2003).

Maier, Gary J., and Louis Fulton. 1998. "Inpatient Treatment of Offenders with Mental Disorders." In Robert M. Wettstein, ed., *Treatment of Offenders with Mental Disorders,* 126–67. New York: Guilford.

Marks, Malcolm J. 1988. "Remorse, Revenge, and Forgiveness." *Psychotherapy Patient* 5:317–30.

Marshall, William L., D. R. Laws, and Howard E. Barbaree, eds. 1990. *Handbook of Sexual Assault: Issues, Theories, and Treatment of the Offender.* New York: Plenum.

Martinson, Robert. 1974. "What Works? Questions and Answers About Prison Reform" *Public Interest* 35:22–45.

Maruschak, Laura, and Allen J. Beck. 2001. *Medical Problems of Inmates, 1997.* Washington, D.C.: Department of Justice, Bureau of Justice Statistics.

Mary and Crystal v. Ramsden, 635 F.2d 590 (7th Cir. 1980).

Maslin, Janet. 2003. "Krakauer Digs Deep into Mormon Extremism." *Providence (R.I.) Journal,* July 24, G-1.

Matza, David. 1964. *Delinquency and Drift.* New York: Wiley.

Maxson, Cheryl L. 1999. "Gang Homicide." In M. Dwayne Smith and Margaret A. Zahn, eds., *Studying and Preventing Homicide,* 197–220. Thousand Oaks, Calif.: Sage.

Maxwell, Gabrielle M., and Allison Morris. 1992. *Family Participation, Cultural Diversity, and Victim Involvement in Youth Justice: A New Zealand Experiment.* Wellington, N.Z.: Victoria University of Wellington, Institute of Criminology.

——. 1993. *Family, Victims, and Culture: Youth Justice in New Zealand.* Wellington, N.Z.: Victoria University of Wellington, Institute of Criminology.

Maxwell, Kimberly. 2002. "Friends: The Role of Peer Influence Across Adolescent Risk Behaviors." *Journal of Youth and Adolescence* 31:267–78.

McCloskey, H. J. 1965. "A Non-Utilitarian Approach to Punishment." *Inquiry* 8:239–55.

McCullough, Michael E., C. Garth Bellah, Shelley Dean Kilpatrick, and Judith L. Johnson. 2001. "Vengefulness: Relationships with Forgiveness, Rumination, Well-being and the Big Five." *Personality and Social Psychology Bulletin* 27:601–10.

McGuire, James, ed. 1995. *What Works? Reducing Reoffending.* Chichester, Eng.: Wiley.

McSwain v. Stricklin, 540 So. 2d 81 (Ala. Civ. App. 1989).

"Menendez Brothers Escape Death Sentence." 1996. *CNN Interactive,* April 17. Available at: http://www.cnn.com/US/9604/17/menendez.2/ (May 27, 2003).

Meriwether v. Faulkner, 821 F.2d 408 (7th Cir. 1987).

Merton, Robert K. 1957. *Social Theory and Social Structure*. New York: Free Press.

Metzner, Jeffrey L., Fred Cohen, Linda S. Grossman, and Robert M. Wettstein. 1998. "Treatment in Jails and Prisons." In Robert M. Wettstein, ed., *Treatment of Offenders with Mental Disorders*, 211–64. New York: Guilford.

Miller, Walter. 1958. "Lower Class Cultures as a Generating Milieu of Gang Delinquency." *Journal of Social Issues* 14:5–19.

Mississippi State Board of Psychological Examiners v. Hosford, 508 So. 2d 1049 (Miss.1987).

Molesky v. Walter, 931 F. Supp. 1506 (E.D. Wash. 1996).

Monahan, John. 1981. *Predicting Violent Behavior: An Assessment of Clinical Techniques*. Beverly Hills, Calif.: Sage.

Monahan, John, and Henry J. Steadman, eds. 1994. *Violence and Mental Disorder: Developments in Risk Assessment*. Chicago: University of Chicago Press.

Mondimore, Francis Mark. 1995. *Depression: The Mood Disease*. Rev. ed. Baltimore: Johns Hopkins University Press.

Mooney, Tom. 2002. "Now Free, Mollicone Must Lecture on His Misdeeds." *Providence (R.I.) Journal*, July 25, A-1, A-13.

Moore, David B., with L. Forsythe. 1995. *A New Approach to Juvenile Justice: An Evaluation of Family Conferencing in Wagga Wagga*. Wagga Wagga, New South Wales, Australia: Charles Sturt University.

Moore, David W., George H. Gallup, and Robert Schussel. 1995. *Disciplining Children in America: A Gallup Poll Report*. Princeton, N.J: Gallup Organization.

Moore, Michael S. 1995. "The Moral Worth of Retribution." In Jeffrie G. Murphy, ed., *Punishment and Rehabilitation*, 94–130. 3d ed. Belmont, Calif.: Wadsworth.

Morris, Herbert. 1972. "Persons and Punishment." In Gertrude Ezorsky, Gertrude, ed., *Philosophical Perspectives on Punishment*, 116–18. Albany: State University of New York Press.

Mumola, Christopher J. 1998. *Substance Abuse and Treatment of Adults on Probation, 1995*. Washington, D.C.: Department of Justice, Bureau of Justice Statistics.

———. 1999. *Substance Abuse and Treatment, State and Federal Prisoners, 1997*. Washington, D.C.: Department of Justice, Bureau of Justice Statistics.

Murphy, Jeffrie G. 1995. "Getting Even: The Role of the Victim." In Jeffrie G. Murphy, ed., *Punishment and Rehabilitation*, 132–51. 3d ed. Belmont, Calif.: Wadsworth.

Murphy, John E. 1991. "An Investigation of Child Sexual Abuse and Consequent Victimization: Some Implications of Telephone Surveys. In Dean D. Knudsen and Joann L. Miller, eds., *Abused and Battered: Social and Legal Responses to Family Violence*, 79–87. New York: Aldine de Gruyter.

Nathanson, Donald L. 1992. *Shame and Pride: Affect, Sex, and the Birth of the Self*. New York: Norton.

National Center on Elder Abuse. 1998. *National Elder Abuse Incident Study: Final Report*. Washington, D.C.: Department of Health and Human Services, Administration for Children and Families and Administration on Aging.

National Commission on Correctional Health Care. 1995. "Position Statement: Correctional Health Care and the Prevention of Violence." *Journal of Correctional Health Care* 2:71–74.

———. 1997. *Standards for Health Services in Prisons*. Chicago: National Commission on Correctional Health Care.

National Fire Protection Association. 2003. "Arson Is Not a Victimless Crime." Available at: http://www.usfa.fema.gov/downloads/pdf/mediakit03.pdf (January 19, 2004).

National Institute for Occupational Safety and Health. 1996. *Violence in the Workplace.* Washington, D.C.: National Institute for Occupational Safety and Health.

National Research Council. 1999. *Pathological Gambling: A Critical Review.* Washington, D.C.: National Academy Press.

Nedopil, Norbert. 2000. "Offenders with Brain Damage." In Sheilagh Hodgins and Rudiger Muller-Isberner, eds., *Violence, Crime, and Mentally Disordered Offenders: Concepts and Methods for Effective Treatment and Prevention,* 39–62. Chichester, Eng.: Wiley.

Nelson, Charles. 1980. "Victims of Rape: Who Are They?" In Carmen G. Warner, ed., *Rape and Sexual Assault: Management and Intervention,* 9–11. Germantown, Md.: Aspen.

New Hampshire v. Costello, 643 A.2d 531 (N.H. 1994).

Oakland Prosecutor v. Dep't. of Corrections, 564 N.W.2d 922 (Mich. Ct. App. 1997).

O'Connor, Matt. 2003. "White Supremacist Held in Murder Plot." *Newsday.com,* January 9. Available at: http://www.newsday.com/news/nationworld/nation/sns-hale,0,5654751. story?coll=ny-nationalnews-headlines (January 26, 2004).

Ohio v. Green, 683 N.E.2d 23 (Ohio Ct. App. 1996).

Ohio v. Johnson, 512 N.E.2d 652 (Ohio 1987).

Ohio v. Lanzy, 569 N.E.2d 468 (Ohio 1991).

Palmer, Ted. 1975. "Martinson Revisited." *Journal of Research in Crime and Delinquency* 12:133–52.

———. 1992. *The Re-Emergence of Correctional Intervention.* Newbury Park, Calif.: Sage.

Paludi, Michele A., ed. 1999. *The Psychology of Sexual Victimization: A Handbook.* Westport, Conn.: Greenwood.

Park, Robert E. 1952. *Human Communities.* Glencoe, Ill.: Free Press.

Parker, Robert N., and R. S. Cartmill. 1998. "Alcohol and Homicide in the United States, 1934–1995, Or One Reason Why U.S. Rates of Homicide May Be Going Down." *Journal of Criminal Law and Criminology* 88:1369–98.

Partridge v. Two Unknown Police Officers of Houston, 791 F.2d 1182 (5th Cir. 1986).

Paternoster, Raymond. 1991. *Capital Punishment in America.* New York: Lexington.

Pelka, Fred. 1995. "Raped: A Male Survivor Breaks His Silence." In Patricia Searles and Ronald J. Berger, eds., *Rape and Society: Readings on the Problem of Sexual Assault,* 250–56. Boulder, Colo.: Westview.

People v. Adams, 581 N.E.2d 637 (Ill. 1991).

People v. Calahan, 649 N.E.2d 588 (Ill. App. Ct. 1995).

People v. Catron, 246 Cal. Rptr. 303 (Cal. Ct. App. 1988).

People v. Villaneuva, 528 N.Y.S.2d 506 (N.Y. Sup. Ct. 1988).

Permanent Deacons of Paterson, New Jersey. 1998. "Capital Punishment Undermines the Sacredness of Life." In Mary E. Williams, ed., *Capital Punishment,* 50–53. San Diego: Greenhaven.

Petersilia, Joan. 2003. *When Prisoners Come Home: Parole and Prisoner Reentry.* New York: Oxford University Press.

Peterson, Ruth D., and William C. Bailey. 1988. "Murder and Capital Punishment in the Evolving Context of the Post-*Furman* Era." *Social Forces* 66:774–807.

Pettiway, Leon E. 1987. "Arson for Revenge: The Role of Environmental Situation, Age, Sex, and Race." *Journal of Quantitative Criminology* 3:169–84.

Phillips, Susan, and Barbara Bloom. 1998. "In Whose Best Interest? The Impact of Changing Public Policy on Relatives Caring for Children with Incarcerated Parents." *Child Welfare* 77:531–41.

Piper, August. 1996. *Hoax and Reality: The Bizarre World of Multiple Personality Disorder.* Northvale, N.J.: Aronson.

Platt, Anthony. 1974. "Prospects for a Radical Criminology in the United States." *Crime and Social Justice* 1:2–10.

Pollack, Otto. 1950. *The Criminality of Women.* New York: Barnes.

Pomeroy, Sarah B. 1975. *Goddesses, Whores, Wives, and Slaves: Women in Classical Antiquity.* New York: Schocken.

Porter, Louise E., and Laurence J. Alison. 2001. "A Partially Ordered Scale of Influence in Violent Group Behavior: An Example from Gang Rape." *Small Group Research* 32:475–97.

Powell, Thomas A., John C. Holt, and Karen M. Fondacaro. 1997. "The Prevalence of Mental Illness Among Inmates in a Rural State." *Law and Human Behavior* 21:427–38.

Powell v. Coughlin, 953 F.2d 744 (2d Cir. 1991).

Pranis, Kay. 1997. "Rethinking Community Corrections: Restorative Values and an Expanded Role for the Community." *International Community Corrections Association (ICCA) Journal on Community Corrections* 8:36–39, 43.

Preston, Marjorie. 2001. "Rape Was Just the Beginning of My Ordeal." In Mary E. Williams, ed., *Rape,* 123–27. San Diego: Greenhaven.

Price v. Sheppard, 239 N.W.2d 1136 (8th Cir. 1973).

Prochaska, James O., John C. Norcross, and Carlos C. DiClemente. 1995. *Changing for Good.* New York: Morrow.

Quinney, Richard. 1970. *The Social Reality of Crime.* Boston: Little, Brown.

———. 1974. *Critique of Legal Order: Crime Control in Capitalist Society.* Boston: Little, Brown.

———. 1977. *Class, State, and Crime: On the Theory and Practice of Criminal Justice.* New York: McKay.

———. 1979. *Criminology.* 2d ed. New York: McGraw-Hill.

Quinsey, Vernon L. 1998. "Treatment of Sex Offenders." In Michael Tonry, ed., *The Handbook of Crime and Punishment,* 403–25. New York: Oxford University Press.

Radelet, Michael L. 1981. "Racial Characteristics and the Imposition of the Death Penalty." *American Sociological Review* 46:918–27.

Radelet, Michael L., Hugo Adam Bedeau, and Constance E. Putnam. 1992. *In Spite of Innocence: Erroneous Convictions in Capital Cases.* Boston: Northeastern University Press.

———. 1995. "In Spite of Innocence: Erroneous Convictions in Capital Cases." In Robert M. Baird and Stuart E. Rosenbaum, eds., *Punishment and the Death Penalty: The Current Debate,* 141–49. Amherst, N.Y.: Prometheus.

Raeder, Myrna S. 1995. "The Forgotten Offender: The Effect of the Sentencing Guidelines and Mandatory Minimums on Women and Their Children." *Federal Sentencing Reporter* 8:157–62.

Rafter, Nicole Hahn. 1998. "Prisons for Women, 1790–1980." In Timothy J. Flanagan, James M. Marquart, and Kenneth G. Adams, eds., *Incarcerating Criminals: Prisons and Jails in Social and Organizational Context,* 30–45. New York: Oxford University Press.

Random House Webster's College Dictionary. 1991. New York: Random House.

Rathbone, Daniel B., and George C. Huckabee. 1999. *Controlling Road Rage: A Literature Review and Pilot Study.* Washington, D.C.: AAA Foundation for Traffic Safety.

Reamer, Frederic G. 1983. "The Free Will-Determinism Debate and Social Work." *Social Service Review* 57:626–44.

———. 1989. "Toward Ethical Practice: The Relevance of Ethical Theory." *Social Thought* 15:67–78.

———. 1990. *Ethical Dilemmas in Social Service.* 2d ed. New York: Columbia University Press.

———. 1993. *The Philosophical Foundations of Social Work.* New York: Columbia University Press.

———. 1998a. *Ethical Standards in Social Work: A Review of the NASW Code of Ethics.* Washington, D.C.: NASW Press.

———. 1998b. *Social Work Research and Evaluation Skills.* New York: Columbia University Press.

———. 2003a. *Criminal Lessons: Case Studies and Commentary on Crime and Justice.* New York: Columbia University Press.

———. 2003b. *Social Work Malpractice and Liability: Strategies for Prevention.* 2d ed. New York: Columbia University Press.

Reckless, Walter C. 1961. *The Crime Problem.* 3d ed. New York: Appleton-Century-Crofts.

Reid, Sue Titus. 1999. *Crime and Criminology.* New York: McGraw-Hill.

Reid, William H., ed. 1981. *The Treatment of Antisocial Syndromes.* New York: Van Nostrand Reinhold.

Reitz, Kevin R. 1998. "Sentencing." In Michael Tonry, ed., *The Handbook of Crime and Punishment,* 542–62. New York: Oxford University Press.

Rennison, Callie. 2002. *Criminal Victimization: 2001.* Washington, D.C.: Department of Justice, Bureau of Justice Statistics.

Rennison, Callie, and Michael R. Rand. 2003. *Criminal Victimization, 2002.* Department of Justice, Bureau of Justice Statistics. Available at: http://www.ojp.usdoj.gov/bjs/pub.pdf/cv02.pdf (January 19, 2004).

Robinson, Walter V. 2002. "Scores of Priests Involved in Sex Abuse Cases." *Boston Globe,* January 31. Available at: http://www.boston.com/globe/spotlight/abuse/stories/013102_priests.htm (January 19, 2004).

Rogers, Jeffrey, and Joseph D. Bloom. 1982. "Characteristics of Persons Committed to Oregon's Psychiatric Security Review Board." *Bulletin of the American Academy of Psychiatry and the Law* 10:155–64.

———. 1985. "The Insanity Sentence: Oregon's Psychiatric Security Review Board." *Behavioral Sciences and the Law* 3:69–84.

Rogers, Richard, and James Cavanaugh. 1981. "A Treatment Program for Potentially Violent Offender Patients." *International Journal of Offender Therapy and Comparative Criminology* 25:53–59.

Ross, Colin A. 1996. *Dissociative Identity Disorder: Diagnosis, Clinical Features, and Treatment of Multiple Personality.* New York: Wiley.

Ross, Robert R., and Elizabeth Fabiano. 1985. *Time to Think: A Cognitive Model of Offender Rehabilitation and Delinquency Prevention.* Johnson City, Tenn.: Institute of Social Sciences and Arts.

Rothman, David J. 1998. "The Invention of the Penitentiary." In Timothy J. Flanagan, James M. Marquart, and Kenneth G. Adams, eds., *Incarcerating Criminals: Prisons and Jails in Social and Organizational Context,* 15–23. New York: Oxford University Press.

Rubinstein, Gwen. 2001. *Getting to Work: How TANF Can Support Ex-Offender Parents in the Transition to Self-Sufficiency.* Washington, D.C.: Legal Action Center.

Rudolph v. Alabama, 375 U.S. 889 (1963).

Russell, Diane E. 1975. *The Politics of Rape: The Victim's Perspective.* New York: Stein and Day.

———. 1983. "The Incidence and Prevalence of Intrafamilial and Extrafamilial Sexual Abuse." *Child Abuse and Neglect* 7:133–46.

———. 1984. *Sexual Exploitation: Rape, Child Sexual Abuse, and Workplace Harassment.* Beverly Hills, Calif.: Sage.

Russell, Diane E., and Rebecca M. Bolen. 2000. *The Epidemic of Rape and Child Sexual Abuse in the United States.* Thousand Oaks, Calif.: Sage.

Ryan, T. A. 1998. "Literacy Training and Reintegration of Offenders." In Timothy J. Flanagan, James M. Marquart, and Kenneth G. Adams, eds., *Incarcerating Criminals: Prisons and Jails in Social and Organizational Context,* 194–207. New York: Oxford University Press.

Sack, William H. 1977. "Children of Imprisoned Fathers." *Psychiatry* 40:163–74.

Sampson, Robert. 1992. "Family Management and Child Development: Insights from Social Disorganization Theory." *Advances in Criminological Theory* 3:63–93.

Sandin v. Conner, 115 S. Ct. 2293 (1995).

Santamour, Miles B. 1989. *The Mentally Retarded Offender and Corrections.* Washington, D.C.: Saint Mary's Press.

Saunders, Benjamin E., et al. 1999. "Prevalence, Case Characteristics, and Long-term Psychological Correlates of Child Rape Among Women: A National Survey." *Child Maltreatment* 4:187–200.

Scarce, Michael. 2001. "Uncovering Male-on-Male Rape." In Mary E. Williams, *Rape,* 42–58. San Diego: Greenhaven.

Schafer, Stephen. 1976. *Introduction to Criminology.* Reston, Va.: Reston.

Schmalleger, Frank M. 2001. *Criminology Today.* Englewood Cliffs, N.J.: Prentice-Hall.

Schrag, Clarence. 1971. *Crime and Justice: American Style.* Washington, D.C.: Government Printing Office.

Schur, Edwin M. 1969. "Reactions to Deviance: A Critical Assessment." *American Journal of Sociology* 75:309–22.

———. 1971. *Labeling Deviant Behavior.* New York: Harper & Row.

Schwartz, Barbara K., and Henry R. Cellini, eds. 1995. *The Sex Offender.* Vol. 1, *Corrections, Treatment, and Legal Practice.* Kingston, N.J.: Civic Research Institute.

———. 1997. *The Sex Offender.* Vol. 2, *New Insights, Treatment Interventions, and Legal Developments.* Kingston, N.J.: Civic Research Institute.

———. 1999. *The Sex Offender.* Vol. 3, *Theoretical Advances, Treating Special Populations, and Legal Developments.* Kingston, N.J.: Civic Research Institute.

Scully, Diana, and Joseph Marolla. 1995. "'Riding the Bull at Gilley's': Convicted Rapists Describe the Rewards of Rape." In Patricia Searles and Ronald J. Berger, eds., *Rape and Society: Readings on the Problem of Sexual Assault,* 58–73. Boulder, Colo.: Westview.

Searles, Patricia, and Ronald J. Berger, eds. 1995. *Rape and Society: Readings on the Problem of Sexual Assault.* Boulder, Colo.: Westview.

Sedlak, Andrea, and Diane D. Broadhurst. 1996. *Third National Incidence Study of Child Abuse and Neglect: Final Report.* Washington, D.C.: Department of Health and Human Services.

Sellin, Thorsten. 1959. *The Death Penalty.* Philadelphia: American Law Institute.

Seton, Paul H. 2001. "On the Importance of Getting Even: A Study of the Origins and Intentions of Revenge." *Smith College Studies in Social Work* 72:77–97.

Shaffer, Howard J., Sharon A. Stein, Blase Gambino, and Thomas N. Cummings, eds. 1989. *Compulsive Gambling: Theory, Research, and Practice.* Lexington, Mass.: Lexington.

Shaw, Clifford R., and Henry D. McKay. 1942. *Juvenile Delinquency and Urban Areas.* Chicago: University of Chicago Press.

Sheley, Joseph F. 2000. *Criminology: A Contemporary Handbook.* 3d ed. Belmont, Calif.: Wadsworth.

Sheridan, Lorraine, and Graham M. Davies. 2001. "Stalking: The Elusive Crime." *Legal and Criminological Psychology* 6:133–47.

Sherif, Muzafer, and Carolyn W. Sherif. 1964. *Reference Groups.* New York: Harper & Row.

Sherman, Edmund, and William J. Reid, eds. 1994. *Qualitative Research in Social Work.* New York: Columbia University Press.

Sherman, Lawrence. 1993. "Defiance, Deterrence, and Irrelevance: A Theory of the Criminal Sanction." *Journal of Research in Crime and Delinquency* 30:445–73.

Shinnar, Shlomo, and Reuel Shinnar. 1975. "The Effects of the Criminal Justice System on the Control of Crime: A Quantitative Approach." *Law and Society Review* 9:581–611.

Shover, Neal. 1998. "White-Collar Crime." In Michael Tonry, ed., *The Handbook of Crime and Punishment,* 133–58. New York: Oxford University Press.

Siegel, Judith M., et al. 1987. "The Prevalence of Childhood Sexual Assault: The Los Angeles Epidemiologic Catchment Area Project." *American Journal of Epidemiology* 126:1141–53.

Siegel, Larry J. 2000. *Criminology.* Belmont, Calif.: Wadsworth.

Simourd, David J., and P. Bruce Malcolm. 1998. "Reliability and Validity of the Level of Service Inventory-Revised Among Federally Incarcerated Sex Offenders." *Journal of Interpersonal Violence* 13:261–75.

Smith, M. Dwayne, and Margaret A. Zahn, eds. 1999. *Studying and Preventing Homicide.* Thousand Oaks, Calif.: Sage.

Smith, Michael, and Walter Dickey. 1998. "What If Corrections Were Serious About Public Safety?" *Corrections Management Quarterly* 2:12–30.

Sorenson, Susan B., and Richard A. Berk. 2001. "Handgun Sales, Beer Sales, and Youth Homicide, California, 1972–1993." *Journal of Public Health Policy* 22:182–97.

Souder v. McGuire, 423 F. Supp. 830 (M.D. Pa. 1976).

Spelman, William. 2000. "What Recent Studies Do (and Don't) Tell Us About Imprisonment and Crime." In Michael Tonry, ed., *Crime and Justice: A Review of Research,* 27:419–94. Chicago: University of Chicago Press.

Spergel, Irving. 1995. *The Youth Gang Problem: A Community Approach.* New York: Oxford University Press.

Stanton, Ann M. 1980. *When Mothers Go to Jail.* Lexington, Mass.: Lexington.

Steadman, Henry, Stanley Fabisiak, Joel Dvoskin, and Edward Holohean. 1989. "A Survey of Mental Disability Among State Prison Inmates." *Hospital and Community Psychiatry* 38:1086–90.

Stuckless, Noreen, and Richard Goranson. 1994. "A Selected Bibliography of Literature on Revenge." *Psychological Reports* 75:803–11.

Sullivan, Dennis, and Larry Tifft. 2001. *Restorative Justice: Healing the Foundations of our Everyday Lives.* Monsey, N.Y.: Willow Tree Press.

Sutherland, Edwin H. 1947. *Principles of Criminology.* 4th ed. Philadelphia: Lippincott.

Sykes, Gresham. 1958. *The Society of Captives: A Study of a Maximum Security Prison.* Princeton, N.J.: Princeton University Press.

Talbot, Margaret. 2003. "The Executioner's IQ Test." *New York Times Magazine*, June 29, 30–35, 52, 58–60.

Tannenbaum, Frank. 1938. *Crime and the Community.* Boston: Ginn.

Tatara, Toshio. 1995. "Elder Abuse." In Richard L. Edwards, ed., *Encyclopedia of Social Work*, 1:834–42. 19th ed. Washington, D.C.: National Association of Social Workers.

Taylor, Richard. 1991. *Metaphysics.* 4th ed. Englewood Cliffs, N.J.: Prentice-Hall.

Teplin, Linda A. 1990. "The Prevalence of Severe Mental Disorder Among Male Urban Jail Detainees: Comparison with the Epidemiologic Catchment Area Program." *American Journal of Public Health* 80:663–69.

Terris, William, and John Jones. 1982. "Psychological Factors Related to Employees' Theft in the Convenience Store Industry." *Psychological Reports* 51:1219–38.

Thomas, William I. 1923. *The Unadjusted Girl.* New York: Harper & Row.

Thompson v. County of Mediana, Ohio, 29 F.3d 238 (6th Cir. 1994).

Thornhill, Randy, and Craig T. Palmer. 2000. *The Natural History of Rape: Biological Bases of Sexual Coercion.* Cambridge, Mass.: MIT Press.

Tittle, Charles R. 1978. "Restitution and Deterrence: An Evaluation of Compatibility." In Burt Galaway and Joe Hudson, eds., *Offender Restitution in Theory and Action*, 33–58. Lexington, Mass.: Lexington.

Tjaden, Patricia, and Nancy Thoennes. 1998. *Prevalence, Incidence, and Consequences of Violence Against Women: Findings from the National Violence Against Women Survey.* Washington, D.C.: Department of Justice, National Institute of Justice.

Toch, Hans. 1975. *Men in Crisis: Human Breakdowns in Confinement.* Chicago: Aldine de Gruyter.

——. 1977. *Living in Prison.* New York: Free Press.

——. 1992. *Living in Prison.* Rev. ed. Washington, D.C.: American Psychological Association.

Toch, Hans, and Kenneth Adams, with J. Douglas Grant. 1991. *Coping: Maladaptation in Prisons.* New Brunswick, N.J.: Transaction.

Tonry, Michael. 1998a. "Intermediate Sanctions." In Michael Tonry, ed., *The Handbook of Crime and Punishment*, 683–711. New York: Oxford University Press.

——, ed. 1998b. *The Handbook of Crime and Punishment.* New York: Oxford University Press.

Tonry, Michael, and Joan Petersilia. 1999. "American Prisons at the Beginning of the Twenty-first Century." In Michael Tonry and Joan Petersilia, eds., *Prisons*, 1–16. Chicago: University of Chicago Press.

Travis, Jeremy. 2000. *But They All Come Back: Rethinking Prisoner Reentry.* Washington, D.C.: National Institute of Justice.

Tunick, Mark. 1992. *Punishment: Theory and Practice.* Berkeley: University of California Press.

Turner, John C., et al. 1987. *Rediscovering the Social Group: A Self-Categorization Theory.* London: Blackwell.

Tyler, Tom, and Steven Blader. 2000. *Cooperation in Groups: Procedural Justice, Social Identity, and Behavioral Engagement.* Philadelphia: Psychology Press.

Umbreit, Mark S. 1994. *Victim Meets Offender: The Impact of Restorative Justice and Mediation.* Monsey, N.Y.: Criminal Justice Press.

———. 2000. *Family Group Conferencing: Implications for Crime Victims.* Washington, D.C.: Department of Justice, Office for Crime Victims.

———. 2001. *The Handbook on Victim-Offender Mediation: An Essential Guide for Practice and Research.* San Francisco: Jossey-Bass.

Umbreit, Mark S., and Robert B. Coates. 1992. *Victim-Offender Mediation: An Analysis of Programs in Four States of the U.S.* Minneapolis: Citizens Council Mediation Services.

———. 2000. *Multicultural Implications of Restorative Justice: Potential Pitfalls and Dangers.* Washington, D.C.: Department of Justice, Office for Crime Victims.

Umbreit, Mark S., with Robert B. Coates and Boris Kalanj. 1994. *Victim Meets Offender: The Impact of Restorative Justice and Mediation.* Monsey, N.Y.: Criminal Justice Press.

Umbreit, Mark S., Robert B. Coates, Betty Vos, and Katherine Brown. 2002. *Victim-Offender Dialogue in Crimes of Severe Violence: A Multi-Site Study of Programs in Texas and Ohio.* St. Paul, Minn.: Center for Restorative Justice and Peacemaking.

Umbreit, Mark S., Betty Vos, Robert B. Coates, and Katherine A. Brown, eds. 2003. *Facing Violence: The Path of Restorative Justice and Dialogue.* Monsey, N.Y.: Willow Tree Press.

United States v. Perez, 28 F.3d 673 (7th Cir. 1994).

Unrau, Yvonne A., and Heather Coleman. 1997. "Qualitative Data Analysis." In Richard Grinnell Jr., ed., *Social Work Research and Evaluation,* 501–26. 5th ed. Itasca, Ill.: Peacock.

van den Haag, Ernest. 1995. "On Deterrence and the Death Penalty." In Robert M. Baird and Stuart E. Rosenbaum, eds., *Punishment and the Death Penalty: The Current Debate,* 125–35. Amherst, N.Y.: Prometheus.

Van Ness, Daniel. 1986. *Crime and Its Victims: What We Can Do.* Downers Grove, Ill.: Intravarsity Press.

Van Ness, Daniel, and Karen Heetderks Strong. 1997. *Restoring Justice.* Cincinnati: Anderson.

Van Ness, Daniel, and Pat Nolan. 1998. "Legislating for Restorative Justice." *Regent University Law Review* 10:53–110.

Vidmar, Neil. 2001. "Retribution and Revenge." In Joseph Sanders and Hamilton V. Lee, eds., *Handbook of Justice Research in Law,* 31–63. Dordrecht: Kluwer Academic.

Vitek v. Jones, 445 U.S. 480 (1980).

Volberg, Rachel A. 1994. "The Prevalence and Demographics of Pathological Gamblers: Implications for Public Health." *American Journal of Public Health* 84:237–41.

von Hirsch, Andrew. 1998. "Penal Theories." In Michael Tonry, ed., *The Handbook of Crime and Punishment,* 659–82. New York: Oxford University Press.

Wald, Patricia M. 1995. "'What About the Kids?' Parenting Issues in Sentencing." *Federal Sentencing Reporter* 8:137–41.

Walgrave, Lode, and Gordon Bazemore, eds. 1998. *Restoring Juvenile Justice.* Monscy, N.Y.: Criminal Justice Press.

Ward, David A., and Kenneth F. Schoen, eds. 1981. *Confinement in Maximum Custody.* Lexington, Mass.: Heath.

Warner, Carmen G. 1980a. "Rape and Rape Laws in Historical Perspective." In Carmen G. Warner, *Rape and Sexual Assault: Management and Intervention,* 1–7. Germantown, Md.: Aspen.

————, ed. 1980b. *Rape and Sexual Assault: Management and Intervention*. Germantown, Md.: Aspen.

Warr, Mark. 1993. "Parents, Peers, and Delinquency." *Social Forces* 72:247–64.

Washington v. Harper, 494 U.S. 210 (1990).

Washington v. Olivas, 856 P.2d 1076 (Wash. 1993).

Washington v. Ward, 869 P.2d 1062 (Wash. 1994).

Weisburd, David, Elin Waring, and Ellen Chayet. 1995. "Specific Deterrence in a Sample of Offenders Convicted of White-Collar Crimes." *Criminology* 33:587–607.

Wettstein, Robert M., ed. 1998. *Treatment of Offenders with Mental Disorders*. New York: Guilford.

Wexler, David. n.d. "Therapeutic Jurisprudence: An Overview." Available at: http://www.law.arizona.edu (September 15, 2002).

Wexler, Harry K. 1994. "Progress in Prison Substance Abuse Treatment: A Five-Year Report." *Journal of Drug Issues* 24:349–60.

White, Ellen E. 1996. "Profiling Arsonists and their Motives: An Update." *Fire Engineering* 149:80–85.

Wiehn, Paul J. 1982. "Mentally Ill Offenders: Prison's First Casualties." In Robert Johnson and Hans Toch, eds., *The Pains of Imprisonment*, 221–37. Beverly Hills, Calif.: Sage.

Williams, Mary E., ed. 1998. *Capital Punishment*. San Diego: Greenhaven.

————. 2001. *Rape*. San Diego: Greenhaven.

Wilson, James Q. 1975. *Thinking About Crime*. New York: Basic Books.

Wilson, James Q., and Joan Petersilia, eds. 2002. *Crime: Public Policies for Crime Control*. San Francisco: ICS Press.

Wolfe, Jean, and Virginia Baker. 1980. "Characteristics of Imprisoned Rapists and Circumstances of the Rape." In Carmen G. Warner, ed., *Rape and Sexual Assault: Management and Intervention*, 265–78. Germantown, Md.: Aspen.

Wolff v. McDonnell, 418 U.S. 539 (1974).

Wright, Martin. 1990. *Justice for Victims and Offenders: A Restorative Response to Crime*. Winchester, Mass.: Waterside.

————. 2002. "The Court as Last Resort: Victim-Sensitive, Community-Based Responses to Crime." *British Journal of Criminology* 42:654–67.

Wyatt, Gail E. 1985. "The Sexual Abuse of Afro-American and White-American Women in Childhood." *Child Abuse and Neglect* 9:507–19.

Young, C. 1932. *Women's Prisons: Past and Present*. Elmira, N.Y.: Summary.

Youngberg v. Romeo, 457 U.S. 307 (1982).

Zahn, Margaret A., and Patricia L. McCall. 1999. "Homicide in the Twentieth-Century United States: Trends and Patterns." In M. Dwayne Smith and Margaret A. Zahn, eds., *Studying and Preventing Homicide*, 10–30. Thousand Oaks, Calif.: Sage.

Zamble, Edward, and Frank J. Porporino. 1988. *Coping, Behavior, and Adaptation in Prison Inmates*. New York: Springer.

Zehr, Howard. 1990. *Changing the Lenses*. Scottdale, Pa.: Herald Press.

Zimring, Franklin E., and Gordon Hawkins. 1986. *Capital Punishment and the American Agenda*. New York: Cambridge University Press.

————. 1995. *Incapacitation: Penal Confinement and Restraint of Crime*. New York: Oxford University Press.

Index